The Chinese Yuan

Internationalization and Financial Products in China

The Chinese Yuan

Internationalization and Financial Products in China

PETER G. ZHANG

WITH THOMAS CHAN

WILEY

John Wiley & Sons (Asia) Pte. Ltd.

Other Wiley Editorial Offices
John Wiley & Sons, 111 River Street, Hoboken, NJ 07030, USA
John Wiley & Sons, The Atrium, Southern Gate, Chichester, West Sussex, P019 8SQ,
    United Kingdom
John Wiley & Sons (Canada) Ltd., 5353 Dundas Street West, Suite 400, Toronto, Ontario,
    M9B 6HB, Canada
John Wiley & Sons Australia Ltd., 42 McDougall Street, Milton, Queensland 4064, Australia
Wiley-VCH, Boschstrasse 12, D-69469 Weinheim, Germany

Library of Congress Cataloging-in-Publication Data
ISBN 978–0–470–82737–6 (Hardback)
ISBN 978–0–470–82739–0 (ePDF)
ISBN 978–0–470–82738–3 (Mobi)
ISBN 978–0–470–82740–6 (ePub)

Typeset in 10/12pt Sabon by Thomson Digital, India
Printed in Singapore by Toppan Security Printing Pte. Ltd.
10 9 8 7 6 5 4 3 2 1

Contents

CHAPTER 19

CHAPTER 20

Foreword

The emergence of China as a leading exporter and "factory to the world" was arguably the most significant development of the late 20th and early 21st century. By opening the country to outside investment, and unleashing the potential of China's own entrepreneurs and state-owned enterprises, China's government has been able to achieve in thirty years what many developed countries have achieved over centuries.

China's impressive economic achievements derived from the reforms of the 1980s and 1990s, were accompanied by government's management of the Chinese yuan (CNY) exchange rate and the country's capital account. As a consequence, the rapid growth of the export driven economy, has been accompanied by the United States trade deficit with China increasing from just US$6 million in 1985 to US$173 billion for the first six months of 2010.[1] Over this period, the exchange rate to the US dollar has gradually been adjusted from CNY1.50 in 1980 to CNY8.62 by 1994, favoring China's exporters, although more recently it has appreciated to CNY6.66. While in 2005 the peg to the US dollar was replaced by a market floating exchange rate referenced to a basket of foreign currencies, the peg was reintroduced in 2008 in response to the worsening global financial crisis. In June 2010, the CNY was allowed once again to float within a basket of foreign currencies but the boundaries remain tight, with its value significantly below the expectation of western countries.

Despite these measures, the CNY has undoubtedly started down the path of internationalization. Recent steps include the setting up of a number of bilateral currency swap agreements which allow certain countries and areas, including Argentina, Belarus, Indonesia, Malaysia, South Korea and Hong Kong to exchange substantial amounts of their own currency into CNY at times when they are under strong selling pressure in the international markets. Another step towards internationalization are the pilot schemes for cross border trade financing which allow manufacturers and importers based in southern China to settle their cross border transactions in CNY. This step is important because it allows the manufacturers to transfer their foreign exchange risk to their overseas customers. Meanwhile, Hong Kong has been established as a test center for capital markets activities in CNY through the issue of CNY denominated securities by certain banks in Hong Kong, and China's agreement with the IMF in 2009 that China may use CNY to purchase special drawing rights. All the above arrangements have strengthened the influence of CNY internationally.

While the above steps represent significant progress, there remains a significant length of road to be traveled before the yuan can be called a truly international currency. There are a number of reasons why China's government has not allowed the CNY to float freely and appreciate rapidly. One of the most important is the impact which any significant appreciation in the yuan would have on the already fragile export market which is still suffering from a combination of increasing labor and production costs, and weakened consumer sentiment in the developed west. Over the past few months, the calls for China to make further currency reforms have become even louder. There are also voices from within China who see appreciation of the CNY as being necessary to take some of the pressure off the asset bubbles which are becoming apparent in many areas of the economy, and in particular the property market.

The arguments and counter-arguments concerning the respective merits of relaxing China's currency and capital account controls will be familiar to anyone who has opened a newspaper or watched a financial news program in the past 10 years. However, in analyzing the current role and performance of CNY dominated products in financial markets in China and overseas, the authors of this book have focused on the lesser-discussed aspects of this debate. Namely that while the years of government's management over the CNY have undoubtedly played an important role in China's recent economic successes, they have also contributed to the relatively underdeveloped state of China's financial markets. If China is to further liberalize its foreign currency markets, and allow the CNY to become an international currency, then it must as a matter of urgency improve the liquidity of CNY denominated financial instruments, and promote further innovation in CNY denominated financial products. With a broader range of CNY denominated financial products, Chinese companies and overseas investors will be able to more effectively control the increased risks which would arise from a relaxation of the controls over China's capital account and the exchange rate. Such innovation will also further support the government's stated strategy of establishing Shanghai as an international financial centre. Financial institutions in Shanghai will also be able to compete more effectively with their counterparts in New York or London.

By providing readers with such an informative overview of the developments in China's financial markets to date, this book highlights the work which still needs to be done, and in doing so provides an effective roadmap for the future direction which further development of CNY-denominated financial products is likely to take.

Simon Gleave
Regional Head of Financial Services, KPMG ASPAC
Head of Financial Services, KPMG China

ENDNOTE

1. US Census Bureau Foreign Trade Statistics.

Preface

The Seventeenth Central Committee of the Communist Party of China (CPC), held in October 2007, called for the whole party and people of all ethnic groups to vigorously enhance the spirit of reform and innovation, thoroughly pursue rational development, improve the capability of independent innovation, and build an innovative country. The report of the Seventeenth CPC Central Committee pointed out that China should stick to the road of independent innovation with Chinese characteristics, and carry out independent innovation in various aspects of modernization. The report clearly requires the financial sector to sharpen the competitiveness of the banking, securities, and insurance industries.

Sharpening the competitiveness of the financial sector is, in effect, increasing its innovative capabilities. China's economy has recorded remarkable achievements in 30 years of reform and opening-up, with its innovative capability being further enhanced each year. Though the pace of economic and financial globalization has been affected to varying degrees by the international financial crisis, the wheel will continue to move forward. Given the increasingly international status of its economy, China should look to identify gaps and areas for improvement in its current performance, comparing this both with its own historical achievements and with the performance of developed and developing countries.

With the steady growth of China's economy and its higher global ranking, Chinese companies will gradually accelerate their expansion overseas and foreign enterprises will increase their investments in China. This will result in foreign currency business accounting for a higher proportion of China's financial sector. However, as the vast majority of the assets of Chinese financial institutions will still be denominated in Chinese yuan (CNY), the key to financial innovation in Chinese institutions in the foreseeable future will lie in innovating CNY products. With gradual progress in the internationalization of the CNY, demand for innovative CNY products from both Chinese and foreign investors will continue to increase. Financial innovation is all about innovative ideas, mechanisms, and risk management. Nevertheless, the performance and profitability of financial institutions depends on products and services; so financial innovation is, in effect, product innovation. Therefore, creating innovative CNY products is the key to China's financial innovation.

China made tremendous progress in its economic development in the 30 years from 1978, when the reform and opening-up program began, recording an average annual real GDP growth rate of almost 10 percent. Even in 2009, when the world economy was in the grip of the global financial crisis, it achieved 8.7 percent growth, reflecting the effectiveness and timeliness of the various measures it had taken to combat the worst effects of the crisis.

Besides the great achievements in economic development, China has also made good progress in developing its financial market in the past decade or so, particularly in the interbank marketplace, with more and more new products. The first new business in the banking industry was the foreign exchange forward settlement, launched in April 1997, after the

People's Bank of China issued "The Tentative Administrative Methods for Renminbi (CNY) Forward Settlement" in January that year. CNY bond forwards, foreign exchange forward trading, foreign exchange swaps, interest rate swaps, and forward rate agreements were introduced in the inter-bank marketplace consecutively from 2005. These new products have developed reasonably well in the past few years, providing market participants with instruments to hedge foreign exchange and interest rate risk.

Despite good progress in product innovation and market development in the financial market, financial futures are still absent from the organized exchanges, and options are absent from both exchanges and the inter-bank marketplace in mainland China. Although the above-mentioned over-the-counter (OTC) products have come into play in the past few years, market liquidity has been rather low, with international weights much lower than the corresponding GDP global weight for each of these products. Risk management cannot be practiced satisfactorily without there being sufficient liquidity for these instruments.

Further, the financial market cannot serve the underlying economy well enough without sufficient development. For example, promotion of the CNY to settle international trade is highly necessary, and the experimental implementation of settlement in 2009 was very timely. Yet, the fact that settlement volume has not been significantly high implies that market foundations, such as CNY foreign exchange risk management, have to be strengthened. Thus, CNY foreign exchange forward and swaps markets need sufficient liquidity for market participants to hedge the related foreign exchange risk.

The financial crisis has taught us many lessons since September 2008. Financial derivative products have been widely blamed for having "caused" the crisis, or at least made it worse. However, we have not seen any serious problems with any derivatives trading in any organized exchanges or most OTC derivatives (other than credit default swaps) worldwide, despite moderate declines in trading values of futures and options trading worldwide from the second half of 2008 and 2009. Futures and options trading in exchanges and most OTC derivative products have well-defined functions in the financial system and the whole economy, so that the underlying economy cannot do well without the necessary financial products and sufficient market liquidity for these products. China has achieved tremendous economic development in the last three decades and has developed its financial markets significantly. Yet many necessary financial products are still absent from the market and the liquidity of most existing segments of the financial market is relatively low. It is highly necessary for China to accelerate the development of its financial market in order to serve its economy better.

While there have been many studies on different aspects of the Chinese economy, there are comparatively few on the current conditions of the financial market, particularly on the specific status of major components of the inter-bank market. The purpose of this book is to provide readers with a detailed description and analysis of the current status of Chinese financial markets, products, liquidities, and potential problems.

The book is divided into four parts. Part I provides an introduction to the Chinese economy and financial markets, covering such aspects as the macroeconomy; the banking industry, and corresponding regulatory bodies; the capital market and corresponding regulatory bodies; and the foreign exchange system and China's international investment positions. Part II introduces the major components of China's inter-bank market; the foreign exchange forward, and swaps markets; the CNY bond forward and interest rate swaps markets; forward rate agreements; and wealth management and other OTC products.

Part III covers offshore CNY products, principally those being traded in the Hong Kong Special Administrative Region. These include CNY non-deliverable foreign exchange forwards, CNY non-deliverable options, non-deliverable foreign exchange swaps, and non-deliverable CNY interest rate swaps. It also introduces H-share stock index futures and CNY bonds in Hong Kong.

In Part IV, we explore CNY product innovation and market development in line with the increasing internationalization of the CNY in the coming decades. We analyze major international currencies and their major markets, and examine the current status of the internationalization process and the need for risk management. In the final chapter, we round things off by looking at the potential development trends for major CNY derivatives markets that will accompany the gradual internationalization of the CNY over the coming decade.

In April 2009, the Chinese State Council released an important set of guidelines to accelerate its stated intention to build Shanghai into an international financial center by 2020 in line with China's economic status. International participation and the internationalization of the CNY are necessary conditions if this aim is to be achieved. We strongly believe that the Chinese financial market, particularly the inter-bank market, will grow steadily so that its major components will occupy similar weights in the global inter-bank marketplace to the weight that the Chinese economy will occupy in the world economy in the coming decades.

We hope that this book can help readers understand the current status of the major Chinese inter-bank market and its future development. We wish to emphasize, however, that the views expressed are those of the authors alone, and not those of the institutions for whom they work.

Peter G. Zhang
with Thomas Chan
November 2010

Acknowledgments

We would like to thank those who have contributed much research work for the completion of this book, in particular, Luo Pengyu of Bank of China, Zhang Zhiqiang of Zendai Investment Management Company, Ms. Ge Chongyang of China Life Asset Management Co. Ltd., Ms. Song Xiaoling of Goldman Sachs International Bank, as well as Du Han, Huang Xindong, Liu Huai-yuan, Sun Yinho, and Xiao Lijuan of the Graduate School of the People's Bank of China. We would also like to thank partners and staff of KPMG China. KPMG Partners Nelson Fung and Terence Fong provided invaluable advice and comments, while Wayne Tsang, Tom Jenkins, Michael Hurle, Fiona Yan, Maggie Ji, Ian Xu, Ryan Ren, Allen Cui, Christina Yu, Teresa Shang, Coco Yang, Andrew Chen, Ada He, Ivor Cheung, Isabel Wu, and Chris Guo all assisted with the editing and translation of the book.

We hereby express our sincere gratitude for their contribution and professional work. At the same time, it is necessary to stress that all the views in this book are expressed in an academic context and do not represent the views of the units or corporations to which the above people belong.

PART One

The Chinese Economy and Financial Markets

As the wheel of history has turned, Chinese culture has expanded from the Yellow River valley to the seven seas. At every phase of history, China has had to face other people and their cultures. Numerous contacts and exchanges, whether positive or negative, have brought about changes in the cultures of China and its neighbors. [D]uring this process the "us" and "them" have merged into a new "us."

—From *A Long River of History* by Cho-Yun Hsu

One of the important lessons to emerge from the recent financial crisis is that the entire purpose of the financial industry is to serve its underlying economy. The dangers of allowing the financial industry to stray too far from the needs of its underlying economy have been all too evident over the past few years. With this as our starting point, we begin by introducing the underlying Chinese economy and its major financial markets before examining the major products in the Chinese inter-bank markets.

CHAPTER 1

The Chinese Economy

Since a country's economy involves many areas, a systematic and in-depth description and analysis of China's economy is beyond the scope of this book. In this chapter, we will focus on describing and analyzing the key aspects of the economy, including its tremendous achievements in the past 30 years and its current problems.

POPULATION AND HUMAN RESOURCES

Human resources are the most important components of economic development as people are the carriers of culture and genes, the subject of social production, practices and consumption, and the subject of succession, learning and innovation in thinking, science and technology. As long as there are people capable of embracing and learning from outstanding cultures created by peoples around the world, and with the courage to explore new territories, anything is possible.

Population Growth Since the Reform and Opening-up

In the 30 years following China's first census in 1953, the population grew from 594 million to more than a billion. Recognizing the potential problems associated with rapid population growth, in the early 1970s the Chinese government had begun to search for appropriate measures to control such growth. In December 1973, the State Council Leading Group Office of Family Planning proposed a policy of "late, rare and low" fertility. In September 1982, the Twelfth Central Committee of the Communist Party of China (CPC) confirmed "family planning" as a basic national policy. In the *Constitution of the People's Republic of China* passed by the National People's Congress (NPC) in December that year, the words "China shall carry out family planning and control population growth to tie in with economic and social development" were added. The family-planning policy, which has now been implemented for more than 20 years, has been a significant factor in controlling the growth of China's population.

Effectiveness of Family-planning Policy and Corresponding Problems

Practice has proved China's family-planning policy to be very successful. As shown in Figure 1.1, after 1980, the annual population growth rate was controlled within

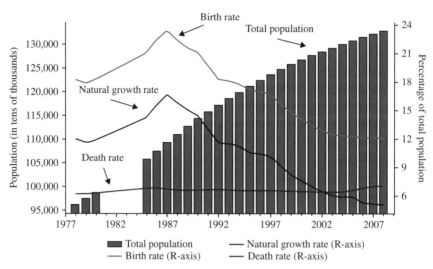

FIGURE 1.1 China's population and population growth rate, 1978–2008

2 percent and, since 1998, it has been within 1 percent, far below the growth rate experienced from the 1950s to the 1970s. However, the family-planning policy has also had many negative effects, the most serious of which is the ageing of the population. The fifth national census conducted at the end of November 2000 showed that the number of people aged 65 and above had reached 88.11 million, accounting for 6.96 percent of the population, and people aged over 60 had reached 130 million, 10.2 percent of the population. By international standards, China has become an ageing society. According to one commentator, "The speed of aging is faster than economic development in China, resulting in the phenomenon of 'getting old before getting rich.'"[1] A State Council white paper also reveals that, in the twenty-first century, the ageing of China's population is growing at an annual rate of about 3 percent.[2] By the end of 2005, there were some 144 million people over the age of 60, accounting for more than 11 percent of its population.[3]

The ageing of the population will have a profound impact on China's economy, requiring further improvement in the social security and healthcare systems. Economists term the positive role of changes in demographic structure as the "demographic dividend." An empirical study (Cai) shows that from 1982 to 2000, the demographic dividend contributed about 27 percent to China's economic growth. However, a research report published in late 2006 pointed out that demographic dividends would only contribute to China's economy for another five to 10 years.[4] After the "demographic dividend" phase, China will enter the "demographic burden" phase, many features of which have been seen in the Japanese economy since the 1990s.

Investment in Education

Since the reform and opening-up in 1978, China has made great achievements in education. In the early stages of the reform period, the government was aware of the problems in the education system during the late stage of the Cultural Revolution (1966–76). In 1977, universities introduced a unified national entrance examination for high school graduates and

TABLE 1.1 Annual enrolments of university students in China, 1991–2008

Year	Master's Students Enrolled	Master's Graduates	Undergraduate Students Enrolled (thousands)	Graduates (thousands)
1991	88,128	32,537	2,044	614
1992	94,164	25,692	2,184	604
1993	106,771	28,214	2,536	571
1994	127,935	28,047	2,799	637
1995	145,443	31,877	2,906	805
1996	163,322	39,652	3,021	839
1997	176,353	46,539	3,174	829
1998	198,885	47,077	3,409	830
1999	233,513	54,670	4,134	848
2000	301,239	58,767	5,561	950
2001	393,256	67,809	7,191	1,036
2002	500,980	80,841	9,034	1,337
2003	651,260	111,091	11,086	1,877
2004	820,000	151,000	13,335	2,391
2005	978,610	189,728	15,618	3,068
2006	896,615	219,655	17,388	3,774
2007	972,539	270,375	18,848	4,477
2008	1,046,429	301,066	20,210	5,119

Source: China Statistical Yearbook (1991–2009).

students who had missed the chance to go to university during the Cultural Revolution. At the same time, a large number of students and scholars were sent abroad to study in developed countries and regions.

In China's history, there have never been so many students admitted to such a wide range of vocational schools, colleges, universities and research institutes as there are now. As Table 1.1 shows, the number of college students at the end of 2008 was nearly 10 times the figure in 1991.

Though China's education system has developed rapidly since 1978, there is still a considerable gap in funding when measured against international standards. In 1999, the most recent year for which UNESCO statistics including China are available,[5] total public expenditure on education in China was 1.9 percent, compared to 4.5 percent for Germany and India, 5 percent for Thailand and 5.1 percent for the United States.

While China has undoubtedly made great strides in education in the past 30 years, many acute problems remain, including a lack of emphasis on vocational training. In addition, investment in human capital in different regions, especially the distribution between rural and urban areas in the same district, is uneven and inefficient. Local governments are the chief sources of education funding; however, the subsidies provided by many provinces are very low. Education penetration nationwide is uneven and expenditure per student varies greatly by region. The central government has recognized these problems and is expected to solve them gradually in the Twelfth Five-Year Plan from 2011 to 2016.

Section Summary

When Peter Zhang was sent to study in the United States in the late 1980s, he asked a Jewish-American friend whether he thought that Jewish people were smarter than others. He responded wittily that wisdom and beauty are distributed normally; thus there are handsome and intelligent individuals in every country. Based on this assumption of normal distribution, China, with the highest population base, should possess the world's largest reserve of human intelligence. This is why a large population is a valuable asset for China. For China's long-term economic and social development, it is vital that it develops, and uses, its intellectual resources, stimulates, creativity and explores, the potential of the entire community through establishing an education and training system that is more internationalized, innovative and in line with China's international economic status. The continued development of its economy requires the support of a certain level of labor force. Hence, it is necessary to maintain a certain level of population growth. Particularly with diminishing tangible resources per capita in the future, developing and using the nation's enormous human resources effectively for more efficient use of natural resources will become increasingly important and urgent.

FOREIGN DIRECT INVESTMENT

Since the reform and opening-up process began at the end of the 1970s, foreign direct investment (FDI) has played an important role in China's economic development. Since that time, China has gradually evolved from a closed, planned economic system to a market-oriented open economy with sustainable growth. As Table 1.2 shows, the amount of

TABLE 1.2 Foreign direct investment in China, 1981–2010 (US$ billion)

Year	FDI	Annual Growth Rate (%)	Year	FDI	Annual Growth Rate (%)
1981	0.2	100.0	1996	41.7	11.2
1982	0.4	100.0	1997	45.3	8.6
1983	0.6	50.0	1998	45.6	0.7
1984	1.3	116.7	1999	40.4	−11.4
1985	1.7	30.8	2000	40.8	1.0
1986	1.9	11.8	2001	47.0	15.2
1987	2.3	21.1	2002	52.7	12.2
1988	3.2	39.1	2003	53.5	1.4
1989	3.4	6.3	2004	60.6	13.3
1990	3.5	2.9	2005	72.4	19.4
1991	4.4	25.7	2006	69.5	−4.1
1992	11.0	150.0	2007	74.8	19.0
1993	27.5	150.0	2008	92.4	23.6
1994	33.8	22.9	2009	90.0	−2.6
1995	37.5	11.0	2010Q1*	23.4	7.7

*Rate for 2010Q1 is the annual growth rate of 2010Q1 compared to the same period in 2009.
Source: China Statistical Yearbook and the Ministry of Commerce website (www.mofcom.gov.cn).

FDI inflow to China over the period from 1981 to 2008 reached US$877.4 billion. It is clear from the table that the FDI inflow experienced several growth phases: one in the early years of reform between 1981 and 1984, growing at an annual rate of 100 percent; another from 1991 to 1993 when the reform deepened and the socialist market economic system was established. From 1998 to 2000, following the East Asian financial crisis, China recorded less than 1 percent in annual FDI growth rate or negative growth. In 2005, the annual FDI growth rate was close to 20 percent, the highest in 10 years, chiefly thanks to foreign investment in the financial sectors, such as banking, insurance and securities. According to the FDI data of the Ministry of Commerce in 2006, total foreign investment in the financial sector in 2005 stood at US$12.083 billion. In anticipation of an appreciation of the CNY, a significant amount of hot money flew into China in the form of FDI in 2007, resulting in an annual growth rate of nearly 20 percent. With the onset of the international financial crisis in 2008, capital flew out of China, resulting in lower FDI growth in 2008 and a 2.6 percent decline in 2009. However, FDI recorded 7.7 percent growth in the first quarter of 2010 compared to the same quarter of 2009.

INTERNATIONAL TRADE

The import and export markets have played an important role in China's economic growth in the past 30 years, especially over the most recent decade. This section introduces the development of China's foreign trade, and analyzes the impact of the import and export markets on China's employment, taxes, prices, international balance of payments and GDP.

China's Import and Export Markets

With huge FDI inflows and improved production and management capabilities, China's production capacity has been enhanced and increasingly internationalized, with foreign trade playing an ever more important role in the country's economic growth. Table 1.3 summarizes China's import and export data and the proportion of the total trade to GDP from 1979 to 2009.

Growth of Foreign Trade and Dependence on Trade

China's foreign trade in 1978 was a mere US$20.6 billion, and it took 10 years for the figure to exceed US$100 billion for the first time. Table 1.3 shows that it took only six years for this to double. In the three-year period from 1993–96, it rose from nearly US$200 billion to almost US$300 billion. Since joining the World Trade Organization (WTO) in 2001, the growth in China's foreign trade had accelerated noticeably to new levels almost every year until 2008. In 2009 total foreign trade recorded its first decline since 1999 because of the financial crisis, yet it returned to growth in the first quarter of 2010, with a quarterly growth rate as high as 44 percent in the first quarter of 2010 compared to Q1 2009.

The level of dependence on foreign trade (that is, the proportion of foreign trade to GDP) in 1978 was a mere 9.6 percent. In 1994, the ratio topped 40 percent for the first time. Following China's entry into the WTO, the dependence on foreign trade rose continuously to

TABLE 1.3　Foreign trade in China, 1979–2010 (US$ billion)

Year	Exports	Export Growth Rate (%)	Imports	Import Growth Rate (%)	Differential (%)	Total Trade	Trade Growth Rate (%)	Total Trade/GDP (%)
1979	13.7	40.1	15.7	44.0	−3.9	29.3	42.1	11.3
1980	18.3	33.7	19.6	24.7	9.1	37.8	28.9	14.3
1981	22.0	20.5	22.0	12.6	7.8	44.0	16.4	15.4
1982	22.3	1.4	19.3	−12.4	13.8	41.6	−5.5	14.8
1983	22.2	−0.4	21.4	10.9	−11.3	43.6	4.8	17.0
1984	26.1	17.6	27.4	28.1	−10.6	53.6	22.8	21.8
1985	27.4	4.6	42.3	54.1	−49.5	69.6	30.0	22.8
1986	30.9	13.1	42.9	1.5	11.6	73.9	6.1	25.0
1987	39.4	27.5	43.2	0.7	26.7	82.7	11.9	25.7
1988	47.5	20.5	55.3	27.9	−7.4	102.8	24.4	25.6
1989	52.5	10.6	59.1	7.0	3.6	111.7	8.7	24.8
1990	62.1	18.2	53.4	−9.8	28.0	115.4	3.4	29.7
1991	71.9	15.8	63.8	19.6	−3.8	135.7	17.6	33.3
1992	84.9	18.1	80.6	26.3	−8.2	165.5	22.0	34.2
1993	91.7	8.0	104	29.0	−21.0	195.7	18.2	32.6
1994	121.0	31.9	115.6	11.2	20.7	236.6	20.9	43.7
1995	148.8	22.9	132.1	14.2	8.7	280.9	18.7	40.8
1996	151.1	1.5	138.8	5.1	−3.6	289.9	3.2	36.1
1997	182.8	21.0	142.4	2.5	18.5	325.2	12.2	36.9
1998	183.7	0.5	140.2	−1.5	2.0	324	−0.4	34.8
1999	194.9	6.1	165.7	18.2	−12.0	360.6	11.3	37.0
2000	249.2	27.8	225.1	35.8	−8.0	474.3	31.5	44.5
2001	266.2	6.8	243.6	8.2	−1.4	509.8	7.5	44.1
2002	325.6	22.3	295.2	21.2	1.2	620.8	21.8	49.6
2003	438.4	34.6	412.8	39.8	−5.2	851.2	37.1	51.9
2004	593.4	35.4	561.4	36.0	−0.6	1,154.8	35.7	59.8
2005	762.0	28.4	660.1	17.6	10.8	1,422.1	23.2	63.1
2006	969.1	27.2	791.6	19.9	7.3	1,760.7	23.8	67.0
2007	1,218.00	25.7	955.8	20.7	4.9	2,173.8	23.5	64.2
2008	1,428.50	17.3	1133.1	18.4	−1.3	2,561.6	17.8	58.2
2009	1,201.66	−15.9	1005.6	−11.2	−4.7	2,207.3	−13.8	45.0
2010Q1*	316.10	28.7	301.6	64.6	35.9	617.7	44.0	52.3

*Rate for 2010Q1 is the annual growth rate of 2010Q1 compared to the same period in 2009.
Source: Data from 1979 to 2001 from the Foreign Trade and Economic Corporation (www.moftec.gov.cn/moftec.cn); other data from the Ministry of Commerce website (www.mofcom.gov.cn).

above 60 percent from 2005 to 2007, before falling to 58.2 percent in 2008 and below 50 percent for the first time since 2003 because of the financial crisis in 2009.

Table 1.3 shows the increasing impact of foreign trade on China's economy. From 1978 to 2008, China recorded an average annual growth rate of 17.9 percent in foreign trade, which was much higher than the corresponding GDP growth rate.

Table 1.4 shows the dependence of the G7 and the BRIC (Brazil, Russia, India and China) countries on foreign trade from 1997 to 2008. It is evident from this that in 2008

TABLE 1.4 Historical changes in major countries' dependence on foreign trade (%)

Year	1997	1998	1999	2000	2001	2002	2003	2004	2005	2006	2007	2008
Canada	65.1	68.1	69.3	71.9	68.1	65.3	59.6	60.0	60.2	58.3	56.3	65.5
US	19.1	18.6	18.9	20.8	18.8	18.1	18.5	20.1	21.2	22.4	23.1	24.2
France	41.2	42.6	44.0	50.0	48.6	45.2	43.8	44.8	45.1	45.7	45.1	49.0
Germany	44.3	46.4	47.4	55.0	55.9	54.6	55.4	59.1	62.6	69.1	71.8	79.5
Italy	37.7	38.1	37.9	43.5	43.0	41.0	39.5	41.0	42.6	46.1	47.0	51.6
Japan	17.8	17.3	16.6	18.4	18.4	19.2	20.2	22.1	24.4	28.1	30.4	30.5
UK	43.2	40.9	39.7	42.8	41.9	39.9	37.8	37.2	39.4	43.1	37.7	49.9
Brazil	13.3	13.3	17.0	17.7	21.1	21.8	22.4	24.6	22.2	21.5	21.5	24.2
India	18.7	18.6	18.8	20.3	19.8	21.4	22.9	26.4	30.9	33.8	32.8	38.1
Russia	40.0	49.0	58.8	57.8	50.8	48.8	49.1	47.4	48.3	47.3	44.7	62.1
China	34.1	31.8	33.3	39.6	38.5	42.7	51.9	59.8	63.6	66.2	64.3	52.2

Source: Trade of goods and services in selected regions and countries, the WTO.

Germany had the highest level of dependence on foreign trade (79.5 percent) followed by Canada (65.5 percent), Russia (62.1 percent), Italy (51.6 percent), the United Kingdom (49.9 percent), and France (49.0 percent). Surprisingly, Japan, the second-largest economy and the fourth-largest export country in 2008, registered only 30.5 percent, and the United States—the largest economy—24.2 percent. Meanwhile, China ranked first for dependence on foreign trade among the BRIC countries in 2007, yet her dependence declined 12.1 percent from 2007 to 2008, reflecting export declines in 2008.

China's Major Trading Partners

Table 1.5 shows China's top 10 trading partners in the first 10 months of 2008. The European Union was China's largest trading partner, accounting for 16.4 percent of China's total foreign trade volume in the period.

TABLE 1.5 China's top trading partners, January–October 2008 (US$ billion)

Ranking	Country (Region)	January–October	Year-on-year Increase (%)	Percentage of Total Trade (%)
1	EU	359.37	25.0	16.4
2	US	281.32	13.6	12.9
3	Japan	225.86	17.7	10.3
4	ASEAN	199.07	21.6	9.1
5	Hong Kong	172.44	8.7	7.9
6	Korea	162.33	25.4	7.4
7	Taiwan	114.79	13.8	5.2
8	Australia	51.00	45.7	2.3
9	Russia	47.96	21.8	2.2
10	India	45.52	49.5	2.1
	Total	2,188.67	24.4	100.0

Source: Ministry of Commerce website (www.mofcom.gov.cn).

TABLE 1.6 Leading exporting and importing countries, 2008 and 2009 (US$ billion)

Country	2008 Export	2009 Export (January–August)	2008 Import	2009 Import (January–August)	2008 Trade	2009 Trade (January–August)
Germany	1,466.1	705.3	1,204.2	602.7	2,670.3	1,307.9
US	1,299.9	669.1	2,164.8	993.3	3,464.7	1,662.4
China	1,428.6	730.9	1,133.1	607.4	2,561.6	1,338.2
Japan	781.4	410.3	762.5	400.3	1,543.9	810.6
France	594.9	304.1	695.5	351.3	1,290.4	655.3
Italy	539.6	259.6	553.2	263.2	1,092.8	522.8
UK	459.3	221.7	636.0	304.5	1,095.3	526.3
Canada	455.7	202.1	408.3	206.6	864.0	408.6

Source: 2008 data from the WTO website, and 2009 data from China Economic Statistics Data Base.

China's Positions in World Trade

According to WTO statistics (www.wto.org), China's export volume jumped from third to second place in 2008, accounting for 8.9 percent of the total world export volume, just 0.2 percent lower than Germany's; China's import volume reached third place in 2008, accounting for 6.9 percent of the total world import volume, 0.4 percent lower than Germany's 7.3 percent. On January 11, 2010 the *Washington Post* reported that China had surpassed Germany as the world's top exporter in 2009 with exports to the value of US$1.20 trillion, slightly higher than Germany's US$1.17 trillion. Also in 2009, the total value of China's imports, at US$1.01 trillion, made China the world's second-largest importing country, second only to the US. If we subtract the export and import contributions of foreign enterprises in China, China's positions in world exports and imports would be substantially lower than those given above.

Table 1.6 gives the export and import data of the top eight trading countries in 2008 and 2009. It shows that China became the largest exporter in the first eight months of 2009, from second position in 2008, and the second-largest importer in the first eight months of 2009, from third in 2008. China's position with respect to the total value of its foreign trade moved up from third place in 2008 to second in the first eight months of 2009.

Impact of Foreign Trade on Employment, Taxes, Prices and International Balance of Payments

Foreign trade has a significant impact on China's economy. In the following paragraphs, we will briefly analyze the specific impact of foreign trade—especially exports—on employment, taxes, prices and international balance of payments, by using the methodology adopted by the National Bureau of Statistics of China (NBS)[6] and, based on this methodology, provide updates on the book's results.

Impact of Foreign Trade on Employment Empirical results show that imports and exports directly stimulated the employment rate to grow by 9.1 percent from 1978 to 2002, making a contribution of 10.8 percent. More specifically, exports directly created 370 million job opportunities, while imports cut 335 million. Without taking technical factors into consideration, overall, imports and exports stimulated the growth of employment by 70.8 percent, making a contribution of 84.6 percent in the period. Meanwhile, imports and exports saved labor input by 26 percent, offsetting the contribution by 31.1 percent. As a result, overall, imports and exports stimulated the growth of employment by 44.8 percent, making a contribution of 53.6 percent.

Impact of Foreign Trade on Prices   Empirical studies have shown that there is no relationship between the export prices of commodities and the consumer price index (CPI), the retail price index (RPI) and the production price index (PPI) in China. Whilst there obviously is some relationship between commodity export prices and the domestic prices of investment goods, the impact is insignificant. Provided that all other conditions remain constant, a 1 percent increase in imports will cause the domestic CPI and RPI to fall by 0.306 percent and 0.339 percent respectively.

Impact of Foreign Trade on the International Balance of Payments   Empirical studies have also shown that China's foreign trade is a decisive factor in causing variations in the current account given that its balance mainly depends on trade balance. Between 1978 and 1994, the proportion of trade balance to the balance of the current account was below 100 percent when both recorded favorable balances. However, from 1997 to 2002, the proportion rose to 155.3 percent on average, indicating the significant impact of the trade balance on the balance of the current account. From 2003 to 2006, the proportion fell sharply to approximately 30 percent on average. This is in effect related to the transfer of foreign capital into China through the current account by both domestic and foreign enterprises aiming to profit from the continuous appreciation of the CNY since 2003. The relationship between domestic and overseas CNY products amid the appreciation pressure on the CNY will be discussed further later.

There is a causal relationship between imports and exports and the capital account. The two affect each other directly or indirectly through direct investment and foreign exchange rates. Empirical studies show that changes in the amount of direct investment by foreign enterprises trigger changes in net exports, rather than the other way round. Regressive analysis of the data for the period between 1982 and 2003 shows a negative relationship between direct investment and the net exports of the current period, indicating that a substantial part of direct investment was spent on importing the required equipment and raw materials. A positive relationship between the previous period's direct investment and the current period's net exports indicates the strong export orientation of foreign enterprises. An increase in investment by foreign enterprises can fuel the growth of exports.

Impact of Foreign Trade on Tax Revenue   Studies show that the tax revenue directly related to imports, including import linkage tax and tax on exported goods, was CNY335.5 billion (US$40.6 billion) in 2002, accounting for 19 percent of the total tax revenue for that year. From 1999 to 2002, an increase of export value by CNY1 increased the total tax revenue by CNY0.4–0.5.

Impact of Foreign Trade on Domestic Productivity and GDP   Empirical studies show that from 1978 to 2003, an increase in exports by one unit increased the related period's imports by 0.617 units, investment by 0.539 units, consumption by 0.128 units, and GDP by 1.050 units ($0.539 + 0.128 + 1.000 - 0.617 = 1.050$). Incidentally, if we take into account the weakening impact of imports on domestic consumption, the export multiplier will be 0.667. An increase in the import of industrial products by 1 percent fueled GDP growth by 0.14 percent. This gives a correlation of approximately 46 percent between foreign trade and productivity.

FOREIGN EXCHANGE RESERVES AND FOREIGN DEBT

Foreign exchange reserves have accumulated along with the steady growth of imports and exports. While soaring foreign exchange reserves reflect China's enhanced national power to some extent, it is considered to be a major cause of increasing appreciation pressure on the CNY.

Changes in China's Foreign Exchange Reserves

China had little by way of foreign exchange reserves in the early stage of the reform and opening-up process. However, the reserves boomed from US$167 million at the end of 1978 to over US$10 billion by the end of 1990, to more than US$100 billion at the end of 1996 and over US$1 trillion at the end of 2006. The total foreign reserves reached US$2.273 trillion in the third quarter of 2009. Table 1.7 shows the growth of China's foreign exchange reserves from 1978 to 2009.

As the table shows, with the exception of 1992 China's foreign exchange reserves continued to increase every year from 1987 to 2009. Foreign exchange reserves grew very slowly from 1977 to 1986 as China recorded six annual declines compared to just three instances of year-on-year growth in the nine-year period. However, China's foreign exchange reserves grew

TABLE 1.7 China's foreign exchange reserves, 1978–2009 (US$ billion)

Year	Amount	Growth Rate (%)	Year	Amount	Growth Rate (%)
1978	0.17	−82.50	1994	51.62	143.50
1979	0.84	403.00	1995	73.60	42.60
1980	−1.30	−254.30	1996	105.05	42.70
1981	2.71	−309.00	1997	139.89	33.20
1982	6.99	158.10	1998	144.96	3.60
1983	8.90	27.40	1999	154.68	6.70
1984	8.22	−7.70	2000	165.57	7.00
1985	2.64	−67.80	2001	212.17	28.10
1986	2.07	−21.60	2002	286.41	35.00
1987	2.92	41.10	2003	403.25	40.80
1988	3.37	15.40	2004	609.93	51.30
1989	5.55	64.60	2005	818.87	34.30
1990	11.09	99.90	2006	1,066.34	30.20
1991	21.71	95.70	2007	1,528.25	43.32
1992	19.44	−10.50	2008	1,946.03	27.34
1993	21.20	9.00	2009	2,399.15	23.28

Source: 1978 to 1999 data from the State Administration of Foreign Exchange website (www.safe.gov.cn); 2000 to 2007 data from the People's Bank of China website (www.pbc.gov.cn).

significantly from 1993 to 1997, with an average annual growth rate of 98.6 percent. The years 1996 and 2001 are considered milestones in that the reserves surpassed US$100 billion and US$200 billion respectively. From 2000 to 2009, China saw steady growth, with an average annual growth rate of 34.6 percent, and at the end of February 2006, it surpassed Japan to become the largest holder of foreign exchange reserves in the world. At the end of 2009, these amounted to US$2.399 trillion. At the end of March 2010, total foreign reserves reached US$2.447 trillion. The overwhelming increase in the reserves has become a major cause of the pressure for the CNY to appreciate, which is now a key issue for China's work in the areas of macroeconomic control and financial market regulation. This issue will be discussed further in later chapters.

Foreign Debt as a Proportion of Foreign exchange Reserves

Table 1.8 shows the balance of China's foreign debt and its proportion to the foreign exchange reserves from 1985 to 2009. It is evident that in 1986 and 1987, foreign debt was more than 10 times the total foreign exchange reserve at the year end. In the 11 years between 1985 and 1996, the proportion of foreign debt remained at more than 100 percent of the reserve. Despite the continuous growth in foreign debt, its proportion to the reserve fell significantly from 1999 onward, sliding to below 50 percent for the first time in 2003, and 24.45 percent and 19.3 percent at the end of 2007 and 2008, respectively.

The level of a nation's foreign exchange reserves is, to some extent, a reflection of its power; though a high level of reserves is not always desirable. In fact, excessive reserves will not only induce the appreciation of the domestic currency but also raise the problem of how

TABLE 1.8 Foreign debt, foreign exchange reserves and the proportion of foreign debt to foreign reserves, 1985–2009 (US$ billion)

Year	Foreign Debt	Foreign Exchange Reserves	Foreign Debt/ Foreign Exchange Reserves (%)	Year	Foreign Debt	Foreign Exchange Reserves	Foreign Debt/ Foreign Exchange Reserves (%)
1985	15.83	2.64	598.7	1998	146.04	144.96	100.7
1986	21.48	2.07	1,036.7	1999	151.83	154.68	98.2
1987	30.2	2.92	1,033.2	2000	145.73	165.57	88
1988	40	3.37	1,186.2	2001	170.11	212.17	80.2
1989	41.3	5.55	744.1	2002	171.36	286.41	59.8
1990	52.55	11.09	473.7	2003	193.63	403.25	48
1991	60.56	21.71	278.9	2004	228.6	609.93	37.5
1992	69.32	19.44	356.5	2005	281.05	818.87	34.3
1993	83.57	21.2	394.2	2006	322.99	1,066.34	30.3
1994	92.81	51.62	179.8	2007	373.62	1,528.25	24.4
1995	106.59	73.6	144.8	2008	374.66	1,946.03	19.3
1996	116.28	105.05	110.7	2009	428.65	2,399.15	17.9
1997	130.96	139.89	93.6				

Source: 1978–2002 and 2005–07 data from the State Administration of Foreign Exchange website (www.safe.gov.cn); 2003–04 data from the Ministry of Commerce website (www.mofcom.gov.cn); 2009 data from State Administration of Foreign Exchange data released on April 6, 2010.

to use the reserve effectively. Empirical studies (Zhang 2008, for example) show that the demand from other parts of the world for the CNY to be appreciated is basically the result of China's ever-increasing foreign exchange reserves. In the face of such demands, China has had to come up with a feasible approach to using the reserves effectively. The seriousness of the issue was reflected in the fact that it was made an important agenda item for the third round of the National Financial Work Conference ending in January 2006. In September of the following year, China Investment Co., Ltd. was established, an indication that China was taking action.

GDP AND GDP PER CAPITA

China has made remarkable progress in economic development and construction, not least in the contribution made to the economy by the growth in GDP, both overall and per capita, as shown in Table 1.9.

From the data in Table 1.9, we can conclude that during the 30 years from 1978 to 2009, the average annual growth rates of real GDP and nominal GDP were 9.82 percent and 16.29 percent respectively. A growth rate above 9.8 percent for 30 years is rare, not only in Chinese history but in the economic history of the world. If Japan's 9.71 percent average annual growth rate of real GDP over the 15 years of post-war reconstruction from 1955 to 1970 is regarded as remarkable, then China's 30-year growth may be seen as miraculous.

China's economic development since the reform and opening-up process began has been tremendous, particularly since 1992, when the CPC Central Committee determined that "the goal of China's economic system reform is to establish a socialist market economic system." From 1992 to 1996, for example, GDP grew by more than 10 percent annually. This performance was matched by another five-year period of annual growth above 10 percent from 2003 to 2007. In 1986, China's GDP exceeded CNY1 trillion and it took just another 16 years for this to balloon to more than CNY10 trillion. In 2006, China's GDP surpassed CNY20 trillion, and in 2008 exceeded CNY31 trillion.

Comparisons with Other Major Economies

As shown in Table 1.10, IMF data for 2009 reveal that China's GDP amounted to US$4.4 trillion, accounting for 7.3 percent of the world total and thus narrowing the gap with the US, Japanese and Eurozone economies. In fact, if we were to use the Chinese National Bureau of Statistics figures for 2008, Chinese GDP would be about US$120 billion higher than the US$4,402 billion shown in Table 1.10, and the Chinese share of world GDP would be about 7.4 percent.

China's Contribution to the World Economy

From the IMF data for 2006 to 2008, we can calculate that China contributed 11.92 percent and 17.42 percent to global economic growth in 2007 and 2008, respectively, as compared to the corresponding US contributions of 10.35 percent and 7.82 percent. Although the GDP of the United States was more than three times that of China in 2008, China surpassed the United States in its contribution to global economic growth since the combination of its

TABLE 1.9 China's GDP and annual growth rate, 1978–2009

Year	GDP (CNY billion)	Real Growth Rate (%)	Per capita GDP (CNY)	GDP (US$ billion)	Per capita GDP (US$)
1978	362.4	11.7	376	229.8	239
1979	403.8	7.6	417	269.9	279
1980	451.8	7.8	458	295.2	299
1981	486.2	5.2	489	278.6	280
1982	529.5	9.1	525	275.4	273
1983	593.5	10.9	580	299.6	293
1984	717.1	15.2	692	256.5	248
1985	896.4	13.5	847	305.3	288
1986	1,020.2	8.8	956	295.5	277
1987	1,196.3	11.6	1,104	321.4	297
1988	1,492.8	11.3	1,355	401.1	364
1989	1,690.9	4.1	1,500	449.1	398
1990	1,854.8	3.8	1,622	387.4	339
1991	2,161.8	9.2	1,867	406.1	351
1992	2,663.8	14.2	2,273	483.1	412
1993	3,463.4	14.0	2,922	601.1	507
1994	4,675.9	13.1	3,901	542.5	453
1995	5,847.8	10.9	4,828	700.3	578
1996	6,788.5	10.0	5,547	816.5	667
1997	7,446.3	9.3	6,023	898.2	727
1998	7,834.5	7.8	6,280	946.3	758
1999	8,206.8	7.6	6,524	991.4	788
2000	8,946.8	8.4	7,059	1,080.7	853
2001	9,731.5	8.3	7,625	1,175.7	921
2002	10,517.2	9.1	8,188	1,270.7	989
2003	11,739.0	10.	9,084	1,418.3	1,098
2004	13,687.6	10.1	10,530	1,653.7	1,272
2005	18,386.8	10.4	14,061	2,229.5	1,705
2006	20,940.7	10.7	15,931	2,668.1	2,030
2007	25,730.6	13.0	19,474	3,382.4	2,560
2008	30,067.0	9.6	23,648	4,520.0	3,404
2009	33,535.3	8.7	25,127	4,909.0	3,678

Source: GDP data in CNY from National Bureau of Statistics of China, per capita GDP in CNY calculated using the GDP data and population data from National Bureau of Statistics of China; 2009 per capita data are calculated according to the average CNY/US$ exchange rate and population data; US data from the IMF database.

nominal GDP growth and CNY appreciation exceeded the nominal GDP growth of the United States.

Per capita GDP

Although China has seen rapid and sustained GDP growth in the past 30 years, its GDP per capita still remains rather low. Table 1.9 showed that in 1978 China's per capita GDP was only CNY379 (US$239). The figure exceeded CNY1,000 for the first time in 1987 and, by

TABLE 1.10 GDP of major economies and their respective shares of world total, 1995-2009 (US$ billion)

Year	World	Eurozone		US		Japan		China	
1995	29,621	7,279	24.6%	7,398	25.0%	5,278	17.8%	728	2.50%
1996	30,336	7,359	24.3%	7,817	25.8%	4,638	15.3%	856	2.80%
1997	30,221	6,726	22.3%	8,304	27.5%	4,264	14.1%	953	3.20%
1998	29,951	6,902	23.0%	8,747	29.2%	3,872	12.9%	1,020	3.40%
1999	31,085	6,872	22.1%	9,268	29.8%	4,384	14.1%	1,083	3.50%
2000	31,942	6,264	19.6%	9,817	30.7%	4,669	14.6%	1,199	3.80%
2001	31,707	6,337	20.0%	10,128	31.9%	4,098	12.9%	1,325	4.20%
2002	32,988	6,917	21.0%	10,470	31.7%	3,925	11.9%	1,454	4.40%
2003	37,087	8,531	23.0%	10,961	29.6%	4,235	11.4%	1,641	4.40%
2004	41,728	9,766	23.4%	11,686	28.0%	4,608	11.0%	1,932	4.60%
2005	45,090	10,151	22.5%	12,422	27.5%	4,561	10.1%	2,236	5.00%
2006	48,761	10,734	22.0%	13,178	27.0%	4,364	8.9%	2,658	5.50%
2007	54,841	12,312	22.4%	13,808	25.2%	4,384	8.0%	3,383	6.20%
2008	60,690	13,633	22.5%	14,265	23.5%	4,924	8.1%	4,402	7.30%
2009	57,937	16,447	28.4%	14,256	24.6%	5,059	8.7%	4,909	8.50%

Source: IMF database.

2004, had surpassed CNY10,000 (US$1,208). In 2008, the figure had reached CNY23,648 (US$3,405). During the 30 years from 1978 to 2008, average per capita GDP growth was 15.35 percent annually, less than 1 percent lower than the nominal GDP growth rate of 16.29 percent. In October 2007, the Sixteenth CPC Central Committee set the strategic target to "double GDP per capita of 2000 by 2020." As Table 1.9 showed, however, it accomplished this with ease, some 12 years ahead of schedule.

In 2003, China's per capita GDP reached US$1,000 for the first time and it took only three years more to double that. In 2008, the figure exceeded US$3,300. During the 30 years from 1978, China's per capita GDP calculated in US dollars grew 9.50 percent (the average annual growth rate would be 9.67 percent if the newly adjusted GDP data are used) annually on average, far lower than the rate calculated in CNY.

Even though China's per capita GDP was undoubtedly rising, it was still low by global standards. For instance, the figure of US$2,560 for 2007 was little more than a third of the global level of US$7,377. Based on our model, China's per capita GDP is expected to reach US$4,000 in 2010, which will be around half of the world level. Table 1.11 provides a comparison of China's per capita GDP figures with those of the members of the Organization for Economic Cooperation and Development (OECD) for 2006 and 2007.

The table shows that China's per capita GDP in 2007 was less than 10 percent of those of the G7, and less than a quarter of those of developing countries such as Hungary, Poland, and Slovakia. There is a tough road ahead if China is to bridge the gap with the more-developed economies and to redress the imbalances within its own borders. While coastal areas in China are booming and prospering rapidly, the vast central and western regions lag behind.

Contribution of Foreign Enterprises to China's GDP

It is evident from the previous analysis of foreign investment and foreign trade that the two factors were extremely important in China's reform and opening-up process. In

TABLE 1.11 A per capita GDP comparison (US$)

Country	2006 Per capita GDP	%	2007 Per capita GDP	%
Canada	38,388	5.29	37,970	7.30
Mexico	7,749	26.22	13,149	21.08
US	44,138	4.60	46,098	6.01
Australia	37,290	5.50	34,090	8.13
Japan	33,960	6.00	34,749	7.98
Korea	18,310	11.10	24,838	11.16
New Zealand	25,215	8.10	24,332	11.39
Austria	38,787	5.20	36,353	7.63
Belgium	37,333	5.40	35,575	7.79
Czech Republic	13,767	14.80	22,575	12.28
Denmark	51,224	4.00	36,139	7.67
Finland	39,781	5.10	35,139	7.89
France	36,450	5.60	32,857	8.44
Germany	35,275	5.80	34,977	7.93
Greece	27,722	7.30	27,612	10.04
Hungary	11,314	18.00	16,839	16.46
Iceland	55,263	3.70	32,857	8.44
Ireland	52,876	3.80	38,299	7.24
Italy	31,267	6.50	30,220	9.17
Luxembourg	81,154	2.50	66,590	4.16
Netherlands	40,097	5.10	40,278	6.88
Norway	71,336	2.90	53,861	5.15
Poland	8,889	22.90	15,493	17.89
Portugal	18,395	11.00	21,904	12.66
Slovakia	10,179	20.00	19,523	14.20
Spain	26,901	7.60	30,819	8.99
Sweden	42,300	4.80	37,323	7.43
Switzerland	50,634	4.00	43,825	6.33
UK	38,761	5.20	35,842	7.73
China	2,032	—	2,772	—

Source: OECD website (www.oecd.org).

recent years, foreign enterprises have accounted for nearly 60 percent of the foreign trade and more than half of net exports, indicating their substantial contribution to China's GDP growth. Unfortunately, given the lack of reliable statistics, an accurate estimate of this contribution is difficult to make. Based on the NBS's results for the period 1978–2003, foreign trade accounted for 66.7 percent of GDP growth. Multiplying this by their 60 percent share of exports means that foreign enterprises can be said to have contributed about 40 percent to the GDP growth in the period. Given that the contribution of exports to the GDP growth continued to climb up from 2004 to 2007, the contribution of foreign investment to the GDP growth may well have exceeded 40 percent in that period.

Contribution of the Service Sector

The service sector is of great importance to a nation's economy, for it not only meets people's basic needs and offers enormous job opportunities, but also stimulates the primary and secondary industries by providing various services. China's service sector has been the focus of rapid restructuring and development since the 1990s in China's bid to accelerate economic development. In 2003, the State Council conducted a comprehensive nationwide census to help formulate development plans and policies for the service sector and publish reliable basic data, details of which became available in December 2005. Amongst other things, the results of the first national economic census revealed that more than 150 million people were employed in the service sector. Table 1.12 shows the steadily increasing share made to GDP by the service sector and its key components from 1978 to 2007.

TABLE 1.12 Service-sector output and contribution to GDP, 1978–2007 (CNY100 million)

Year	GDP	Tertiary-industry GDP	Percentage
1978	3,645.22	872.48	23.9
1979	4,062.58	878.89	21.6
1980	4,545.62	982.03	21.6
1981	4,891.56	1,076.60	22.0
1982	5,323.35	1,162.95	21.8
1983	5,962.65	1,338.06	22.4
1984	7,208.05	1,786.26	24.8
1985	9,016.04	2,585.04	28.7
1986	10,275.18	2,993.79	29.1
1987	12,058.62	3,573.97	29.6
1988	15,042.82	4,590.26	30.5
1989	16,992.32	5,448.40	32.1
1990	18,667.82	5,888.42	31.5
1991	21,781.50	7,337.10	33.7
1992	26,923.48	9,357.38	34.8
1993	35,334.00	11,915.73	33.7
1994	48,198.00	16,179.76	33.6
1995	60,794.00	19,978.46	32.9
1996	71,177.00	23,326.24	32.8
1997	78,973.00	26,988.15	34.2
1998	84,402.00	30,580.47	36.2
1999	89,677.00	33,873.44	37.8
2000	99,215.00	38,713.95	39.0
2001	109,655.00	44,361.61	40.5
2002	120,333.00	49,898.90	41.5
2003	135,823.00	56,004.73	41.2
2004	159,878.30	64,561.29	40.4
2005	183,217.40	73,432.87	40.1
2006	211,923.50	84,721.40	40.0
2007	257,306.00	103,880.00	40.4

Source: National Bureau of Statistics website (www.stats.gov.cn). Statistics for 2008 are not yet available.

Compared to countries with a similar per capita income, the service sector's share of China's GDP is very low.[7] In the early 1960s, the economic structure of major developed countries tended to shift from industry-based to service-based. Nowadays, the added value in the global service industry accounts for more than 60 percent of the world's GDP; the figure exceeds 70 percent in developed countries and stands at 43 percent in lower middle-income countries. Thus, the Chinese service sector's share of GDP is lower than lower middle-income economies and the global average.

ENORMOUS CONSUMPTION POTENTIAL

Insufficient Consumption

Analysis of consumption as a percentage of GDP clearly highlights China's problem of insufficient consumption. Figure 1.2 sets out the proportion of consumption and investment in China's economy from 1978 to 2008. It is clear from this that although the share of consumption in GDP increased slightly from 1995 to 2000, it has maintained a general declining trend since 1981 (peaking at 67.1 percent), slipping as low as 48.59 percent in 2007. By contrast, the percentage of investment in GDP grew from 35 percent to 44 percent.

Positive Consumption Policy

A positive consumer policy is one which rebates a percentage of the consumption amount to consumers in order to stimulate consumption and boost domestic demand. The rebate ratio is the core of a positive consumption policy; the higher the ratio, the higher the consumption enthusiasm.

It is never easy to stimulate consumption, as the experience of Japan in the past decade and more has shown. Traditionally, governments stimulate consumption by reducing tax rates to raise the levels of disposable income. However, such an approach has limited effect

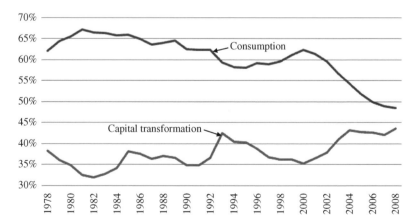

FIGURE 1.2   Consumption and capital formation trends, 1978–2008
Source: National Bureau of Statistics of China website (www.stats.gov.cn).

in China since most people pay very little individual income tax, and the tax levy on the high-income group is not strictly enforced. It is therefore difficult to stimulate consumption without offering special incentives, and more than CNY10 trillion of the net balance between deposits and loans will remain idle. For consumption rebates, the government undertakes to rebate a percentage of consumption, say 10 or 15 percent, on certain types of consumption on verification of presented receipts. For example, to develop the level of access to information technology in China, the government could introduce a 15 percent rebate on computer prices, equivalent to a 15 percent discount to consumers, which would provide an immense boost to computer sales. Such a policy would have a wide range of benefits compared to discounts.

Of course, the higher the proportion of rebates, the greater the stimulatory effect on the economy and the greater the burden on the government. In contrast, a small percentage rebate may not arouse the interest of consumers, and thus has little stimulus effect. An appropriate rebate should be determined based on the forecast increase in the overall tax revenue resulting from the increased consumption; that is, the rebate should correspond with the increased tax revenue. The implementation of this policy should create a benign economic cycle as a whole. In addition to higher tax revenue, an increase in income for enterprises will raise employment, thus reducing the government's costs in promoting employment. Therefore, to obtain the maximum stimulatory effect, the rebate ratio can be increased to take into account the social costs of employment.

Rebates form the core of a positive consumption policy, which can take many forms and generate different results. The most direct form is for the government to provide consumers with cash rebates, but this is not realistic and puts the government under financial pressure. It can also take the form of rebating cash from the tax revenues at the year end, but this is again not the best way. We believe the best method is to rebate the agreed amount to consumers' social security accounts. Consumers can withdraw the sum in the form of a pension after retirement. This will serve to both stimulate consumption and strengthen the social security system. A detailed discussion is beyond the scope of this book and readers interested in the policy and its related mathematical model may wish to refer to Zhang (2003a).

Urgent Need for a Positive Consumption Policy

China's economy maintained a five-year continuous high growth rate of 10 percent from 2003 to 2007. From the exchange rate reform in July 2005 to the end of 2008, the CNY appreciated 21.1 percent against the US dollar. China's exports maintained an annual growth rate of nearly 30 percent in 2005 and 2006, and the trade surplus for these two years soared 218 percent and 74 percent year-on-year, respectively.

The sub-prime crisis has caused the real estate market in the United States to slow down, and the country's economic growth fell significantly in 2007 and 2008. The global economic downturn has greatly affected China's exports. Amid a decline in the macro efficiency of investment and the global economic downturn, there is an urgent need to take more vigorous stimulus measures; that is, to create a positive consumption policy to stimulate consumption and maintain steady economic growth.

A positive consumption policy can stimulate consumption, but the most important foundation and premise for stimulating consumption is to improve the three factors that constrain consumption; namely, the social security system, the medical system and the education system. Without effective improvement in these three areas, no policy can stimulate consumption in China effectively.

PROBLEMS IN CHINA'S ECONOMIC DEVELOPMENT

China's GDP surged nearly 82-fold from 1978 to 2008, at an average annual growth rate of 9.86 percent. Over this period, per capita GDP also showed a 12-fold increase, from US$240 to US$3,314, at an average annual growth rate of 9.17 percent. Sustained economic growth has appreciably enhanced China's overall standing in the world. However, there remain many profound problems which, if not resolved promptly and effectively, may cause China's economy to struggle to maintain sustained, healthy, and harmonious growth for a period of time. While a systematic discussion of these issues is beyond the scope of this book, the following provides a brief outline of some of these problems.

Trade Surpluses, Foreign exchange Reserves, and Pressure on the CNY

The continued expansion of imports and exports has brought sustained growth in China's trade surplus, which in turn has led to excess liquidity and rapid growth in foreign exchange reserves. All of this has put pressure on the Chinese government to appreciate the CNY. At the same time, the growth in net exports has led to biased growth in domestic investment, resulting in rapid economic growth and further increased pressure on the currency. This has now become the most acute problem in China's financial system and macroeconomy. The analysis of Yu Xuejun (2007) indicates that net exports and exchange rates are the root causes of China's macroeconomic problems. Using data presented earlier in the chapter, Table 1.13 compares China's foreign exchange and net export figures from 1996 to the first quarter of 2010.

The table shows that, from 1999 to 2004, the growth in foreign exchange reserves was significantly higher than the corresponding increase in net exports; however, from 2005 to 2007, increments in the foreign exchange reserves lagged behind the corresponding increases in net exports. Net exports continued to decline from 1999 to 2001, seeing no significant change from 1997 to 2004. However, net exports soared nearly 218 percent, to US$102 billion, in 2005 from US$32.09 billion in 2004, with a further growth of 74 percent from 2005 to 2006. There was no significant change in the growth of foreign investment from 2001 to 2006, thus there was no dramatic change in the capacity of the import and export of foreign enterprises, which accounted for about 60 percent of China's imports and exports. As a result, an average annual growth rate of more than 100 percent for net exports from 2004 to 2007 was a clear indication of the seriousness of the net export problems (Wang 2006; Yu 2007; Li and Ma 2007).

The contribution of China's net exports to growth in the foreign exchange reserves rose from a mere 15.5 percent in 2004 to more than 70 percent in 2006 and 2008, indicating that the trade surplus was the chief reason for the growth in foreign exchange reserves in recent years. Net exports, through exchange, directly contributed to excess liquidity and rapid growth in the foreign exchange reserves, leading to frequent trade frictions and increased pressure on the CNY. With a systematic analysis of the changes in China's trade surplus and

TABLE 1.13 Comparative performance of China's foreign exchange reserves and net exports, 1996–2010 (US$ billion)

Year	Balance of Foreign Exchange Reserves	Changes of Foreign Exchange Reserves	Net Exports	Annual Rate of Increase of Net Exports (%)	Foreign Direct Investment	Difference Between Increase in Foreign Exchange Reserves and Net Exports Plus Foreign Investment	Share of Net Exports to Increase in Foreign Exchange Reserve Changes (%)
1996	105.05	31.453	12.22	−26.8	54.80	−35.57	38.9
1997	139.89	34.84	40.42	230.8	64.41	−69.99	116.0
1998	144.96	5.07	43.47	7.5	58.56	−96.96	857.4
1999	154.68	9.72	29.23	−32.8	52.66	−72.17	300.7
2000	165.57	10.89	24.11	−17.5	59.36	−72.58	221.4
2001	212.17	46.60	22.55	−6.5	49.67	−25.62	48.4
2002	286.41	74.24	30.43	34.9	55.01	−11.20	41.0
2003	403.25	116.84	25.47	−16.3	53.51	37.86	21.8
2004	609.93	206.68	32.09	26	60.63	113.96	15.5
2005	818.87	208.94	102.0	217.9	72.41	34.53	48.8
2006	1,066.34	247.47	177.47	74.0	69.47	0.53	71.7
2007	1,528.25	461.91	262.2	47.7	74.77	124.94	56.8
2008	1,946.03	417.78	297.25	13.4	92.40	28.13	71.1
2009	2,399.15	453.12	196.07	−34.0	90.00	167.05	43.3
2010Q1	2,447.08	47.93	14.53	−76.7	23.40	10.00	30.3

Source: Calculated using the data from Tables 1.5 and 1.9.

the major items in the international balance of payments since 1996, we detected an outflow of capital from 1997 to 2001 arising from the impact of the East Asian financial crisis and resulting in the net exports exceeding the growth of foreign exchange reserves in this period. However, each year from late 2002 to 2007, with the pressure on the CNY (which will be discussed and analyzed in detail in Chapter 12), China saw a significant increase in the influx of international speculative money.

Energy Consumption

With sustained economic growth, energy consumption has become an increasingly important factor. According to customs statistics, in 2004 China imported a total of 120 million tons of crude oil (up 34.8 percent, the largest increase in four years) with an import value of US$33.91 billion—an increase of 71.4 percent. This made China the world's second-largest importer of crude oil after the United States. The growth rate of crude-oil imports in recent years has outstripped China's GDP growth rate. While the surge in demand indicates the rapid growth of the Chinese economy, it also suggests that China is inefficient in using oil compared with other countries. China's GDP was less than half that of Japan, but its oil consumption far surpassed Japan's in 2004 and 2005.

Based on 2009 data from the OECD and the International Energy Agency (IEA), we calculated the consumption of oil for the generation of every unit of GDP by different countries in 2006 and the corresponding proportion for China (as shown in Table 1.14).

TABLE 1.14 Energy consumption in major countries at the end of 2006 (tons per unit GDP)

US	0.21	Canada	0.32
Japan	0.10	India	0.80
Germany	0.17	Mexico	0.27
UK	0.14	Russia	1.81
France	0.19	Brazil	0.29
Italy	0.16	China	0.90
Spain	0.20		

Source: Statistics of OECD and IEA 2009.

As the table shows, China's consumption of 0.90 tons of standard oil to generate US$1,000 of GDP (given constant prices in 2000) was lower only than Russia's. Japan, as the most energy-efficient country, consumed just one-ninth of China's figure.

The Chinese government has long recognized that there is enormous room for improvement in its energy efficiency. In June 2005, for example, Premier Wen Jiabao presided over a national conference on the subject of building a conservation-minded society. Shortly before this, the State Council had approved the National Development and Reform Commission document *Regarding the Recent Key Work of Building a Conservation-Minded Society*; and the CPC Central Committee considered "How to establish a resource-saving economic system and society." Nevertheless, it will take some time for the construction of a resource-saving society in China.

Serious Environmental Pollution

Accompanying China's sustained economic growth, environmental pollution is becoming an increasingly serious problem. According to the *Statistical Yearbook 2009* of the NBS, China's industrial wastewater emissions reached 24.6 billion tons in 2007; sewage emissions 31 billion tons; and industrial gaseous waste emissions 38.9 trillion cubic meters. In addition, pollution involving hazardous waste, industrial solid waste, smoke and dust emissions is very serious. Although the measures taken by the government in recent years have shown some positive results, they have not proved overly effective as yet. Enhancing environmental awareness and strengthening environmental protection is the foundation and prerequisite for sustainable economic development and for ensuring people's health.

Capacity for Independent Innovation

According to the Ministry of Science and Technology, China's total expenditure on research and development (R&D) for 2007 placed it fourth after the United States, Japan, and Germany. As Figure 1.3 indicates, its expenditure amounted to only 14.2 percent of that of the United States. As a proportion of GDP, China's R&D expenditure lags a long way behind developed countries, equaling only 43.9 percent of Japan's, which ranked first.

The absolute value of R&D personnel in China reached 1.73 million man-years in 2007, ranking first in the world. However, China ranked lowest in terms of the number of R&D personnel per 10,000 labor force (see Figure 1.4).

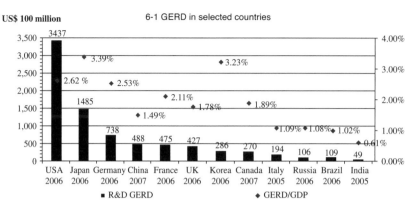

FIGURE 1.3 International comparisons of gross expenditure on R&D (GERD)
Source: MOST; Main Science and Technology Indicators 2008/1(OECD) RICYT; UNESCO.

These data show that China employs a large number of R&D personnel, but that it has yet to catch up with other countries to become a power in science and technology.

Differences in Income Distribution

A fair income distribution is of great help in improving people's material living conditions, and unequal distribution usually leads to conflict. The inequality of income distribution in China has become more marked in recent years, with the Gini coefficient close to, or even higher than, than in some developed countries. Internationally, the Gini coefficient is generally used to determine the extent of equality in income distribution. The Gini coefficient varies from 0 to 1, with a value below 0.2 representing perfect equality; between 0.2 and 0.3 representing relative equality; between 0.3 and 0.4 representing reasonable distribution; between 0.4 and 0.5 representing relative inequality; and above 0.5 representing absolute

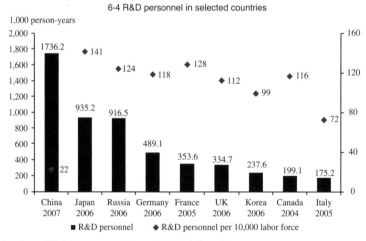

FIGURE 1.4 Number of R&D personnel per 10,000 labor force
Source: MOST; Main Science and Technology Indicators 2008/1(OECD).

inequality. At the beginning of the reform and opening-up period, the distribution of income in China was more equal, with the Gini coefficient at 0.330 in 1980. Since the 1990s, the trend towards inequality has worsened, with the Gini coefficient rising to 0.496 in 2006. An income gap is the inevitable outcome of a market economy, since equal income distribution is detrimental to the enthusiasm of market participants. On the other hand, a large disparity in income distribution is harmful to social stability and inconsistent with the objectives of harmonious social development; therefore, it has to be reversed.

Lack of Brands

China has exported processed goods for a long time but it still lacks internationally recognized brands. Brand names represent image and quality, which could bring higher added value. Brand-building is very important in establishing an international image and global "brand value." In the absence of internationally recognized brands, China's exports can only compete at the low-end, low value-added and labor-intensive level. Japan focused on establishing international brands long before the rapid development of its economy. Brands like Sony, Toshiba, Mitsubishi, and Toyota became world-renowned and consumers around the world soon stopped looking down on goods labeled "Made in Japan." Brand-building has to go through a process. A major exporter is not a real major exporter without high-technology and brand names.

Many other important issues relating to the Chinese economy are worth exploring, but are beyond the scope of this book. We are pleased that in the report of the Seventeenth CPC Central Committee issued in October 2007, President Hu Jintao presented a comprehensive and systematic exposition on the problems of China's economy and society, providing specific guiding ideology for addressing these issues in a way that will enable China's economy to take further strides towards establishing a sustainable, harmonious and stable future.

More recently, at the annual economic meeting in December 2009, the central government gave further recognition to the problems outlined above and will take more concrete measures to tackle these issues in 2010 and beyond. We look forward to seeing improved economic performance with higher efficiency in the coming years.

DEVELOPMENT FORECASTS

The problems described above that can affect or hinder the sustainability of China's economic development can be summarized as follows:

- controlling foreign exchange capital inflows to gradually improve the CNY exchange rate formation mechanism
- constraining the growth of the foreign exchange reserves and improving the utilization of foreign currency assets
- improving the utilization of energy, water, and other raw materials
- enhancing the capability of independent innovation
- increasing the income of farmers and other low-income earners to reduce income disparities
- improving the social security, medical, and education systems to stimulate consumption.

If these problems are resolved promptly and effectively, China's economy will maintain a relatively high growth rate over the next decade, and a growth rate higher than the global level over the next two decades or even longer.

International Forecasts for the Chinese Economy

In October 2003, Jim O'Neill, Managing Director and Head of Global Economic Research of Goldman Sachs, forecast that within 40 years, the GDP of the BRIC countries was likely to exceed that of the G6 (the United States, Japan, Germany, France, Italy, and the United Kingdom). By 2041, he said the global economic pattern would have changed drastically, with China likely to be the world's largest economic power. In May 2006, when Jim O'Neill visited China again, he revised his original projections as being too conservative. Based on more recent developments, he predicted Brazil, Russia, India and China would become established among the six major economic powers much earlier than he had forecast in 2003. China was likely to surpass the United States and become the world's largest economy by 2032.[8]

Goldman Sachs's study of the BRIC countries was based on a specific economic model and has received a lot of attention worldwide. We should point out that any model is built on a number of assumptions, and the accuracy of these projections depends largely on the time taken to solve China's economic problems, as well as the development of the world economy over the next few decades.

Potential and Development Conditions

It wasn't until the early twentieth century that the developed countries began to publish GDP statistics, making it difficult to find data and comparative figures from earlier periods. However, Professor Angus Maddison's well-known book *The World Economy: A Millennial Perspective* (2001) provides good estimates for GDP, population, and per capita GDP in major countries and regions from year one to 1998. This study revealed some interesting statistics regarding China's economic status from past eras. For example, in 1600 (during the reign of Emperor Wanli of the Ming Dynasty), China's GDP accounted for 29.1 percent of the world total. But, as a result of the internal and external turmoil in the late Ming Dynasty and the change of power in late seventeenth century, this fell to 22.3 percent by 1700. By 1820 (the twenty-fifth year of the reign of Emperor Jiaqing of the Qing Dynasty), China's population accounted for 36.6 percent of the world total, with its 32.9 percent share of world GDP, making it the world's largest economy. By 1870, China's share of GDP had dropped to 17.2 percent and continued to do so, to the point where, by 1913, it was just 8.9 percent. By contrast, the Reformation and the Renaissance in Europe laid the ideological groundwork for the Industrial Revolution, which delivered unrivalled economic and military power into the hands of Europe and the United States. Consequently, Western Europe's share of global GDP rose from 8.7 percent in 1000, to 23.6 percent in 1820 and then to 33.6 percent in 1870.

As we saw from Tables 1.9 and 1.10, China's real adjusted GDP growth rate of 8.7 percent gave it a GDP figure of more than US$4.91 trillion in 2009, which was very close to that of Japan (US$5.06 trillion). Given the fact that the Chinese economy grew at 11.9 percent in the first quarter of 2010, the annual GDP growth rate should be around 10 percent in 2010. Japanese GDP is expected to grow a few percent for the same year, and China is almost certain to become the world's second-largest economy in 2010. Nevertheless, China's per capita GDP would be just over 10 percent that of Japan's in 2010, and energy efficiency, technology innovation, and other measures would still be much lower in China than the corresponding measures in Japan. Therefore, there is still a long way for China to go even after becoming the world's second-largest economy.

By 2020, China's share of GDP is expected to account for about 15 percent of the world total. Besides the efficiency of the macro factors discussed above, the most important condition for economic growth is innovation in science and technology, mechanisms and systems, and culture and ideas. The level of science and technology is a chief indicator of how developed a country is; the efficiency of mechanisms and systems is a major condition that ensures a country's economy reaches a world-class level; an innovative culture and ideas are the forces that drive a country to maintain this level. Whether China can reclaim its status as the world's largest economy depends on the speed, intensity, and extent of innovation in these three areas. To achieve this goal, it needs to draw on the experience of other countries in these areas and, by building on existing achievements, restructure and refine these ideas.

CONCLUSION

By 2008, after 30 years of reform and opening-up, China's real economy had grown more than 80-fold, at an average annual rate of over 9.86 percent. Its per capita GDP had increased more than 10-fold and its global economic status had improved significantly. Despite these widely recognized achievements, its per capita GDP was little more than a quarter of the world's average level. There is still a long way to go in the journey to build an affluent society.

The vast human resources and intellectual reserves of China's large population need to be exploited through effective education and vocational training. Having such resources will enable China to seek out and assimilate the latest materials and cultural knowledge to assist in its innovation and progress. A large population also gives huge potential for consumption. By gradually improving the social security, medical, and education systems, as well as taking appropriate and effective measures to stimulate consumption to offset the adverse impact of the slowing international market, China can ensure sustained, efficient, harmonious and sound economic growth.

Since its entry into the WTO in 2001, China's dependence on foreign trade has increased sharply, surpassing the majority of developed and developing countries in 2007. While it maintained an annual growth rate of over 9.8 percent from 1978 to 2008, this achievement was not always reflected in its international competitiveness ranking, which fell from thirty-third in 2002 to forty-ninth in 2005.[9] By 2007, it had improved its position to thirty-fourth among the 131 economies surveyed,[10] but there was still a considerable disparity with its overall GDP ranking. The chief reason for this, according to one commentator was that "China is still subject to a variety of institutional defects and many challenges, such as the lack of modern pension systems, adequate unemployment insurance and other social security nets." What China needs, the analyst said, is "to strengthen its economic system pillars, improve the quality of its education system and better serve the public with improved public health services. China is facing severe challenges in education, which is crucial to the development of a country's innovative potential."[11] To maintain sustainable economic growth, ongoing efforts and improvements in many areas are required.

Over the next 20 years, China's GDP is expected to rise to 20 percent of the world total. Establishing a sound market mechanism will help achieve this. Only through adjusting and refining its policies on science and technology, and redesigning and regulating the entire financial and economic system, can it expect to achieve a balance in its foreign trade and capital accounts.

As the ratio of China's per capita GDP to the world average increases, the nation's international status will gradually rise and the international competitive environment will undergo a series of significant changes. This chapter gives only a brief introduction and analysis of the key aspects of China's economy; many other important areas worth exploring are beyond the scope of this book. In the following chapters, we will introduce China's banking sector, capital market, and foreign exchange market.

ENDNOTES

1. *Characteristics and Problems of China as an Ageing Society, and Countermeasures*, Zhu Qingfang: Chinese Sociology website.
2. Development of China's Undertakings for the Aged.
3. *Financial Times*, December 23, 2006: 1.
4. "Demographic Dividends Drive Asset Prices," by Dr Jiming Ha *et al.*, China International Capital Co. Ltd., December 27, 2006.
5. Data Centre, UNESCO Institute for Statistics.
6. "Empirical Analysis on Influence of Foreign Trade on China's Economy," National Bureau of Statistics of China, 2005.
7. See the *Blue Book of Finance and Economy 2007—IFTE Report Series on Service Industry in China, No.5 – Reform and Renovation of Chinese Service Industry*, 2007.
8. "'BRICs' grow at 'ultra-high-speed'," *Reference News*, August 9, 2007: 9.
9. See *The Global Competitiveness Report 2005–2006*, released by the World Economic Forum on September 28, 2005.
10. See *The Global Competitiveness Report 2007–2008*, released by the World Economic Forum on October 31, 2007.
11. "Why Has China's Ranking Declined to 49th in *The Global Competitiveness Report 2005–2006*?", Zhongguang.net, October 12, 2005.

CHAPTER 2

China's Banking System

China's financial system is, like the systems of Japan and Germany, dominated by banks, with bank loans accounting for more than 75 percent of total corporate financing. As at the end of the first quarter 2010, the total assets of banking financial institutions in both local and foreign currencies topped CNY84.3 trillion (US$12 trillion), more than double the gross domestic product of 2010. The Chinese banking industry has performed better than that of most other countries and regions during the financial crisis because of clear improvements in management, risk management, and supervision that have taken place in the past few years. However, in previous decades, China's banking industry shouldered a heavy historical burden; it suffered from a high level of strategic non-performing loans (NPLs) and was less competitive than its counterparts in developed countries. Since China's reform and opening-up, its banking industry has accelerated its own reform, enjoying declining NPL ratios and increasing profitability. Currently, four out of the five state-owned banks have completed their restructuring and are listed on the stock exchange. Joint stock commercial banks have also reformed their shareholding systems, and rural credit cooperatives and city commercial banks have also begun fast-track reforms.

REGULATORY BODIES

The regulatory agencies which oversee China's banking system include the People's Bank of China (PBC) and the China Banking Regulatory Commission (CBRC).

The People's Bank of China

The PBC was established on December 1, 1948 with the consolidation of the Huabei Bank, the Beihai Bank and the Xibei Farmers' Bank. With the gradual liberation of the country, the PBC took over all the assets of banks and other financial institutions.

In 1953, the PBC merged all Chinese banking institutions and bank assets, and became the only bank in China. At that time, the PBC provided loans to agriculture, industry, and commerce departments, taking up the functions of retail and wholesale banking as well as acting as the central bank.

Since 1978, as a part of China's gradual market-oriented reform program, the function and status of the PBC and the corresponding bank management system have changed. The PBC has undertaken drastic reforms, resulting in changes to China's entire financial system.

In February 1979, the Agricultural Bank of China (ABC) was re-established and took over all of the PBC's savings and credit operations in rural areas. In March 1979, the Bank of China (BOC) was separated from the PBC and ran the foreign exchange businesses independently. The People's Construction Bank of China, which changed its name to China Construction Bank (CCB) in 1996, was also separated from the Ministry of Finance in the same year to take part in a pilot scheme to replace investment funding in the construction sector with loans.

A major change in China's financial system took place in 1983. In September that year, the State Council assigned the functions of the central bank to the PBC. In January 1984, the Industrial and Commercial Bank of China (ICBC) was established to take up all of the PBC's industrial and commercial loan business as well as its urban deposit business. The PBC thus became the specialized central bank.

In 1998, the China Insurance Regulatory Commission (CIRC) was formally established and took over the PBC's function as insurance regulator.

In March 2003, the State Council established the CBRC in a move to separate monetary policy from banking supervision, transferring regulatory functions from the PBC to the CBRC.

These new changes further strengthened the crucial role of the PBC as China's central bank in implementing financial macro-control, maintaining currency stability, promoting sustainable economic growth and guarding against systemic financial risks.

The China Banking Regulatory Commission

The CBRC is responsible for supervising and managing banks, financial asset management companies, investment trust companies and other deposit-taking financial institutions to safeguard the legitimate and stable operation of the banking industry. The CBRC has formally performed its duties since April 28, 2003.

The regulatory objectives of the CBRC are:

> . . . *protecting the interests of depositors and consumers through prudent and effective supervision; maintaining market confidence through prudent and effective supervision; enhancing public knowledge of modern banking financial products and services and identifying corresponding risks through publicity, education and information disclosure; and making efforts to combat banking financial crimes and to maintain financial stability.*

Since its establishment, the CBRC has recorded some remarkable achievements. Through the enactment of the *Administration of Capital Adequacy Ratios of Commercial Banks*, the CBRC has set a new precedent for further regulation designed to ensure that banks have reliable profit-reporting mechanisms and maintain a designated capital-adequacy ratio. In this way, the CBRC has urged banks to enhance the accuracy of loan classifications, to increase loss provisions, to intensify efforts to verify debts, to improve the authenticity of profits, and to implement plans to meet capital-adequacy requirements. Strengthened capital regulation addresses both symptoms and root causes. At the heart of the CBRC's regulatory efforts is the need to improve corporate governance and internal control mechanisms, which have lifted the legal supervisory system to a new level.

FINANCIAL INSTITUTIONS IN CHINA

Type and Quantity

Financial institutions can be divided into banks and non-bank financial institutions. Table 2.1 sets out the number of each type of corporate financial institution and their employees as at the end of 2008. From the beginning of the first quarter of 2007, the CBRC has counted the Bank of Communications as a large-sized bank, rather than a joint stock bank.

As at the end of 2008, of the total of 5,634 financial institutions, 88.13 percent were rural credit cooperatives. Of these, 464 were banks, of which nearly 60 percent were rural banks. (These figures do not include group finance companies, trust companies, financial leasing companies and other non-bank financial institutions.) The five major state-owned banks between them employed almost 55 percent of the total number of people working in banking institutions. China has fully opened its banking sector to the outside world since December 2006. The business scale of foreign banks has expanded rapidly such that at the end of 2008 the 32 foreign corporate financial institutions had an average annual growth rate of 28.96 percent and employed almost 28,000 people. These figures are expected to increase.

Asset Allocation

Table 2.2 shows the distribution of assets and liabilities of China's leading banking financial institutions. As at the end of 2008, the total assets of banking financial institutions had risen

TABLE 2.1 A breakdown of China's financial institutions, 2008

Type of Institution	Number of Employees	Number of Corporate Financial Institutions
Policy banks	56,483	3
Large commercial banks	1,483,250	5
Joint stock commercial banks	167,827	12
City commercial banks	150,920	136
Urban credit cooperatives	7,080	22
Rural credit cooperatives	583,767	4,965
Rural commercial banks	38,526	22
Rural cooperative banks	63,770	163
Town banks	1,629	91
Loan companies	45	6
Rural credit union funds	52	10
Enterprise group finance companies	4,879	84
Trust companies	4,916	54
Financial leasing companies	552	12
Automotive finance companies	1,539	9
Currency brokerage firms	144	3
Postal savings banks	116,759	1
Asset management companies	8,907	4
Foreign financial institutions	27,812	32
Total	2,718,857	5,634

Source: China Banking Regulatory Commission Annual Report (2008); CBRC website (www.cbrc.gov.cn).

TABLE 2.2   Assets and liabilities of China's major financial institutions, 2008

	Assets			Liabilities		
Type of Institution	Amount (CNY trillion)	Growth (%)	Proportion of Industry Total (%)	Amount (CNY trillion)	Growth (%)	Proportion of Industry Total (%)
Policy banks	5.65	31.96	9.05	5.26	34.30	8.98
Large commercial banks	31.84	13.67	51.03	29.88	13.03	50.99
Joint stock commercial banks	8.81	21.52	14.12	8.37	21.09	14.28
City commercial banks	4.13	23.69	6.62	3.87	22.62	6.60
Rural commercial banks	0.93	52.39	1.49	0.88	51.84	1.49
Rural cooperative banks	1.00	55.32	1.61	0.94	55.06	1.60
Urban credit cooperatives	0.08	−38.73	0.13	0.08	−39.33	0.13
Rural credit cooperatives	5.21	19.98	8.35	4.99	20.03	8.51
Non-bank financial institutions	1.18	21.46	1.89	0.95	19.23	1.62
Postal savings banks	2.22	25.30	3.55	2.19	24.90	3.74
Foreign banks	1.34	7.37	2.16	1.20	5.95	2.05
Total	62.39	18.61	100.00	58.60	18.23	100.00

Source: China Banking Regulatory Commission Annual Report (2008); CBRC website (www.cbrc.gov.cn).

by 18.61 percent over the previous year, while their liabilities went up 18.23 percent. The combined assets and liabilities of the five large commercial banks accounted for 51.03 percent and 50.99 percent of the respective totals. However, a year-on-year decline in this proportion indicates a downward trend in the concentration of the banking industry. Foreign banks accounted for just 2.16 percent and 2.05 percent of the totals.

TABLE 2.3   Net profit of major financial institutions in China, 2007 and 2008

	2007		2008	
Type of Institutions	Amount (CNY billion)	Share of Total (%)	Amount (CNY billion)	Share of Total (%)
Policy banks	48.93	10.95	22.98	3.94
Large commercial banks	246.60	55.20	354.22	60.72
Joint stock commercial banks	56.44	12.63	84.14	14.42
City commercial banks	24.81	5.55	40.79	6.99
Rural commercial banks	4.28	0.96	7.32	1.25
Rural cooperative banks	5.45	1.22	10.36	1.78
Urban credit cooperatives	0.77	0.17	0.62	0.11
Rural credit cooperatives	19.34	4.33	21.91	3.76
Non-bank financial institutions	33.38	7.47	28.45	4.88
Postal savings banks	0.65	0.15	0.65	0.11
Foreign banks	6.08	1.36	11.92	2.04
Total	446.73	100.00	583.36	100.00

Source: CBRC Annual Report (2008) and website (www.cbrc.gov.cn).

Profitability

Table 2.3 shows the net profit of major financial institutions in China in 2007 and 2008. In 2008, the after-tax profit of the top five commercial banks surged by almost 44 percent over the previous year and accounted for almost 80 percent of the total after-tax profit of the banking financial institutions. The fact that, in 2008, 32 foreign banks achieved a combined after-tax profit 15 percent higher than that of the 163 cooperative banks in rural areas indicates that China's rural banks are small-scale and have low profit margins.

COMMERCIAL BANKS

Overview of the Banking Sector
The Sector's Significant Status Figure 2.1 shows the amount of bank loans, including loans made by non-financial institutions, as a proportion of total financing, from the fourth quarter of 2002 to the first quarter of 2009. From this it is clear that bank lending is the primary source of corporate finance. Although China's capital market developed well in 2007 and the total financing amount reached CNY653.2 billion, the stock market only provided 13.11 percent of the amount. Bank loans accounted for as much as 83.11 percent of the total in 2008. In view of the recession in 2009, China has actively invested in fixed assets such as infrastructure projects to stimulate economic growth. The total bank loans for the first quarter of 2009 amounted to CNY4,523.5 billion, accounting for 90.73 percent of the total in 2008. This shows that the banking sector occupies a position of absolute dominance in China's financial markets, and that this status is likely to be maintained for some time to come.

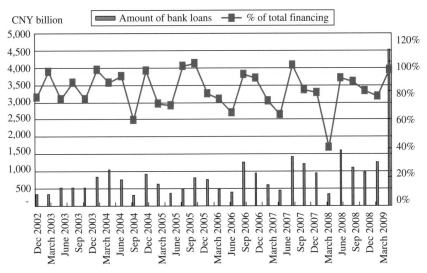

FIGURE 2.1 Amount of bank loans and their contribution to total financing
Source: Essence Securities.

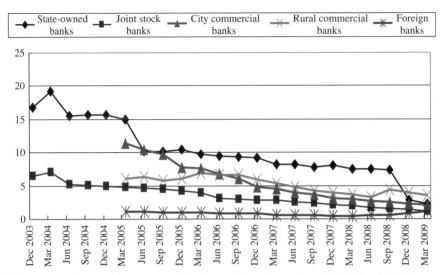

FIGURE 2.2 Non-performing loan ratios of banks in China, December 2003–March 2009
Source: Essence Securities.

Asset Quality

Figure 2.2 shows the NPLs of various types of banks in China from December 2003 to March 2009. The chart shows that, before shareholding reform, the overall NPL ratio of state-owned banks was high, peaking at nearly 20 percent. After the completion of shareholding reform, the NPL ratio has steadily declined year-by-year as corporate governance and profitability have improved. As at March 2009, the NPL ratio of state-owned banks stood at 2.3 percent. The NPL ratio of rural commercial banks, which had yet to achieve the desired results in corporate governance, was higher. The NPL ratio of joint stock commercial banks dropped steadily and has been maintained at a relatively low level of 1.5 percent. The loan quality of foreign banks was generally higher than that of Chinese banks thanks to their flexible control mechanisms and better risk management.

Policy Banks

The China Development Bank (CDB) was established under the State Council in March 1994. Currently, it has 34 branches and two representative offices. Its main role is to support the development of infrastructure, basic industries, and pillar industries, and to promote the coordinated growth of regional economies. In December 2008, the CDB received approval from the State Council to restructure itself into the China Development Bank Corporation, with a registered capital of CNY300 billion (US$44.8 billion) injected by the Ministry of Finance and the Central Huijin Investment Co., Ltd., with respective shareholdings of 51.3 percent and 48.7 percent. The China Development Bank Corporation will be fully regulated as a commercial bank with a capital restraint mechanism established. Its capital-adequacy ratio is 11.3 percent.

Headquartered in Beijing, the Export–Import Bank of China was established in 1994 under the leadership of the State Council. Currently, there are more than 10 domestic

TABLE 2.4 Key financial indicators of three policy banks, 2008

	China Development Bank	Export–Import Bank of China	Agricultural Development Bank of China
Total assets (CNY billion)	2,894.70	566.73	1,354.65
Equity	349.40	9.47	22.69
Operating income	74.41	23.37	34.89
Net profit	29.60	0.20	0.63
Loans	2,272.00	451.24	1,206.90
NPL ratio (%)	0.64	1.52	3.80

Source: China Development Bank Annual Report (2007), *Export–Import Bank of China Annual Report* (2008) and *Agricultural Development Bank of China Annual Report* (2008).

branches and representative offices, and overseas representative offices in Eastern and Southern Africa, Paris and St. Petersburg. It has established agency relationships with more than 300 banks. The Export–Import Bank of China is an important force in supporting trade, and a key component of the financial system. It is the chief policy financing channel for the import and export of machinery and electronic products, complete sets of equipment and high-tech products, foreign-contracted projects, and all kinds of overseas investment. It is the major on-lending bank of foreign government loans and is the loan provider of the Chinese government's preferential loans to foreign companies. It plays an increasingly important role in promoting the development of an open economy in China.

The Agricultural Development Bank of China was founded in November 1994 under the leadership of the State Council, with registered capital of CNY20 billion (US$2.4 billion). It has 30 provincial branches, 330 second-tier branches and more than 1,800 sub-branches at the county level. Its primary responsibilities are to raise funds using the state's credit rating; to undertake agricultural policy credit businesses as specified by the government; and to serve as an agent for the state treasury to allocate special funds to support agriculture in accordance with state laws, regulations and policies. In this way, it promotes the development of China's agriculture and rural economy.

The key financial indicators of the three policy banks are set out in Table 2.4.

Large Commercial Banks

The ICBC, the ABC, the BOC, the China Construction Bank (CCB) and the Bank of Communications (BOCOM) are the five key components of China's banking system. With the exception of the ABC, all have become listed companies, improving their corporate governance and significantly enhancing their competitiveness. According to the 2008 global bank rankings by *The Banker* magazine in the United Kingdom, the total assets and tier-1 capital of the ICBC were ranked nineteenth and eighth, respectively; those of the ABC were twenty-seventh and seventy-first; those of the BOC were ranked twenty-eighth and tenth respectively; the CCB's were ranked twenty-third and thirteenth respectively; while BOCOM was ranked sixty-sixth and fifty-fourth respectively in these categories.

Since the reform process began, the five previously state-owned banks have made a substantial contribution to the country's sustained economic growth and, with their dominant role in China's banking system, remain the backbone of its financing system. As at April 2009, collectively they accounted for 58 percent of private deposits and 44 percent of total loans.

In June 2004, BOCOM completed its divestiture of non-performing assets, received capital injections from the government and completed financial restructuring for its share reform. In August that year, The Hong Kong and Shanghai Banking Corporation Limited (HSBC) invested a total of CNY14.461 billion (around US$1.747 billion) for a 19.9-percent stake in the bank, making it BOCOM's second-largest shareholder. In June 2005, BOCOM became the first of its domestic counterparts to be successfully listed in Hong Kong. When it listed its A-shares on the Shanghai Stock Exchange in May 2007, they closed more than 70 percent higher than the issue price.

National Joint Stock Commercial Banks

In addition to the five large commercial banks, a number of joint stock commercial banks and city commercial banks thrive in China. Table 2.5 shows the performance and global rankings of China's major joint stock commercial banks and city commercial banks in 2007. Thanks to the flexibility of their share structure and their ability to raise additional capital, these joint stock banks have developed rapidly in recent years. As at April 2009, the assets of 14 national joint stock commercial banks accounted for 17.50 percent of the total financial assets of the banking sector.

Foreign Banks

The reform process of China's banking sector from 1980 to 2006 and the opening up of the banking industry to foreign institutions can be divided into three phases.

TABLE 2.5 Overview of China's Top Ten major joint stock and city commercial banks, 2007

Bank	Ranking of Tier-1 Capital	Ranking of Total Assets	Total Assets (US$ million)	Pre-tax Profits (US$ million)	Return on Total Assets (%)	Capital-adequacy Ratio (%)	NPL Ratio (%)
China Merchants Bank	99	90	179,415	2,881	1.61	10.67	2
China CITIC Bank	138	109	138,438	1,799	1.30	15.27	1
China Minsheng Bank	131	118	125,920	1,261	10.10	10.70	1
Shanghai Pudong Development Bank	176	119	125,261	1,473	1.18	9.15	1
Industrial Bank	147	124	116,548	1,494	1.28	11.90	1
China Everbright Bank	195	134	101,220	1,148	1.13	7.20	5
Huaxia Bank	313	156	81,091	523	0.64	8.27	3
Guangdong Development Bank	272	185	59,897	683	1.14	7.10	4
Bank of Beijing	178	207	48,493	—	—	20.10	2
Shenzhen Development Bank	312	209	48,263	516	1.07	5.60	6

Source: The Bank magazine, 2008.

Phase 1 In 1980, the Export–Import Bank of Japan became the first foreign bank to open a representative office in Beijing. In 1981, Nanyang Commercial Bank (from Hong Kong) was the first foreign bank to set up an operating establishment in Shenzhen following the reforms. In 1983, China promulgated the *Procedures for the Administration of Resident Representative Offices in China Established by Overseas Chinese and Foreign Financial Institutions*. Two years later, it promulgated the *Regulations Governing Foreign Banks and Joint Chinese-Foreign Banks in Special Economic Zones of the People's Republic of China*, allowing foreign banks to establish operations in Shenzhen, Zhuhai, Xiamen, Shantou, and Hainan. In August 1990, China promulgated the *Procedures for the Administration of Foreign Financial Institutions and Joint Chinese-Foreign Financial Institutions in Shanghai*.

Phase 2 In 1994, China promulgated the first comprehensive set of regulations for foreign banks, the *Regulations of the People's Republic of China Governing Foreign Financial Institutions*, which prescribed the market access conditions and regulatory standards for foreign banks wishing to operate there. In 1996, the *Provisional Rules Governing the Conduct of Pilot CNY Business by Foreign Financial Institutions in Pudong, Shanghai*, enabled foreign banks to conduct pilot CNY business targeting foreign enterprises and foreign residents in Pudong. In March 1998, the *Notice on Relevant Issues Concerning Approval for Participation by Foreign Banks in the National Inter-Bank Market* allowed foreign banks to participate in the national inter-bank market and to engage in CNY inter-bank lending and borrowing, as well as spot bond transactions. In August 1998, Shenzhen became the second pilot city to allow foreign banks to conduct CNY business. In July 1999, the *Notice on the Expansion of CNY Business Scope for Foreign Banks in Shanghai and Shenzhen* loosened the geographical restrictions on the customers of CNY business and the scope of CNY business of foreign banks, allowing them to borrow CNY funds with maturities of more than one year in the inter-bank market.

Phase 3 In December 2001, China joined the World Trade Organization and abolished some geographic and customer restrictions, enabling foreign banks to provide foreign exchange services to Chinese enterprises and Chinese residents. CNY businesses in Shanghai, Shenzhen, Tianjin, and Dalian were opened to foreign banks. In January 2002, revised *Rules for Implementing the Regulations of the People's Republic of China Governing Foreign Financial Institutions* were issued, and in December the following year, the *Procedures for the Administration of Equity Investment of Overseas Financial Institutions in Chinese Financial Institutions* prescribed the eligibility conditions and shareholding ratios of foreign investors for investment in Chinese banks. In November 2006, China promulgated the *Regulations of the People's Republic of China Governing Foreign Banks* and the *Rules for Implementing the Regulations of the People's Republic of China Governing Foreign Banks* and followed that up by scrapping the geographic and customer restrictions on foreign banks, allowing them to provide CNY business-related services to all customers. Any non-prudential restrictions on foreign banks' operations in China were also removed.

After the full liberalization of the banking industry, foreign banks have developed rapidly in China. As at the end of 2009, 193 banks from 46 countries and regions had set up 228 representative offices in China; banks from 13 countries and regions had set up 34 fully foreign-funded banks, two joint venture banks and one fully foreign-funded finance company; another 71 foreign banks from 24 countries and regions had set up 95 branches in China. As at the end of 2008, 58 branches of foreign banks and 27 foreign corporate banks were allowed to conduct CNY business and 51 foreign banking institutions were allowed to engage in trading financial derivatives.

As at the end of 2009, the total assets of foreign financial institutions in China stood at CNY1.35 trillion (US$195.5 billion); the total loan balance was at CNY723.6 billion (US$105.9 billion); the total deposit balance was at CNY733.6 billion (US$107.4 billion); the liquidity ratio was at 58.8 percent and the NPL ratio at 0.85 percent. Foreign corporate banks had a capital-adequacy ratio of 17.75 percent and a core capital-adequacy ratio of 17.23 percent on average.

Non-bank Financial Institutions

Currently, there are five major types of non-bank financial institution in China: trust investment companies, enterprise group finance companies, financial leasing companies, auto-financing companies, and currency brokers. By the end of 2009, there were 175 non-bank financial institutions in China with total assets of CNY1.55 trillion (US$227 billion), including 57 trust investment companies with total assets of CNY112.7 billion (US$16.5 billion); 93 finance companies with total assets of CNY1,229.2 billion (US$179.9 billion); 12 financial leasing companies with total assets of CNY160.1 billion (US$23.4 billion); and 10 auto-financing companies with total assets of CNY 48.3 billion (US$7.1 billion).

Over the past decade, non-bank financial institutions have developed rapidly in China's financial industry, but views on their status are divergent and the course of their development has experienced ups and downs.

Introduction of Strategic Investors

Chinese financial institutions in the banking sector have enhanced their corporate governance, operations management, and risk control, and accelerated the pace of financial innovation through the introduction of foreign institutional investors. As at the end of 2008, four large commercial banks—ICBC, BOC, CCB and BOCOM—had introduced nine foreign institutional investors; 24 small and medium-sized commercial banks had taken on 33 foreign institutional investors; and three rural cooperative financial institutions had attracted three foreign institutional investors. The total capital inflow from these foreign investors was US$32.78 billion. In addition, 26 non-bank financial institutions had attracted 25 foreign institutional investors, bringing in US$1.12 billion in capital.

"Going Out" Strategy

In 2008, the Chinese financial institutions in the banking sector continued to increase their overseas presence by setting up establishments and investing in overseas financial institutions. As at the end of that year, five large commercial banks had a total of 78 tier-1 operating establishments overseas and had paid approximately US$7.13 billion to acquire (or invest in) five foreign institutions.

The major overseas acquisitions undertaken by domestic banks in 2008 included:

- In January, the ICBC completed the acquisition of Seng Heng Bank in Macao, holding a 79.9333 percent stake. In March, it also acquired a 20 percent stake in Standard Bank Group at a cost of about CNY40.945 billion (US$5.6 billion). In July, the ICBC announced that it had signed an agreement to acquire 90 percent of Indonesia's Halim Bank. In August, it was reported that the ICBC would acquire 100 percent of Russia's Rosevrobank for between US$800 million and US$850 million.

■ In September, the BOC entered into an agreement with the Rothschild family to acquire a 20-percent stake in the Rothschild bank. Under the deal, the BOC was to take up 663,268 new shares and acquire 577,064 existing shares. (BOC abandoned the plan in April 2009.)

■ In October, China Merchants Bank acquired a 53.12-percent stake in Hong Kong's Wing Lung Bank for HK$30 billion (US$3.8 billion).

In May 2009, according to Thai media reports, the ICBC was in negotiations with the Thai Ministry of Finance to acquire its 30-percent stake in Asia Commercial Bank (ACL) at a price between 100 percent and 200 percent higher than ACL's share price. In April 2010, the ICBC said that it had obtained all the necessary governmental and regulatory approvals to complete the acquisition of all issued shares of Thailand's ACL. In a statement filed with the Hong Kong Exchange, the Beijing-based bank said it had acquired 1.546 billion of ACL's ordinary shares and 282,048 of its preferred shares, which in combination accounted for 97.24 percent of the total issued shares of ACL.[1]

In June 2009, the ICBC announced that it had agreed to acquire a 70-percent stake in a subsidiary of Bank of East Asia Limited in Canada for about HK$567 million. The acquisition will help ICBC to expand its operating network in North America. Twelve months after completing the transaction, Bank of East Asia will have the right to sell the remaining 30-percent stake, while the ICBC will be entitled to acquire an additional 10-percent stake.

INTEREST RATE SYSTEM

China's mechanism for setting interest rates has notable dual characteristics. While the PBC sets lending rates and deposit rates for commercial banks, inter-bank offered and bid rates and interest rates on government bonds are determined by the market. China now understands the role that interest rates play in macroeconomic modulation, and increasingly uses interest rate leverage. As China's economy slipped into deflation in 1998, the government had eight consecutive rate cuts before raising interest rates for the first time in October 2004. By adjusting interest rates, the government adjusts the cost to enterprises of using capital, thereby regulating the economy. The cycle of rate hikes ended in October 2008, with the sub-prime crisis having an impact on the economy. Faced with a sharp reversal in economic development, the government's task turned from restraining overheated investment to promoting the growth of domestic demand. Thus, benchmark interest rates went down, as illustrated in Table 2.6.

Control over interest rates has obvious drawbacks; however, considering the crucial status of the banking system in China's financial system, as well as the banks' ability to manage and take interest risk, the government has adopted a progressive strategy for reforming interest rates. The inter-bank offered and bid rates were deregulated in June 1996, and determined by the demand and supply of funds in the market. An inter-bank bond market was established in June 1997, liberating the interest rates of repurchase and spot bond transactions. In September 1999, government bonds were issued at interest rates determined by tender in the inter-bank bond market.

TABLE 2.6 Adjustments in China's benchmark deposit and loan interest rates (%)

Adjustment Date	One-year Loan Interest Rate	One-year Deposit Interest Rate	Adjustment Date	One-year Loan Interest Rate	One-year Deposit Interest Rate
May 15, 1993	9.36	9.18	April 28, 2006	5.85	2.25
July 11, 1993	10.98	10.98	August 19, 2006	6.12	2.52
January 1, 1995	10.98	10.98	March 18, 2007	6.39	2.79
July 1, 1995	12.06	10.98	May 19, 2007	6.57	3.06
May 1, 1996	10.98	9.18	July 21, 2007	6.84	3.33
August 23, 1996	10.08	7.47	August 22, 2007	7.02	3.60
October 23, 1997	8.64	5.67	September 15, 2007	7.29	3.87
March 25, 1998	7.92	5.22	December 21, 2007	7.47	4.14
July 1, 1998	6.93	4.77	September 16, 2008	7.20	4.14
December 7, 1998	6.39	3.78	October 9, 2008	6.93	3.87
June 10, 1999	5.85	2.25	October 30, 2008	6.66	3.6
February 21, 2002	5.31	1.98	November 27, 2008	5.58	2.52
October 29, 2004	5.58	2.25	December 23, 2008	5.31	2.25

Source: PBC website (http://www.pbc.gov.cn).

In January 2004, the floating range of lending interest rates for financial institutions widened, with the upper limit of commercial banks and urban credit cooperatives increasing to 1.7 times the benchmark rates, and that of rural credit cooperatives to twice the benchmark rates. In principle, ceilings on the lending rates of the financial institutions (excluding urban and rural credit cooperatives) were removed in October 2004. In March 2005, the interest rates of inter-bank deposits were deregulated. In August 2006, the liberalization of the interest rates on commercial individual housing loans was promoted, the lower limit of 0.9 times the benchmark rates being extended to 0.85 times, while the lower limit of other commercial lending rates remained unchanged at 0.9 times.

On January 4, 2007, the Shanghai inter-bank offered rate (Shibor) was officially launched to serve as the benchmark interest rate of China's money market. Subsequently, a variety of financial products which use Shibor as their benchmark have emerged. Interest rate swaps, forward rate agreements, inter-bank borrowings, rediscount, bond trading, wealth management products and inter-bank currency deposits were all introduced successively. Currently, Shibor is playing a significant role in the process of pricing bond issues. A total of 57 fixed rate corporate bonds, worth CNY234.69 billion (US$33.79 billion), were issued in 2008, all of them priced based on Shibor. Some 42 percent of short-term finance notes were also priced based on Shibor. Since the birth of medium-term notes in April 2008, 26 percent of those issued (with a value of CNY44.9 billion or US$ 6.46 billion) were priced with reference to Shibor.

INTER-BANK MARKET

Emergence of the Market

Prior to 1979, credit was allocated vertically; that is, credit was allocated through the PBC, which conducted all financial business at that time. Neither inter-bank transactions nor an inter-bank market existed. The reform linking loans to deposits in 1979 allowed commercial banks to grant loans in line with their deposit-taking ability. An unofficial inter-bank market came into being in 1981.

These horizontal transactions among banking institutions proved to be successful. As a result of early loosening of financial regulations, sporadic special transactions between financial institutions occurred in 1985. The demand for inter-bank transactions increased after the PBC tightened its monetary policy, leading to a shortage of bank liquidity in 1985. Since then, various forms of inter-bank activity have flourished across the country, resulting in many irregular operations. The standard inter-bank trading rules came into effect in 1990. From June 1996, the PBC removed all restrictions on inter-bank interest rates. The re-purchase rates and prices of bonds have been solely determined by demand and supply since the establishment of the inter-bank bond market in 1997.

Market Participants

In recent years, inter-bank market transactions have been very active, with a rapid growth in trading value. Table 2.7 lists the spot trading volume of bonds by China's major financial institutions from 2008 to 2009 in the inter-bank market. The table shows that the total spot trading volume of bonds surged at an annual growth rate of 93.25 percent. Commercial banks are the key players, and their trading volume accounted for more than 75 percent of the total. The share of foreign banks has also continued to rise in recent years.

Market Products

There are four main types of transactions on the inter-bank market: borrowing and lending, bond repurchases, spot bond trading, and interest rate derivative trading.

TABLE 2.7 Spot trading volume of bonds in the inter-bank market (CNY billion)

	2009	2008	2007	2006
Commercial banks	37,379.45	61,384.36	25,347.92	13,283.41
National commercial banks	18,000.63	31,876.32	15,061.41	7,428.36
Foreign banks	3,501.12	6,298.80	2,661.14	862.79
City commercial banks	12,392.28	17,898.55	6,018.66	3,793.53
Rural commercial banks	2,348.17	4,280.87	1,287.65	800.76
Rural cooperative banks	1,133.45	1,029.78	319.05	397.97
Town banks	0.00	0.00	0.00	0.00
Others	0.35	0.04	0.00	0.00
Credit cooperatives	2,381.42	3,211.01	815.42	503.16
Non-bank financial institutions	100.98	341.67	366.00	879.24
Securities firms	3,689.90	5,587.55	2,630.30	1,955.76
Insurance companies	418.26	1,116.56	527.36	394.08
Funds	1,916.58	6,280.92	2,210.31	4,366.09
Non-financial institutions	400.24	995.76	442.12	282.78
Others	0.27	0.36	3.28	7.21
Total	48,868.22	81,653.95	33,182.97	21,865.32

Source: China Bond website (www.chinabond.com.cn).

In 2008, inter-bank lending and borrowing reached a total of CNY15 trillion (US$2 trillion), averaging a daily turnover of CNY60 billion (US$8.6 billion), up 40.2 percent on the previous year. The repurchase volume of bonds totaled CNY58.1 trillion (US$8.4 trillion), averaging a daily turnover of CNY231.6 billion (US$33 billion), up 28.7 percent from 2007. Inter-bank spot bond transactions amounted to CNY37.1 trillion (US$5.3 trillion) in 2008, averaging a daily turnover of CNY147.9 billion (US$21 billion), up 140 percent on the previous year. There were 1,783 Shibor-based interest rate swap transactions with a nominal value of CNY89.919 billion, accounting for 22 percent of the total interest rate swap transactions. There were also 137 forward rate agreement transactions—all based on the three-month Shibor rate—with a nominal value of CNY11.36 billion (US$1.63 billion).

Open market Operations

In June 2002, the PBC issued its first tranche of central bank bills, withdrawing CNY5 billion (US$0.6 billion) from the market. The issue hit a record monthly high of CNY834 billion (US$120 billion) in March 2008 and totaled CNY4,293 billion (US$ 618 billion) for the entire year. The PBC made its first repurchase in January 2004, releasing CNY40 billion (US$4.8 billion) into the market. Since then it has made frequent repurchases in the inter-bank market in a bid to regulate the money supply. The repurchase volume for 2008 totaled CNY3,325 billion (US$478 million).

Figure 2.3 shows the monthly withdrawal and release of money by the PBC through the issuance and repurchase of notes since June 2002. It is clear from the chart that the PBC recalled CNY808.73 billion (US$ 110.88 billion) amid concerns of an overheating economy in 2007, and continued to adopt various means to tighten liquidity in the first half of 2008 when the economy remained overheated. In 2009, the impact of the financial crisis surpassed market expectations. In an effort to stimulate economic growth, the PBC had released more than CNY400 billion

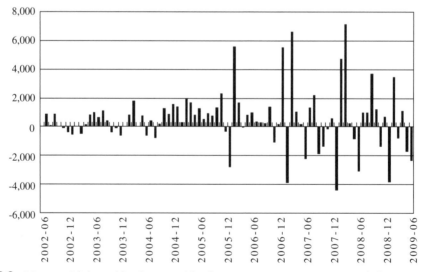

FIGURE 2.3 Money withdrawal by the central bank, June 2002–May 2009 (CNY billion)
Source: Financial China Information.

(US$58.7 billion) by the end of June to facilitate the implementation of various investment policies. As the market mechanism has improved, open market operations have become one of the principal tools for regulating the money supply and their use is set to rise. The inter-bank market, as the carrier of policy tools, needs further development.

CONCLUSION

After several years of hard work, China's banking sector has accumulated considerable experience and achieved remarkable results in its reform, for which it has received wide recognition within the international community. However, the new market structure has raised new requirements for the sector's future development. Given an improved CNY exchange rate formation mechanism, the accelerated liberalization of interest rates, the increasing dependence on trade and rising overseas investment, and the demand for product innovation and stringent risk management, these requirements will have to be met.

As a measure of the great achievements made by China in its banking reform over the past few years, in a ranking of global banks by market value published in February 2009 by the German newspaper *Frankfurter Allgemeine Zeitung*, the ICBC, CCB and BOC were in the top three, with BOCOM in tenth place. While this is, rightly, a source of great pride for China, there is still a long way to go for Chinese banks to catch up with their major international counterparts in profitability, product innovation, risk management, among others. This will require continuous efforts. The products and their corresponding markets for the banking industry will be discussed further in Part 2.

ENDNOTE

1. See "ICBC Says It Obtains All Necessary Approval to Acquire Thai Bank," *People's Daily* online, April 21, 2010.

CHAPTER 3

China's Capital Market

This chapter focuses on China's capital market, which is mainly composed of the stock market, plus the bond and other markets. China's stock and bond markets have developed significantly in recent years. The value of A-shares increased from CNY3.24 trillion (US$397 billion) at the end of 2005 to CNY32.7 trillion (US$4.3 trillion) at the end of 2007, before dropping to CNY12.13 trillion (US$1.75 trillion) as a result of the global financial crisis in 2008. Yet, by the end of 2009 its value was more than double that of the end of 2008. The stock and bond markets have played important roles in China's economy in recent years and have great potential to develop further. Despite significant growth, however, there is still room for improvement to bring them into line with the performance of overseas markets.

STOCK MARKET

Introduction

China's first stock trading can be traced back to the 1890s in Shanghai. A trading center was established in Shanghai in 1920 with active transactions in stocks, bonds, futures and other securities transactions in the 1930s. At that time, Shanghai was the financial center of East Asia. Trading in securities was banned with the setting up of the People's Republic in 1949.[1]

With China's reform and opening-up, over-the-counter stock transactions began in the 1980s. In 1990, stock exchanges were established in Shanghai and Shenzhen. China's capital market has exhibited sustained and stable growth over the past 16 years.

Development of the Securities Market

As the CNY is not completely convertible under capital accounts, shares listed in China are separated into A-shares—initially targeted at domestic investors only—and B-shares, targeting foreign investors. Since February 2001, however, B-shares, which began to be traded soon after A-shares in 1991, have been open to domestic investors, too. However, they account for only a small proportion of the total value of China's stock market, with low liquidity.

According to the China Securities Regulatory Commission (CSRC) website, by the end of March 2010, the number of companies listed in China's A-share and B-share markets amounted to 1,807, and the number of companies listed overseas (the H-share market) amounted to 156. The number of companies listed on both the A-share and H-share markets totaled 36. Growth, both in the overall size of China's stock markets and in the proportion of shares which are tradable, has been significant in recent years. At the end of 2008, the market value of the 1,625 A-share and B-share companies listed on China's stock exchanges had reached CNY12.14 trillion (US$1,747.5 billion), of which tradable shares amounted to CNY4.52 trillion (US$651.01 billion), representing 37.3 percent of the total market value. By the end of 2009, however, the market value of the 1,718 A-share- and B-share-listed companies had reached CNY24.39 trillion (US$3,571.6 billion), of which tradable shares amounted to CNY15.13 trillion (US$2,214.6 billion), representing 62 percent of the total market value. Table 3.1 illustrates the total number, total market capitalization, and annual turnover of listed companies in China's stock markets from 1998 to the end of the first quarter of 2010.

Two Stock Exchanges

The Shanghai Stock Exchange (SSE) began operations in December 1990. After 19 years of exploration and practice, the Shanghai exchange has developed into the largest stock exchange in mainland China in the number of listed companies, the total market value, and the volume of stock and Treasury bonds traded. By the end of 2008, 1,184 types of securities and 908 companies were listed on the exchange, with a total market value of CNY9,725.2 billion (US$1,400 billion), together with 75.53 million registered investor accounts. In 2008 cumulative funds raised through public offerings and new share placings had reached CNY223.816 billion (US$32.23 billion). With the help of the exchange, a large number of key enterprises, infrastructure, and high-tech companies have been able both to raise funds and improve their management mechanisms. Total trading value of the SSE reached US$5,062 billion, which accounted for 6.29 percent of the total value of shares traded around the world in 2009, making it the third-largest stock exchange in the world, behind the NASDAQ and NYSE Euronext (US).

TABLE 3.1 China's stock market capitalization and annual turnover, 1998–2010

Year	Number of Listed Companies (A- and B-share)	Total Market Capitalization (US$ billion)	Tradable Market Capitalization (US$ billion)	Total Funds Raised (US$ billion)	Total Turnover (US$ billion)
1998	851	235.60	69.40	10.15	284.38
1999	949	319.77	99.22	11.41	378.33
2000	1,088	580.92	194.33	25.40	734.76
2001	1,160	525.82	174.74	14.49	462.79
2002	1,224	463.08	150.83	11.62	338.17
2003	1,287	512.96	159.22	16.40	388.01
2004	1,377	447.70	141.22	18.26	511.46
2005	1,381	397.34	130.25	23.06	387.94
2006	1,434	1,121.16	313.56	70.15	1,134.52
2007	1,550	4,303.35	1,224.21	116.53	6,058.36
2008	1,625	1,747.51	651.02	61.40	3,846.06
2009	1,718	3,571.58	2,214.62	83.62	7,847.54
2010Q1	1,807	3,588.16	2,294.02	26.29	1,704.11

Source: Original CNY data are from the CSRC website and the corresponding US$ data are converted using exchange rates in Table 4.1.

The Shenzhen Stock Exchange (SZSE) was also established in December 1990, in the coastal city of Shenzhen in southern China, the frontier of China's reform and opening-up initiative. Although it developed rapidly in the initial stages, it has been somewhat eclipsed by the Shanghai exchange and, in 2008, accounted for 36.9 percent of the total turnover of mainland China's stock markets. Total trading value of the SZSE reached US$2,774 billion, which accounted for 3.45 percent of the total value of the world's share trading in 2009, making the SZSE the sixth-largest stock exchange (behind the NASDAQ and NYSE Euronext, the SSE, the Tokyo Securities Exchange and the London Stock Exchange).

PRICE/EARNINGS RATIO, TURNOVER RATE, AND SECURITIZATION

In the early stage of China's economic reform from a planned economy to a market-oriented economy, most of the shares of listed companies were held by the government or government agencies and were therefore not tradable in the market. Only a few enterprises were free from government shareholding. The reform of the shareholder structure of listed companies has solved a major problem in the mechanisms of China's stock market, leading recently to improvements in the market.

The Price/Earnings Ratio

As illustrated in Table 3.2 and Figure 3.1, during most of its life, the valuation level of China's A-share market has been higher than that in mature or emerging markets, and has approached the level of the Nasdaq Composite Index (Nasdaq) in the United States.

TABLE 3.2   Historical static PE ratios of the world's major stock price indexes

Index	31 Dec 09	31 Dec 08	31 Dec 07	31 Dec 06
AC WORLD	25.7	9.8	16.0	18.0
MSCI EMERGING INX	16.64	7.7	17.4	15.0
DOW JONES INDUS. AVG	15.75	16.0	16.4	17.4
S&P 500	18.00	12.3	20.1	18.2
NASDAQ COMPOSITE IX	33.79	17.7	37.7	40.3
FTSE 100	61.47	7.7	12.4	18
CAC	15.66	7.5	11.6	14.6
DAX	60.24	10.0	13.6	14.3
NIKKEI 225	43.54	12.5	18.2	23.4
S&P/ASX INDEX	14.92	10.4	15.5	16.4
HANG SENG INDEX	15.93	8.7	18.1	14.8
HK CHINA ENT IX	16.28	9.8	24.5	20.4
BOVESPA	20.76	8.5	15.4	14.1
BSE INDEX	18.25	9.8	28.0	23.5
RTS IX	12.67	3.2	13.0	8.7
TAIEX	25.64	8.6	20.3	n.a.
KOSPI	14.49	10.6	17.5	11.8
SH COMPOSITE IX	24.23	14.0	44.3	33.2
SZSE COMPONENT IX	34.42	17.6	61.8	53.0

Source: Bloomberg; strategy reports by the CICC Research Department.

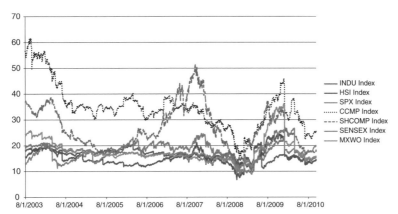

FIGURE 3.1   Trend of historical PE ratios of the world's major stock price indexes
Source: Bloomberg; CICC weekly strategy report on June 22, 2009.

According to the historical figures in Figure 3.1, before 2005, the price/earnings (PE) ratio in the Shanghai Stock Exchange Composite Index was lower than that in the Nasdaq but higher than in any other major market. From 2006, China's A-share market became a bull market and the PE ratio increased rapidly, exceeding that of the Nasdaq. In 2008, the impact of the global financial crisis caused the A-share index to plunge, and the PE ratio was pushed down to approximately the same level as other major world markets. The PE ratio of the A-share market skyrocketed again after a significant rebound in 2009 and almost reached the same level as that of the Nasdaq on June 22, 2009.

Turnover Rate

Turnover rate refers to the frequency with which stock is bought and sold in the market during a certain period and is an indicator of stock liquidity. It can be calculated using the ratio of transaction volume and share issuance amounts, or the ratio of transaction amounts and total market value. The higher the turnover rate, the more actively the stock is being traded and the better its liquidity. As shown in the Table 3.3 the level of activity in the A-share market has increased substantially and, in 2006, the turnover rate of the Shanghai and Shenzhen markets surpassed that of the New York Securities Exchange, and the Shenzhen market even got very close to that of the Nasdaq. In 2007 and 2008, the turnover rates of China's A-shares were also higher than the world average. This is both proof of the active state of China's stock market as a result of its development and a reflection of the intensive speculative culture in China's stock market over the past few years. Whereas most exchanges experienced significant drops in turnover rates, the turnover rates of both Chinese stock exchanges increased by more than 70 percent in 2009, reflecting intense speculation in the market.

Securitization Ratios

The securitization ratio refers to the ratio of the total market value of all kinds of securities to the country's GDP. The total market value of securities is usually represented by

TABLE 3.3 Turnover rates of major countries and regions, 2005–09 (%)

Country (Region)	Stock Exchanges	Turnover Rate				
		2005	2006	2007	2008	2009
Developed Markets						
US	NYSE	99.10	134.30	166.90	240.20	120.00
	Nasdaq	250.40	269.90	625.20	1026.50	716.36
Eurozone	NYSE Euronext	112.80	116.40	136.90	141.80	68.06
	OMX Nordic Exchange	116.70	134.50	137.00	138.00	71.67
UK	London SE	110.10	124.80	154.20	152.70	67.99
Ireland	Irish SE	59.50	59.60	84.00	81.30	42.00
France	Luxembourg SE	0.50	0.30	18.50	11.90	0.16
Germany	Deutsche Börse	149.40	173.70	208.40	264.00	98.76
Norway	Oslo Børs	118.80	144.30	145.40	143.20	87.53
Switzerland	SIX Swiss Exchange	114.70	130.20	121.80	133.90	61.51
Japan	Tokyo SE	115.30	125.80	138.40	151.20	119.24
	Osaka SE	97.70	74.90	127.60	134.10	79.78
Canada	Toronto Stock Exchange	69.20	76.40	83.70	103.80	76.78
Italy	Borsa Italiana	160.00	162.90	204.10	182.30	93.67
Spain	BME Spanish Exchanges	161.20	167.00	191.90	171.40	132.19
Austria	Wiener Börse	41.60	50.20	55.60	65.70	39.34
Israel	Tel-Aviv SE	46.10	46.60	49.60	55.00	66.02
Emerging Markets						
Mexico	Mexican Exchange	27.20	29.60	29.80	29.90	26.31
Brazil	BM&FBOVESPA	42.80	45.50	57.10	66.70	64.95
Chile	Santiago SE	14.80	19.00	22.50	19.90	21.13
Argentina	Buenos Aires SE	11.20	7.20	8.90	7.00	3.58
Greece	Athens Exchange	48.80	58.60	64.00	61.20	65.33
Turkey	Istanbul SE	168.50	141.30	129.70	135.10	165.55
Australia	Australian SE	84.00	88.40	101.60	113.00	73.79
Malaysia	Bursa Malaysia	28.30	36.20	57.10	36.00	23.90
India	National Stock Exchange India	75.60	67.80	67.70	75.70	61.52
	Bombay SE	35.40	31.90	29.40	29.00	19.36
Indonesia	Indonesia SE	54.70	44.80	60.10	43.60	32.74
New Zealand	New Zealand Exchange	43.50	51.60	45.20	45.50	44.59
Thailand	Thailand SE	80.70	72.70	66.60	74.50	62.46
Taiwan	Taiwan SE Corp.	131.40	141.70	153.30	145.50	168.12
Singapore	Singapore Exchange	48.40	58.20	77.60	63.70	46.11
South Korea	Korea Exchange	206.90	171.40	192.60	196.30	148.97
Hong Kong	Hong Kong Exchanges	50.30	62.10	94.10	86.00	66.88

TABLE 3.3 (*Continued*)

Country (Region)	Stock Exchanges	Turnover Rate				
		2005	2006	2007	2008	2009
Philippines	Philippine SE	19.70	21.80	33.00	24.20	19.17
Poland	Warsaw SE	38.70	45.40	43.40	43.60	42.97
Mainland China	Shanghai SE	82.10	153.80	211.00	118.20	207.30
	Shenzhen SE	128.90	251.70	389.20	235.90	408.17

Source: World Federation of Exchanges (WFE), *2009 Annual Report.*

the total market value of stocks. The higher the securitization rate, the more important the role a security market plays in the nation's economy; it is therefore an important index for measuring the market's level of development. Although it has witnessed substantial development in the past decade, the securitization level of China's A-share market is still low and has fluctuated over time. The securitization rate increased from 25.3 percent in 1998 to 54.5 percent in 2000, and then dropped to a low of 17.6 percent in 2005, before rebounding in 2006. Table 3.4 provides a comparison between China's performance and that of other major countries and regions in this regard. The table shows a positive correlation between economic development and the extent of securitization. The securitization level in mature economies is generally higher than that in emerging economies. The securitization rates in the US, the UK, Japan and Canada, for example, all surpassed 100 percent. We can also see that China's securitization level is low even among emerging economies. The development of the economy, especially the capital market, will give the stock market greater development potential.

TABLE 3.4 Securitization ratios of major countries and regions, 2005–09 (%)

Country (Region)	Exchange	Securitization Rate				
		2005	2006	2007	2008	2009
Developed Markets						
US	NYSE	109.2	122.9	113.4	64.6	83.0
	NASDAQ	28.9	33.1	29.1	16.8	22.7
Eurozone	NYSE Euronext	86.4	31.5	34.3	15.4	22.9
	OMX Nordic Exchange	96.5	9.4	10.1	4.1	6.5
UK	London SE	145.0	258.7	137.4	69.9	128.1
Germany	Deutsche Börse	46.1	54.2	63.4	30.3	38.5
Japan	Tokyo SE	107.4	106.6	98.8	63.3	65.2
	Osaka SE	4.4	7.7	4.8	3.0	2.7
Canada	Toronto Stock Exchange	126.1	134.1	152.3	68.4	125.5
Italy	Borsa Italiana	47.7	53.0	50.7	22.6	31.0
Spain	BME Spanish Exchange			123.7	58.8	98.0

(*continued*)

TABLE 3.4 (*Continued*)

Country (Region)	Exchange	Securitization Rate				
		2005	2006	2007	2008	2009
Emerging Markets						
Mexico	Mexican Exchange	30.8	38.8	38.8	21.5	40.2
Brazil	BOVESPA	57.3	56.9	102.7	37.6	85.0
Argentina	Buenos Aires SE	26.9	34.1	21.9	12.2	14.8
Australia	Australian SE	118.2	115.9	142.7	67.7	126.5
Malaysia	Bursa Malaysia	137.8	139.4	174.2	85.1	149.5
India	National Stock Exchange India	65.9	68.9	150.6	49.6	99.1
	Bombay SE	70.6	74.2	165.0	53.5	105.7
Indonesia	Indonesia SE	29.3	29.9	49.0	19.3	39.8
Singapore	Singapore Exchange	220.3	234.4	323.0	145.6	271.7
South Korea	Korea Exchange	90.0	88.2	107.0	49.7	100.3
Hong Kong	Hong Kong Exchanges	591.9	706.4	1282.2	616.4	1093.9
Poland	Warsaw SE	31.2	36.2	49.7	17.3	35.1
China	Shanghai SE	12.6	34.0	109.2	32.4	55.1
	Shenzhen SE	5.1	8.4	23.2	8.0	17.7

Source: IMF International Financial Statistics Yearbook 2005 and exchange members.

CHINA'S EXCHANGE-TRADED FUND

An exchange-traded fund (ETF) is a special open-ended securities investment fund that aims to track the trend of a specific index (referred to as "the target index") by purchasing and redeeming stock portfolios. The funds are divided into shares and traded on securities exchanges. The trading mechanism of ETFs allows room for arbitrage between the primary and secondary markets, and can effectively prevent ETFs being traded at significant discounts, unlike closed-end funds. The trading price of ETFs depends on the value of the underlying stock portfolio; that is, the "unit net value of fund assets."

Since their emergence in the US in 1993, ETFs have developed greatly around the world. By the end of 2008, there were 1,398 ETFs being traded in the major global securities exchanges, with total assets of US$1,776.8 billion. The first ETF in China was the Shanghai Securities Exchange 50 Index Fund, which was introduced in November 2004. Up to the end of 2008, there were five ETFs on the Shanghai and Shenzhen exchanges, with a total transaction value of US$47.35 billion, which accounts for just 0.5 percent of the global total.

SECURITIES COMPANIES

At present, China has no banks that can match the universal concept of an investment bank, so securities transactions are mainly conducted by securities companies. By the end of 2008, there were 165 such companies, with total assets of CNY2.32 trillion, representing just 4.27 percent of the total deposits with banking institutions. Most securities companies are small-scale and their average assets in 2008 were only CNY14.2 billion (US$2.079 billion). In 2008, the total assets of securities companies in China were only equivalent to some 38.4 percent of the total assets of the US investment bank Goldman Sachs.

In an agreement signed on its accession to the WTO, China promised a gradual opening of its financial industry from December 2006. In July, 2006, the CSRC set a risk-control index framework with net assets as the core element and supporting compliant dealers in increasing their capital by means of public offerings, capital injections from specific investors or by introducing strategic investors. As at the end of 2008, there were eight listed securities companies.

HONG KONG STOCK EXCHANGE

For historical reasons, the Hong Kong Stock Exchange (HKEx) was more active than both the SSE and SZSE before 2006. However, in turnover terms it was surpassed by the SSE in 2007 and by the SZSE in 2009. Even so, the HKEx will continue to be a very important market for mainland Chinese companies to raise capital. As one of the major financial centers in the Asia Pacific area, Hong Kong has been offering listing opportunities, which has provided a benchmark for, and accelerated the development of, the mainland's stock markets.

Funds Raised in Hong Kong

By the end of May 2009, there were 150 H-shares (of mainland companies listed on the HKEx) and 87 red-chip stocks (shares of mainland-controlled or related companies that are registered overseas and listed in Hong Kong) trading on the main board of the Hong Kong Stock Exchange, and a further 50 H-shares and four red-chip stocks trading on its Growth Enterprise Market (GEM). Table 3.5 shows the annual funds raised from IPOs and subsequent offerings by H-share and red-chip stock companies from 1993 to 2009.

The funds raised by H-shares and red-chip stocks from 1993 to 2009 amounted to HK$954.5 billion (US$122.4 billion) and HK$1,094.2 billion (US$140.3 billion), respectively. The combined total (US$262.7 billion) has made an important contribution to China's development.

Trading of Stocks

Table 3.6 shows the performance of the H-shares and red-chip stocks over the 17-year period to 2009 and illustrates the increasing importance of mainland companies to the Hong Kong stock market.

Market Value of Mainland Companies

Turnover of H-share and red-chip stocks reached the highest annual growth of 189.2 percent from 2006 to 2007 to HK$10.475 trillion (US$1.343 trillion) in 2007, accounting for 63.44 percent of the total turnover in the exchange. With consecutive declines from 2007 to 2009, the turnover of H-shares and red-chip stocks fell to HK$7.089 trillion (US$908.9 billion) in 2009, accounting for 61.3 percent of the HKEx's total annual turnover. From 1998 to 2005, total

TABLE 3.5 The performance of H-shares and red-chip stocks on the HKEx, 1993–2009 (HK$ million)

	H-shares			Red chips		
Year	IPOs	Public Offerings	Total	IPOs	Public Offerings	Total
1993	8,141.52	—	8,141.52	950.52	14,128.71	15,079.23
1994	9,879.81	—	9,879.81	1,541.37	11,685.17	13,226.54
1995	2,011.35	980	2,991.35	1,569.75	5,103.86	6,673.61
1996	6,834.16	1,037.50	7,871.66	3,427.30	15,581.81	19,009.11
1997	32,037.52	1,046.70	33,084.23	39,394.82	41,589.99	80,984.81
1998	2,072.36	1,480.16	3,552.52	142.38	17,232.47	17,374.85
1999	4,263.69	—	4,263.69	1,985.53	53,191.82	55,177.35
2000	51,750.69	—	51,750.69	44,096.46	249,562.21	293,658.67
2001	5,570.84	497.25	6,068.09	12,060.08	7,021.19	19,081.27
2002	16,873.60	—	16,873.60	20,950.56	31,771.67	52,722.23
2003	46,252.59	592.04	46,844.63	2,962.40	1,930.15	4,892.55
2004	40,016.78	19,229.95	59,246.73	14,548.60	11,816.68	26,365.28
2005	137,184.78	21,493.17	158,677.95	1,037.45	21,352.85	22,390.30
2006	290,026.72	13,796.28	303,823.01	2,763.76	48,004.16	50,767.91
2007	74,773.29	10,868.70	85,641.98	49,592.21	65,381.97	114,974.19
2008	29,488.36	4,618.98	34,107.34	—	223,800.56	223,800.56
2009	114,176.43	7,551.15	121,727.58	8,015.83	69,993.11	78,008.94

Source: Hong Kong Stock Exchange website (http://sc.hkex.com.hk/TuniS/www.hkex.com.hk/chi/stat/smstat/chidimen/cd_fr_c.htm).

TABLE 3.6 Annual turnover and market share of H-shares and red-chip stocks on the Hong Kong Exchange, 1993–2009

	H-Shares		Red Chips		Total	
Year	Turnover (HK$ million)	% of Turnover	Turnover (HK$ million)	% of Turnover	Turnover (HK$ million)	% of Turnover
1993	33,037.82	3.01	88,290.28	8.05	121,328.09	11.07
1994	34,208.97	3.32	57,515.41	5.59	91,724.38	8.91
1995	17,291.65	2.27	45,856.63	6.02	63,148.28	8.29
1996	24,890.36	1.93	135,359.18	10.52	160,249.54	12.45
1997	297,769.58	8.48	1,043,672.51	29.71	1,341,442.09	38.19
1998	73,538.68	4.61	369,386.79	23.13	442,925.47	27.74
1999	102,788.51	5.80	354,818.00	20.01	457,606.51	25.81
2000	164,309.62	5.74	674,856.93	23.60	839,166.55	29.34
2001	245,201.03	13.47	497,246.00	27.31	742,447.03	40.77
2002	139,711.41	9.50	309,354.25	21.04	449,065.66	30.54
2003	501,496.87	22.12	493,945.47	21.79	995,442.34	43.92
2004	933,860.83	27.49	614,727.35	18.10	1,548,588.19	45.58
2005	949,155.23	26.46	603,820.77	16.83	1,552,976.00	43.29

TABLE 3.6 (*Continued*)

	H-Shares		Red Chips		Total	
Year	Turnover (HK$ million)	% of Turnover	Turnover (HK$ million)	% of Turnover	Turnover (HK$ million)	% of Turnover
2006	2,521,764.08	39.26	1,100,508.90	17.13	3,622,272.98	56.39
2007	7,748,899.57	46.93	2,725,604.54	16.51	10,474,504.11	63.44
2008	6,130,592.75	48.53	2,283,227.61	18.08	8,413,820.36	66.61
2009	5,152,805.63	44.56	1,936,589.39	16.75	7,089,395.02	61.30

Source: Hong Kong Stock Exchange website (http://www.hkex.com.hk/data/chidimen/CD_TOs.htm).

turnover of H-shares and red-chip stocks as a percentage of the turnover of A-shares in mainland China increased from 20 percent to 51.3 percent, before dropping to a mere 11.6 percent in 2009.

At the end of 2008, the total market value of H-shares and red-chip stocks on the Hong Kong exchange was HK$5.5 trillion (US$705 billion), which was higher than that of the tradable market capitalization of the A-share market (US$651 billion) and more than 40 percent of the total market capitalization of that market in mainland China. The overseas and domestic stock markets in Hong Kong have played different but complementary roles in promoting China's economic development.

Mainland companies have also listed on other overseas securities exchanges, including in the United States and Singapore. With the further development of China's economy, deepening globalization and China's increasing participation in global capital markets, more mainland companies will pursue listings in major international financial centers, with great potential for developing the domestic stock market.

THE STRUCTURE OF CHINA'S BOND MARKET

Domestic bonds include PBC bills, Treasury bonds, financial bonds, corporate bonds and asset-backed securities. Table 3.7 shows the total face value of the major bonds in the domestic bond market from 2004 to May 2010.

As Table 3.7 shows, PBC bills have developed most swiftly and, with the exception of Treasury bonds and financial bonds (bonds issued by state-sponsored institutions such as the CDB), have become the largest bond type in the domestic market. By the end of May 2010, their face value had reached CNY4.648 trillion (US$680.8 billion), or 24.6 percent of the total market value, placing them just behind Treasury bonds (31 percent) and financial bonds (28.6 percent). Other than the three types of bills and bonds mentioned above, the total value of other bonds only amounted to CNY2.984 trillion (US$437 billion), or 15.8 percent of the total by the end of May 2010.

By the end of 2009, Treasury bonds and financial bonds accounted for 61.8 percent of the total, and amounted to 32.3 percent of GDP for 2009. At the same time, the short-term

TABLE 3.7 Value of the major bonds in domestic bond market, 2004–10 (US$ billion)

Bond Type	2004	2005	2006	2007	2008	2009	End
PBC bills	141.46	272.09	405.06	481.28	692.88	619.67	680.80
Treasury bonds	292.12	331.71	364.27	611.72	701.98	840.42	857.73
Financial bonds, by	175.29	241.19	318.38	424.49	589.88	745.85	790.97
Policy banks	165.89	216.84	286.37	378.64	528.72	651.43	693.43
Commercial banks	7.03	21.87	28.89	41.15	55.97	86.08	89.05
Non-bank financial institutions	2.17	2.21	2.63	4.21	4.75	8.20	8.28
Securities companies	0.21	0.28	0.48	0.50	0.46	0.29	0.22
Corporate bonds	14.90	22.08	35.51	58.17	97.95	160.59	180.81
Short-term financing bills	—	16.92	33.45	42.13	60.52	66.75	87.68
Asset-backed securities	0.21	0.28	2.36	4.26	7.93	5.86	4.17
Foreign bonds	—	0.26	0.38	0.39	0.43	0.59	0.59
Medium-term bills	0.00	0.00	0.00	0.00	24.07	126.19	163.56
Total	623.75	884.25	1,159.39	1,622.45	2,175.66	2,566.13	2,766.60

Source: China Government Securities Depository Trust & Clearing Co., Ltd (CDC); US$ amounts are converted using CNY/US$ exchange rates of Table 4.1.

financing bills and bonds issued by non-financial institutions only accounted for 3.2 percent of the market value. All of this indicates that the scale of the domestic corporate bond market is still limited and there is ample room for development.

PBC BILLS MARKET

As shown in Table 3.7, excluding special Treasury bonds and financial bonds, PBC bills became the largest bond type in the domestic market at the end of May 2010. The PBC has been issuing bills for the past several years with the aim of constraining the excess liquidity arising from foreign exchange translation. The annual trade surplus (calculated by multiplying the monthly trade surplus by the average monthly exchange rate) increased from CNY211.4 billion (US$25.5 billion) in 2003 to CNY2.074 trillion (US$272.8 billion) in 2007, with a compound annual growth rate of 77 percent in the four years from 2003 to 2007. The annual trade surplus as a percentage of the money supply (M1) was only around 20 percent from 2002 to 2004, yet it increased to more than 70 percent from 2005 to 2007, indicating the role of foreign trade in the Chinese market.

TREASURY BOND MARKET

Since 1981, when China's bond market was reopened, the domestic bond market has developed quickly. Currently, there is an inter-bank market for bonds, with some bonds also traded on securities exchanges. By issuer, bonds in China can be divided into three categories: government bonds, financial bonds, and corporate bonds. Government bonds are issued by the Ministry of Finance, financial bonds by government-sponsored financial institutions, and corporate bonds by enterprises. Government bonds play the leading role, while corporate bonds take the lowest share in the domestic market.

Issuance and Outstanding Amounts

Table 3.8 shows the performance of government bond issues from 1981 to May 2010. The amount issued increased steadily from 1984 to 2007, with a compound annual growth rate of 29.83 percent. In 2007, the issuance of government bonds (including special Treasury bonds of CNY1.55 trillion) reached a climax of CNY2.188 trillion (US$287.9 billion) and the related outstanding amount represented 18.07 percent of GDP, almost 5 percent higher than the corresponding rate in 2006. In 2009, with the implementation of the CNY4 trillion economic stimulus packages, the issuance amount was CNY1.621 trillion (US$237.35 billion), 123.75 percent higher than the corresponding issuance in 2008.

TABLE 3.8 Government bond information, 1981–May 2010 (US$ billion)

Year	Issuance Amount	Principal/Interest Payments	Year-end Outstanding Amount	% of GDP
1981	2.79	—	2.79	1.00
1982	2.28	—	4.81	1.70
1983	2.10	—	6.77	2.30
1984	1.52	—	6.32	2.50
1985	2.06	—	8.08	2.60
1986	1.81	0.23	8.45	2.90
1987	3.15	0.62	10.36	3.20
1988	3.55	0.76	13.15	3.30
1989	7.01	0.51	19.49	4.30
1990	4.34	2.50	18.00	4.40
1991	5.28	2.94	17.70	4.40
1992	8.36	6.21	19.23	4.00
1993	6.62	3.89	21.13	3.50
1994	11.93	4.23	21.83	4.00
1995	18.09	9.39	31.23	4.50
1996	22.22	15.23	38.36	4.70
1997	29.10	21.96	45.61	5.10
1998	39.00	27.13	57.54	6.10
1999	44.88	21.65	80.78	8.10
2000	50.22	18.75	112.24	10.40
2001	54.17	23.24	143.20	12.60
2002	53.90	29.81	186.85	15.10
2003	65.76	30.20	232.57	16.50
2004	58.10	29.00	292.11	16.10
2005	61.77	25.99	331.72	13.50

(continued)

TABLE 3.8 (*Continued*)

Year	Issuance Amount	Principal/Interest Payments	Year-end Outstanding Amount	% of GDP
2006	86.94	54.43	364.28	13.10
2007	287.86	61.94	611.72	18.07
2008	104.34	96.78	701.98	16.21
2009	237.35	136.20	840.42	17.12
2010*	76.85	64.98	857.82	—

Source: 2003 China Statistical Yearbook; data for 2004–06 come from the China Bond website, and GDP data come from the National Bureau of Statistics; US$ amounts are converted using CNY/US$ exchange rates of Table 4.1; data for 2010 are from January to May 2010.

Total Transactions and Liquidity

The total transaction amount and liquidity of China's government bond market are shown in Table 3.9.

As shown in the table, in 2003, the transaction amount of China's Treasury bonds exceeded CNY13 trillion (US$1.575 trillion) for the first time, which was equal to more than 96 percent of GDP and 6.78 times greater than the Treasury bond balance for that year. Although the transaction volume reached CNY27.325 trillion (US$4.342 trillion) in 2009, this was just 81.45 percent of GDP that year. Thus, the Chinese Treasury market is rather low in liquidity compared to most developed markets (the US Treasury market, for example, where the total annual turnover of Treasury bonds/GDP ratio has been

TABLE 3.9 Purchase and redemption turnover of China's Treasury bonds, 1997–2009 (CNY billion)

Year	Purchase	Redemption	Total Turnover	Redemption/ Total Turnover (%)	Total Turnover/ Outstanding Amount	Total Turnover/ GDP (%)
1997	335.30	—	—	—	—	—
1998	606.40	—	—	—	—	—
1999	531.70	1,350.50	1,882.20	71.75	2.81	20.99
2000	408.50	2,130.90	2,539.40	83.92	2.73	25.59
2001	530.40	3,680.20	4,210.60	87.40	3.55	38.40
2002	1,142.60	8,604.50	9,747.00	88.28	6.30	81.00
2003	1,395.70	11,645.90	13,041.60	89.30	6.78	96.02
2004	828.00	9,126.40	9,954.40	91.68	4.12	62.26
2005	1,365.20	9,289.50	10,654.70	87.19	3.94	58.15
2006	1,410.90	11,596.30	13,007.30	89.15	4.48	61.38
2007	2,271.40	17,178.60	19,450.00	88.32	4.18	75.59
2008	3,837.60	19,726.90	23,564.50	83.71	4.83	78.37
2009	4,341.53	22,973.38	27,314.91	84.11	4.76	81.45

Source: China Bond website and the National Bureau of Statistics.

at around 1,000 percent in the past few years). As the Treasury market is the most fundamental part of the whole financial system, other fixed income and foreign exchange related markets are dependent on it having sufficient liquidity. Thus, measures to stimulate liquidity are vital to promote the further development of the financial market.

FINANCIAL, CORPORATE, AND OTHER BONDS

Financial Bonds

Financial bonds are debt securities issued by financial institutions registered in the PRC's inter-bank bond market with agreed principal and interest payment terms. Financial bonds in China are mainly issued by policy banks, such as the CDB, and commercial banks. Table 3.10 lists the issuance amounts and trust amounts of the financial bonds issued in China from 1998 to the end of May 2010. As proof of the scale of China's financial bond market, this table shows that the trust amount for the years 2007 to 2009 accounted for 69.4 percent, 84.0 percent, and 88.8 percent, respectively, of corresponding Treasury bonds. This table also shows that the year-end trust amount of financial bonds has grown steadily since 1998 and surpassed CNY1 trillion (CNY1.179 trillion or US$142.45 billion) for the first time in 2003. The year-end trust amount of financial bonds exceeded CNY5 trillion (CNY5.095 trillion or US$745.89 billion) by the end of 2009.

Corporate Bonds

Although China's corporate bond market has been in existence for almost as long as the market for Treasury bonds, its market scale lags far behind both Treasury bonds and

TABLE 3.10 Issuance of financial bonds, 1998–May 2010 (CNY billion)

Year	Times of Issuance	Par Value	Par Value Growth (%)	Number of Bonds in Year-end Stock	Year-end Trust Amount	Growth in Year-end Trust Amount (%)
1998	7	193.00	—	16	510.70	—
1999	20	185.10	−4.10	24	608.90	19.23
2000	17	164.50	−11.13	35	730.10	19.91
2001	28	262.50	59.57	53	841.90	15.30
2002	37	322.00	22.67	83	987.50	17.30
2003	39	462.00	43.48	99	1,179.00	19.39
2004	35	512.30	10.89	124	1,450.80	23.06
2005	53	711.70	38.91	166	1,968.60	35.69
2006	64	922.00	29.55	211	2,538.80	28.96
2007	7	1,190.50	29.12	264	3,227.00	27.11
2008	85	1,178.30	−1.02	321	4,096.80	26.96
2009	105	1,474.91	25.17	380	5,095.23	24.37
May 10	32	506.52	—	396	5,399.73	—

Source: Wind Information.

financial bonds. In 2005, the PBC published a number of measures to fast-track the development of short-term corporate financing bonds and companies have since begun to issue such bonds by submitting memoranda and records under a simplified approval procedure.

However, the amount of capital raised on China's corporate bond market represents only a fraction of the face value of Treasury bonds issued. In the period from 1986 to May 2009, the total amount of capital raised from corporate bonds was less than 30 percent of the total amount of capital raised on the stock market. Although the scale of bond financing has expanded rapidly in recent years (with an average increase of 66 percent over the four-year period since 2005), corporate bonds still face problems that lie outside the scope of this book.

Asset-backed Bonds

Asset securitization—the transformation of certain illiquid credit assets with steady expected future cash flows into tradable securities in the financial market after specific structural arrangement, segregation and reorganization of risks and benefits embodied in the asset—originated in the US in the 1970s and was later developed in Europe and Southeast Asia.

The CDB introduced asset-backed securities in December 2005 and April 2006, with respective financing amounts of up to CNY4.177 billion (US$0.512 billion) and CNY5.73 billion (US$0.70 billion). The CCB introduced the first mortgage loan-backed securities, with a financing amount of CNY2.926 billion (US$0.36 billion). The China Securitization Forum website shows that in 2006 nine securities companies issued asset-backed securities, with a total value of CNY17.637 billion (US$2.22 billion).

Table 3.11 gives the number and amount of issuance of asset-backed securities from 2005 to 2009. After the financial crisis broke out, the securitization experimentation has slowed down.

The emergence of asset-backed securities represents one of the key developments in China's capital market. However, the further development of the market requires certain basic conditions, such as benchmark interest rates and a basic bond-rating system. It will take some time before these conditions are put in place. Therefore, the development of asset-backed securities will be a long-term process.

TABLE 3.11   Annual issuance amount of asset-backed securities 2005–2009

Year	Issuance Amount (CNY billion)	Issuance Amount (US$ billion)	Number of Issues
2005	4.18	0.51	6
2006	11.58	1.45	7
2007	17.81	2.34	16
2008	30.20	4.35	26
2009	0	0	0

Source: Wind Information.

BONDS ISSUED BY OVERSEAS ORGANIZATIONS IN THE PRC AND ISSUED BY PRC ORGANIZATIONS OVERSEAS

Bonds Issued by Overseas Organizations in the PRC

In February 2005 the PBC, the Ministry of Finance, the National Development and Reform Commission, and the CSRC jointly published measures allowing overseas institutions to issue bonds in the PRC. This was seen to be an important initiative in reforming the financial system, in learning from international experience and promoting regulated market development. The initiative was designed to improve the confidence of foreign investors to invest in the PRC and to upgrade China's image overseas while developing the domestic bond market and helping Hong Kong become an international financial center for CNY transactions. At that time, the Ministry of Finance approved three overseas financial institutions to issue bonds: the International Finance Corporation (IFC) under the World Bank; the Asian Development Bank (ADB); and the Japan Bank for International Cooperation (JBIC). With State Council approval, the IFC became the first multinational institution to issue CNY bonds—which became known as "Panda Bonds"—in China, marking another important step in the internationalization of China's markets. In December 2009 the ADB released its second issue of Panda bonds, with a principal amount of CNY1 billion, a bullet maturity of 10 years, and a fixed coupon rate payable annually.

Overseas Bond Issuance by Domestic Institutions

In June 2007, the PBC and the National Development and Reform Commission jointly published measures enabling domestic institutions to issue yuan-denominated bonds in the Hong Kong SAR. The CDB pioneered the venture with its CNY5 billion (US$0.658 billion) bond issue to Hong Kong institutional and individual investors later that month. Hong Kong citizens and organizations showed tremendous enthusiasm for the bonds, pushing the total subscription up to CNY14 billion (US$1.842 billion). Following this lead, the China Import and Export Bank began to issue CNY bonds of CNY2 billion (US$263 million) in Hong Kong and was followed into the market by the Bank of China (BOC) and the CCB. In September 2007, the BOC became the first commercial bank to issue CNY bonds in Hong Kong. In July 2009, following its conversion into a commercial bank, CDB announced the issue in Hong Kong of CNY bonds with a minimum issue size of CNY1 billion.

RELATIONSHIP BETWEEN DIRECT AND INDIRECT FINANCING

Direct financing refers to financing from the stock or bond markets, while indirect financing is that provided by banks.

Based on the financing statistics of the domestic stock market, the Hong Kong stock market and domestic corporate bonds shown earlier, it is possible to calculate the ratio of China's direct financing to indirect financing (bank loans). Table 3.12 shows a breakdown of total domestic financing in the capital market, total bank loans, and the ratio of their respective contributions.

TABLE 3.12 Financing from China's stock and bond markets, 2002–09

Year	Stock Market Financing (CNY billion)	Bond Market Financing (CNY billion)	Mainland Capital Market Financing (CNY billion)	HK Stock Market Financing (CNY billion)	Total Bank Loans Growth (CNY billion)	Mainland Capital Market Financing/ Bank Loans (%)	HK Stock Market Financing/ Bank Loans (%)
2002	96.18	539.02	635.20	73.82	1,800	35.30	4.10
2003	135.78	615.03	750.81	54.97	2,770	27.10	2.00
2004	151.10	797.17	948.27	90.96	2,260	42.00	4.00
2005	188.25	873.02	1,061.27	190.65	2,350	45.20	8.10
2006	559.43	867.02	1,426.45	363.88	3,180	44.90	11.40
2007	885.87	2,623.46	3,509.33	114.97	3,630	96.70	3.20
2008	385.22	1,361.79	1,747.01	223.80	4,910	35.60	4.60
2009	614.27	1,232.00	1,846.27	78.01	10,523	17.55	0.74

Source: Tables 3.1 and 3.6; bank loan information comes from the PBC website.

The table shows that other than in 2007 (when special Treasury bonds were issued), the ratios between direct financing and indirect financing were all below 50 percent. Even when Hong Kong figures are incorporated, the ratios were rarely above 50 percent.

A comparison of China's bond market structure with that of the United States highlights the fact that a low contribution from corporate bonds remains a big problem for China's bond market. The percentage contribution can be raised by developing the corporate bond market through measures such as introducing benchmark interest rates and a corporate credit-rating system; this is likely to be a long journey.

FUND MANAGEMENT

The Status of China's Funds Industry

At the end of 2008, after nearly a decade of development, there were 444 funds in China, with a total net value of CNY1,947.3 billion (US$280.4 billion). The average assets under management in each fund totaled CNY4.3 billion. Among them, the net value of those that were allowed to invest in stocks amounted to CNY1.3473 trillion (US$194 billion), making up 30.38 percent of the tradable market value of China's stock market, 9.11 percent of the market capitalization and 21.52 percent of the total value of residential term deposits. The vast majority of the funds (413) were open-ended. From an investment perspective, there were 210 equity funds (stocks), comprising 45 percent of the total assets, 126 hybrid funds (24 percent), with the balance being made up of assets managed under principal-guaranteed funds, fixed income/bond funds and money market funds, as shown in Tables 3.13 and 3.14.

Equity funds dominated the market during the opening period. Since 2002, when hybrid funds and bond funds were introduced, part of the capital has been diverted from equity funds to these new funds. The hybrid funds, with their flexible arrangements for allocating assets, won the hearts of investors, their market share rising from 5.7 percent in 2002 to 24.28 percent by the end of 2008. Money market funds experienced ups and downs within just a few

TABLE 3.13 Movement of types of funds (by number of funds), 1998–2009

Year	Total funds	Open-end	Closed-end	Equity	Hybrid	Bond	Principal Guaranteed	Money Market
1998	41	0	41	27	1	0	0	0
1999	56	0	56	43	1	0	0	0
2000	46	0	46	45	1	0	0	0
2001	53	3	50	52	1	0	0	0
2002	71	17	54	58	11	2	0	0
2003	113	59	54	70	25	12	1	5
2004	168	114	54	87	53	13	4	11
2005	223	169	54	109	67	15	4	28
2006	311	258	53	151	92	22	6	40
2007	347	313	35	170	107	25	5	40
2008	444	413	32	210	126	61	7	40
2009	557	526	31	235	155	76	6	43

Source: Wind Information.

years of their initial introduction in 2003. During the A-share market downturn in 2004 and 2005, they were popular in the market, with the net assets amounting to CNY195.3 billion (US$23.6 billion), covering 41.8 percent of the whole fund market. However, when the market became bullish in 2006, money market funds shrank to CNY64 billion (US$8.42 billion) in August 2007, with a market share of 3.4 percent, while other funds increased significantly. However, in 2008, the impact of the financial crisis meant that money market funds rose again, gaining a market share of 20 percent by the end of 2008.

TABLE 3.14 Ratio of net fund value to A-share market value, 1998-2009

Year	Tradable Value (CNY billion)	Market Capitalization (CNY billion)	Total Term Deposits (CNY billion)	Net Fund Value (CNY billion)	% of Tradable Value	% of Market Capitalization	% of Term Deposits
1998	576.90	1,948.70	—	10.7	1.90	0.60	—
1999	821.40	2,647.10	—	45.8	5.60	1.70	—
2000	1,608.80	4,809.10	4,614.20	77.5	4.80	1.60	1.70
2001	1,446.30	4,352.20	5,143.50	70.4	4.90	1.60	1.40
2002	1,248.50	3,832.90	5,878.90	95.9	7.70	2.50	1.60
2003	1,317.90	4,2458.00	7,447.70	136.4	10.40	3.20	1.80
2004	1,168.90	3,705.60	8,339.60	231.6	19.80	6.20	2.80
2005	1,063.10	3,243.00	9,691.70	235.5	22.20	7.30	2.40
2006	2,500.40	8,940.40	10,653.60	741.3	29.60	8.30	7.00
2007	9,031.00	39,920.40	4,931.30	3,083.2	34.14	7.72	62.52
2008	4,434.80	14,797.50	6,259.50	1,347.3	30.38	9.11	21.52
2009	15,125.87	24,393.91	8,435.97	2,676.1	17.69	10.97	31.72

Source: Figures are calculated based on Wind Information and statistics from the PBC website. The figures refer to year-end balances.

A Comparison of China's Fund Industry with Mature Markets

China's fund industry has developed rapidly in the past decade, but compared with mature markets it is still in its primary stages. The 2009 report of the authoritative Investment Company Institute (ICI) in the United States, shows that the total assets of the common funds in the world reached US$19 trillion, 51 percent of which was contributed by the United States, 33 percent by Europe, 11 percent by Asia Pacific, and only 1.5 percent by mainland China. From these figures, it is clear that China's fund industry is still in its primary stages and there remains plenty of room for development.

The modern fund industry in the United States has been developing since 1924 and has become mature. By the end of 2008, total assets under management amounted to US$9.6 trillion, or 51 percent of the world total. Of this, 30 percent comes from domestic equity funds; 9 percent from international equity funds; 16 percent from bond funds; 40 percent from money market funds; and 5 percent from hybrid funds. The impact of the financial crisis has meant that the net assets of bond funds and money market funds now constitute more than half of the total as the market share of equity funds shrank. A comparison of the fund structures of the US and China reveals that the percentage shares of China's equity funds and hybrid funds are higher than those of the US. This is because China's stock market is growing rapidly, with more investment opportunities compared with mature markets. On the other hand, a lack of product variety and low turnover in the bond market and money market has dampened capital flows into the two markets. We believe these problems will be solved and capital flows will increase as these markets develop.

Future Developments

After 10 years of development, China's fund industry has played an important role in the capital market. Benefiting from the trend of capital flows from the banking sector to the capital market, the industry has bright prospects. Funds with banking, insurance, and foreign backgrounds will grow rapidly. Qualified Foreign Institutional Investors (QFIIs) and Qualified Domestic Institutional Investors (QDIIs) will also have a large influence on the industry.

The rapid development of China's fund industry has exposed some problems that need immediate resolution. These include limitations in the variety of fees charged that push fund companies to rely on expanding assets under management in order to increase fee revenue; a talent shortage and brain drain caused by insufficient incentives amid fast development; and the convergence of asset allocation and stock pooling as a result of the frequent short-term assessments that fund managers have to undergo, making it hard for them to adhere to a consistent investment style. The degree to which these problems can be solved will have a direct impact on the sustainable development of the fund industry.

CHINA'S INSURANCE INDUSTRY

China's insurance industry began in 1980 and has maintained a high growth rate over the past 30 years. However, its scale is limited when compared to other components of China's financial industry, or the insurance industries of other countries.

Development of the Industry

The launch of the *Insurance Law* in 1995 was a landmark, setting up a legal framework for China's insurance industry. The establishment of the China Insurance Regulatory Commission (CIRC) in November 1998 was another landmark and, since its establishment, the CIRC has promulgated over 200 detailed rules to regulate and supervise the rapidly growing industry. At the end of 1999, the industry's total assets represented just 2.9 percent of GDP. By the end of March 2009, this had risen to more than 11 percent, with an annualized growth rate exceeding 30 percent.

The asset management philosophy of China's insurance industry has also changed. Before December 2004, the share of assets in the form of bank deposits was larger than that in the form of investments. Later, the investment amount began to increase quickly and, by March 2009, was more than double that of bank deposits. From December 1999 to December 2008, the annualized growth rate of investment in the insurance industry was 31.23 percent, far higher than that of assets for the same period. This showed that China's insurance industry had a strong will to invest in an environment where investment avenues were opening up and the capital market was developing rapidly.

By 2002, Sino–foreign joint ventures outnumbered local insurance companies, a special characteristic of the structure of China's insurance industry. However, while the number of the state-owned insurance companies has decreased, they still hold a leading position in the market. By March 2009, the insurance premium income of domestic companies accounted for more than 96 percent of the market total. The dominance of domestic insurance companies is not expected to change in the years ahead.

Bank Equity Holdings

In September 2006, it became possible for insurance companies, insurance group (holding) companies and insurance asset management companies to invest in equities of domestic commercial banks. The idea was to encourage greater investment from insurance companies, large and small. In January 2008, the China Banking Regulatory Commission (CBRC) and the CIRC jointly signed a memorandum strengthening cooperation between the banking and insurance industries and agreeing such things as entry criteria, approval procedures, risk handling, and information exchanges that would be encountered during mutual investments between commercial banks and insurance companies. The memorandum also defined the segregation of duties and respective responsibilities of the two regulatory committees and set down principles of prudent regulation, on-site checks and off-site supervision, risk management procedures, and information exchange.

In May 2008, new rules were issued to regulate the solvency of insurance groups. These defined two structures for China's insurance groups: (i) holding companies (such as Ping An Insurance), where a holding company is set up within the group and a parent and subsidiary framework is formed; and (ii) direct-equity holding (as exemplified by China Life Insurance Company), where the insurance company directly holds the equity of other insurance institutions and expands its business via subsidiaries.

In 2005, China Life Insurance Company purchased 0.4 billion CCB H-shares for US$0.25 billion and later spent a further HK$2.35 billion (US$288 million) to purchase 788.42 million BOC H-shares. In August 2006, China Life Insurance spent CNY0.392

billion (US$49.2 million) to purchase 70 million shares in Industrial Bank via share auctions. Later that year, it spent CNY12 billion (US$1.5 billion) to purchase 3.9 billion shares in ICBC on the Shanghai and Hong Kong stock exchanges, and a further CNY5.67 billion (US$711 million) to purchase 20 percent equity in Guangdong Development Bank.[2]

Ping An Insurance is also a role model for investment in bank equities, having acquired Fujian Asia Bank with HSBC Holding Company, and obtained a banking license through this transaction in 2004. Two years later, it made significant investments in both the H-shares and A-shares of BOC and purchased an 89.24-percent stake in Shenzhen Commercial Bank.[3]

In June 2009, Shenzhen Development Bank announced that it would issue up to 585 million non-public shares to Ping An Life Insurance. At the same time, Ping An declared that it would purchase 16.76 percent of Shenzhen Development Bank's equity from the bank's largest shareholder, Newbridge Capital, no later than December 31, 2010.

Domestic and Overseas Listings

In November 2003, the People's Insurance Company of China listed on the Hong Kong Stock Exchange and became the first state-owned financial enterprise to be wholly listed outside the mainland, marking the beginning of the restructuring and listing process of state-owned insurance companies. The following month, China Life Insurance Company listed on the New York and Hong Kong stock exchanges and became the first Chinese financial company listed both in the US and Hong Kong. In June 2004, Ping An Insurance Company of China, Ltd. was listed in Hong Kong as a financial group. Min An Insurance Company (Hong Kong) Limited, an affiliate of China Insurance Company Limited, announced its listing on the main board of the Hong Kong Stock Exchange in December 2006, so becoming the fourth Chinese insurance company to list in Hong Kong.

With the restarting of the IPO process in the A-share market by the CSRC in May 2006, China Life, China Ping An and China Pacific Insurance were quickly listed and raised a collective CNY97.2 billion (US$12.2 billion). In June 2009, China Pacific Insurance's IPO plan for the H-share market was approved in principle by the board. After a delay caused by adverse market conditions, the IPO was completed in December 2009, raising US$3.575 billion.

QUALIFIED FOREIGN INSTITUTIONAL INVESTORS

After years of preparation, the guidelines governing the investment activities of QFIIs came into force in December 2002. QFIIs can be overseas fund management institutions, insurance companies, securities companies, and other asset management companies. All must be approved by the CSRC to invest in China's capital market and the investment quotas—which can range from US$50 million to US$800 million—are subject to the approval of the State Administration of Foreign Exchange (SAFE). UBS was one of the first QFIIs and its US$800 million investment quota remains the largest approved to date.

By December 31, 2009, a total of 86 QFIIs had been approved for investment, with a combined investment quota of US$16.6 billion. However, even if the quota amount was fully used, this would be equivalent to only 0.5 percent of the total stock market value by the end of 2009; it therefore had a limited impact on China's capital markets.

In May 2007, the second Sino–US Strategic and Economic Dialogue held in Washington resulted in a series of commitments that were beneficial for strengthening and deepening the bilateral economic relationship, including an agreement to increase the QFII investment quota to US$30 billion providing that it would be helpful for the balance of international payments. It will take some time though for these commitments to be fulfilled.

CHINA'S WTO COMMITMENTS

Commitments Made by the Securities and Insurance Industry

Under the terms of the agreement governing China's accession to the WTO, foreign securities organizations can trade directly in B-shares. Their representative offices have become special players in the stock market and foreign investors are allowed to hold a maximum of 33 percent of the shares when establishing joint venture securities companies. Foreign securities organizations are allowed to engage in risk investment, A-share and B-share margin trades, H-share trades, government and corporate bonds and funds. However, individual investments cannot exceed one-third of the total. (For detailed commitments, see the official WTO website or the CSRC official website.) By 2009 nine Sino-foreign securities joint ventures had been established, with one application pending. Foreign investors included Morgan Stanley, UBS, Credit Lyonnais, Daiwa Securities SMBC, Goldman Sachs, UBS, Credit Suisse and Deutsche Bank.

Foreign Investments in China's Funds and Securities

Under the commitments made on entering the WTO, foreign investors have actively invested in China's funds and securities during recent years. By the end of 2007, 28 foreign financial institutions had invested in 28 funds in China.

CONCLUSION

In recent years, the A-share market has experienced a bull market and then an overwhelming bear market. In 2009, it rebounded strongly and the market has now become relatively stable. Although the development of securitization has been promising, we should realize that compared to international markets, listed-company governance and stock market supervision and regulation still have a long way to go. Thanks to the share splitting reform in May 2005 and the reduction of non-public stocks beginning in 2008, the high ratio of state shareholding has been largely resolved. However, further efforts will be needed to solve this problem at its roots. China's fund management market has entered a fast-moving era and the share of fund assets and transaction amounts in the capital market is increasing. The significant fluctuation encountered by the fund industry will not change the overall rapid development trend. During China's more than 30 years of reform, the Hong Kong SAR has performed an important role in the development of China's economy. Compared to the Hong Kong stock market, the financing function of the domestic stock market still needs substantial improvement. Accelerating the enhancement of the domestic stock market's financing function and further raising the ratio of direct financing in the whole financial market will be of great significance for the healthy development of the nation's economy.

During the past two decades, China's bond market has seen considerable development. However, corporate bonds are still growing slowly. Because the exchange market and inter-bank market have not been effectively connected, the yield curves of the two markets exhibit significant variances. These have come to the government's attention and the creation of new bond products is being actively promoted. The introduction of inter-bank Treasury bond forwards is preparation for launching Treasury bond futures, interest swaps, interest options and other related products.

Stock-market and bond-market risks have increased significantly, and the domestic market still lacks the necessary instruments to hedge risks. It will be necessary, therefore, to develop equity and interest rate derivative products to provide the necessary instruments for managing risk. These products are dealt with in Part II of this book.

ENDNOTES

1. For further details, see the Shanghai Stock Exchange website, www.sse.com.cn.
2. For further details, see "Investment on Bank Equity by Insurance Companies," at www.e-chinalife.com.
3. For details of these and other purchases made by Ping An, see "Investment in Bank Equity by Insurance Companies," at www.pa18.com.

CHAPTER 4

China's Foreign Exchange System and International Investment Positions

REFORMING THE FOREIGN EXCHANGE SYSTEM

Since the founding of the PRC, China's foreign exchange regime has experienced four stages of development: the planned economy; the economic transformation; the socialist market economy starting from 1994; and the managed floating exchange rate system with reference to a basket of currencies.

The Planned Economy (1953–78)

In its early years, the PRC suffered from a shortage of foreign exchange. To use its foreign exchange resources effectively to support the country's economic recovery and development, China adjusted the CNY exchange rates flexibly to regulate foreign exchange income and expenditure, and established a centralized management system for its foreign exchange. From 1953, foreign trade was managed exclusively by state-owned companies, while foreign exchange services were centrally operated by the People's Bank of China (PBC). Foreign exchange income and expenditure were subject to mandatory state planning, with earnings being sold to the government, which then arranged and approved the national demand for foreign exchange. Under the planned economy, China's exporting enterprises were not sufficiently competitive in the international market and had little incentive to earn foreign exchange because they had to sell it to the state at a prescribed rate. The resulting insufficient supply of foreign exchange led to increased demand and an overestimation of the exchange rate.

Economic Transformation (1979–93)

To stimulate the enthusiasm of enterprises for foreign exchange, and to expand earnings, China began to implement an exchange retention system from 1979. Using centralized and prioritized management, the retention system for trade and non-trade foreign exchange allowed local governments and enterprises to retain a certain percentage of foreign exchange income, thus providing the foreign capital needed to expand production and incentives to export.

As enterprises had different foreign exchange surpluses and deficits, demand soon rose for methods to transfer foreign exchange. Thus, in late 1980, the Bank of China (BOC) allowed enterprises to sell their surplus foreign exchange to the bank, and to buy the foreign exchange they needed.

Subsequently, two foreign exchange markets coexisted in China: the first being the official exchange rate, which was overestimated at CNY1.5 to US$1. In addition, an internal settlement price was designated in 1981 to stimulate foreign trade. This was calculated based on the country's average export exchange costs plus 10 percent profit, and fixed at CNY2.8 to US$1. This latter rate was used in the foreign exchange swap market. In fact, there was a third market for China's foreign exchange—the black market, where shortages pushed the price much higher than in the official or swap markets.

The two official exchange rate schemes encouraged exports and helped take care of the interests of non-trade business, but their scope was unclear and they failed to resolve a number of complex accounting and management issues. In 1985, the internal settlement price was abolished and replaced by a single exchange rate, also fixed at CNY2.8 to the dollar, and overestimation continued. Subsequently, the exchange rate continued to adjust in accordance with changes in domestic price level, and reached CNY5.22 in November 1990. In 1991, China implemented a managed floating exchange rate regime, and at the same time opened the swap market's foreign exchange rate to fluctuations in supply and demand. The result was volatile exchange rates. By the end of 1993, following PBC intervention, the exchange rate had risen to CNY8.72 to the dollar.

The Socialist Market Economy

In November 1993, the Central Committee of the Communist Party of China (CPC) made the decision to establish a "socialist market economic system" that would reform the system by which foreign exchange was managed. The new system was to be market-based, with a managed floating exchange rate and a standardized foreign exchange market that would gradually transform the CNY into a convertible currency.

On January 1, 1994, the old exchange retention system was replaced by the practice of bank settlement and sale of foreign exchange. However, in order to ensure the supply of foreign exchange, except for the retained part permitted by state regulations that could be stored on foreign exchange accounts, all foreign exchange had to be transferred back promptly and sold to designated domestic banks at market rates. Under the new regime, the dual exchange rates were merged at a set exchange rate of CNY8.70 to the dollar.

On April 1, 1994, the inter-bank foreign exchange market, the China Foreign Exchange Trade System (CFETS), was set up in Shanghai. The CFETS adopted a membership scheme, as well as transaction matching and a centralized clearing system. The PBC was made responsible for any necessary interventions to ensure exchange rate stability.

Through these reforms, in 1994 China achieved conditional CNY current account convertibility. In 1996, it removed the remaining restrictions and, at the end of the year, announced full CNY current account convertibility. In 1998, when the foreign exchange swap center was shut down, all foreign exchange trading for foreign-invested enterprises began to be settled in the banking system.

Since its accession to the WTO in 2001, China's economy has developed rapidly. The foreign exchange management system has been further refined, current account convertibility has continued to improve and there have been steady experiments with capital account convertibility. Some foreign exchange insurance funds are now allowed to invest in offshore securities markets, and individuals are allowed to transfer assets offshore. Investment quotas under the Qualified Foreign Institutional Investors (QFII) scheme have been enlarged. Multinational corporations are now allowed to carry out foreign exchange operations within their group, collecting or transferring foreign exchange funds on a regional or global basis. Regulations have been enacted to prescribe cross-border mergers and acquisitions by domestic residents, as well as mergers and acquisitions of domestic enterprises by foreign investors. Rules have also been put in place concerning domestic residents' equity financing and return investment through overseas special purpose entities.

Managed Floating Exchange Rate System

In July 2005, China further improved its exchange rate system based on market supply and demand with reference to a basket of currencies, which was exactly in line with the reform target set in November 1993. As a matter of fact, the CNY had been under increasing pressure to appreciate since late in 2002, and the 2005 reform served to offset further pressure over the following couple of years.

Since the foreign exchange reform, the state has issued a number of policies to promote the development of the foreign exchange market. These include allowing eligible non-financial enterprises and non-bank financial institutions to enter the spot inter-bank foreign exchange market; introducing US-style market-makers and inquiry-trading mechanisms; permitting all banks to conduct foreign exchange forward settlements and CNY-to-foreign currency swaps; launching forward and swap transactions; implementing a comprehensive position management of bank settlement and increasing the total threshold of the banking system; expanding the volatility scale of non-US-dollar currencies in the inter-bank market; lifting client restrictions on the listed exchange rate floating range of non-US-dollar currencies; expanding the bid-ask spread of foreign exchange cash and transfer; and allowing multiple prices within one day.

The reform has recorded a number of great achievements, including current account convertibility, further improvements to the CNY exchange rate mechanism, and greater innovation in the foreign exchange products introduced by banks. However, if it is to promote the balance of international payments and reduce dependence on foreign trade, China needs to widen the channels of capital inflow and outflow, and gradually realize capital account convertibility for its currency. At the same time, it needs to nurture and develop its foreign exchange market, improve the supervision of cross-border capital flows and guard against financial risks to protect national financial security.

CNY/US$ EXCHANGE RATES

Before looking at China's international positions and various CNY products in the following chapters, we need to say a little about the CNY exchange rate *vis-à-vis* the US dollar over the years. Table 4.1 shows the exchange rates from 1977 to 2010.

TABLE 4.1   CNY/US$ exchange rates, 1977–2010

Year	CNY/US$	Appreciation/ Depreciation (%)	Year	CNY/US$	Appreciation/ Depreciation (%)
1977	173.00	8.69	1995	835.10	3.21
1978	157.71	9.70	1996	831.42	0.44
1979	149.62	5.41	1997	828.98	0.29
1980	153.03	−2.23	1998	827.91	0.13
1981	174.55	−12.33	1999	827.83	0.01
1982	192.27	−9.22	2000	827.84	0.00
1983	198.09	−2.94	2001	827.65	0.02
1984	279.57	−29.14	2002	827.70	−0.01
1985	293.66	−4.80	2003	827.67	0.00
1986	345.28	−14.95	2004	827.65	0.00
1987	372.21	−7.24	2005	816.19	1.40
1988	372.21	0.00	2006	797.42	2.35
1989	376.51	−1.14	2007	760.20	4.90
1991	532.33	−29.27	2008	694.51	9.46
1992	551.46	−3.47	2009	683.11	1.67
1993	576.20	−4.29	2010	682.69	0.06
1994	861.87	−33.15			

Source: Zhang (2008); data from 2005 to 2009 are daily average rates from the SAFE; data for 2010 is the average to June 10, 2010 from the SAFE.

As shown in the table, the exchange rate remained at around 8.28 from 1997 to 2004. The amendments of July 2005 began the appreciation process, with a 1.4-percent appreciation that year (using the average daily exchange rate against the previous year's average). From 2005 to 2009 there was a cumulative appreciation of 21.2 percent, an annual average of 4.71 percent.

FOREIGN EXCHANGE TRADING VALUE

Annual Trading Value

Table 4.2 shows the annual value of China's foreign exchange trade from 1994 to 2009. The PBC has not released the relevant figures since the change of regime in 2005 and the figures shown in the table for the years since then are estimates only.

The good news is that in 2007 the PBC participated for the first time in the Bank for International Settlements (BIS) triennial survey, the data from which shows that the average daily foreign exchange trading value was US$9 billion in April 2007. This comprised US$5.53 billion in spot trading, US$2.82 billion in forward trading, and US$0.67 billion in foreign exchange swap trading. Extrapolating from this (using the conventional method of multiplying the average daily value by the average number of working days in a year, 250), we can say that the annual foreign exchange trading value in China was about US$2,250 billion and the average compound annual growth rate from 2004 to 2007 was 120.8 percent.

TABLE 4.2 China's foreign exchange trade, 1994–2009

Year	Trading Amount (US$ billion)	Annual Growth Rate (%)	Proportion of GDP (%)
1994	40.8	—	7.5
1995	65.5	60.5	9.4
1996	62.8	−4.1	7.7
1997	70.0	11.5	7.8
1998	52.0	−25.7	5.5
1999	31.5	−39.4	3.2
2000	42.2	34.0	3.9
2001	75.0	77.7	6.4
2002	97.2	29.6	7.6
2003	151.1	55.5	10.7
2004	209.0	38.3	12.6
2005*	461.5	120.8	20.7
2006*	1,019.0	120.8	38.2
2007*	2,250.0	120.8	66.5
2008*	3,609.1	60.4	83.4
2009*	5,789.1	60.4	116.3

Source: Foreign exchange trading value from Zhang (2008); GDP data from Table 1.10.
*Indicates estimated figures

Assuming that foreign exchange trading value increased at the same annual compound rate from 2004 to 2007, we can obtain the values for 2005 and 2006 as given in Table 4.2. Assuming an annual growth rate of 60.4 percent from 2007 to 2009, the trading values for 2008 and 2009 are as shown in the table. Based on these figures, it is estimated that total foreign exchange trading value should surpass the Chinese GDP for the first time in 2009.

Foreign Exchange Trading Value and GDP Compared

Table 4.2 shows that the total annual foreign exchange trading value as a percentage of the corresponding GDP was only around 7.5 percent for the nine years from 1994 to 2003. The ratio passed the 10 percent level for the first time in 2003, and it increased steadily to 66.5 percent in 2007. In that year, however, the world foreign exchange trading value was 14.7 times greater than the world GDP figure, while the foreign exchange trading value/GDP ratio in China was a mere 4.5 percent of the world ratio. This was a clear indication that the Chinese foreign exchange market needs to improve its liquidity.

International Comparisons

The BIS survey data for April 2007 show that the average daily foreign exchange trading value in China was only 0.28 percent of the world average. Considering that China's GDP represented 6.2 percent of the global figure, the Chinese foreign exchange market needs to accelerate its liquidity if the CNY is to play a more important role in the world marketplace. The same data show that the average daily foreign exchange trading value in India was 177.8 percent higher than the corresponding Chinese figure for April 2007, even though China's GDP was 188.7 percent higher than India's for that year. We will compare the

CNY foreign exchange market more closely and systematically to those of other currencies in Chapter 20.

INTERNATIONAL INVESTMENT POSITION

Definition

A country's international investment position (IIP) shows its balance of financial assets and liabilities at a given point in time. IMF member countries are required to report these statistics, under clause VIII governing capital account free convertibility. The IIP reflects the level of a country's international assets, industrial distribution, the time structure of

TABLE 4.3 China's international investment position, 2004–2009 (US$ billion)

Item	End of 2004	End of 2005	End of 2006	End of 2007	End of 2008	End of 2009
Net position	276.4	407.7	640.2	1,188.1	1,493.8	1,821.9
A. Assets	929.1	1,223.3	1,690.5	2,416.2	2,956.7	3,460.1
1. Direct investment in foreign countries	52.7	64.5	90.6	116.0	185.7	229.6
2. Securities investment	92.0	116.7	265.2	284.6	252.5	242.8
2.1 Equity securities	0.0	0.0	1.5	19.6	21.4	54.6
2.2 Debt securities	92.0	116.7	263.7	265.0	231.1	188.2
3. Other investment	165.8	216.4	253.9	468.3	552.3	536.5
3.1 Trade credit	43.2	66.1	92.2	116.0	110.2	164.6
3.2 Loans	59.0	71.9	67.0	88.8	107.1	94.2
3.3 Currency and deposits	55.3	67.5	73.6	138.0	152.9	140.9
3.4 Other assets	8.3	10.9	21.0	125.5	182.1	136.8
4. Reserve assets	618.6	825.7	1,080.8	1,547.3	1,966.2	2,451.3
4.1 Monetary gold	4.1	4.2	12.3	17.0	16.9	37.1
4.2 SDR	1.2	1.2	1.1	1.2	1.2	12.5
4.3 Reserve position in the IMF	3.3	1.4	1.1	0.8	2.0	2.5
4.4 Foreign exchange	609.9	818.9	1,066.3	1,528.2	1,946.0	2,399.2
B. Liabilities	652.7	815.6	1,050.3	1,228.1	1,462.9	1,638.1
1. Foreign direct investment in China	369.0	471.5	614.4	703.7	915.5	997.4
2. Securities investment	56.6	76.6	120.7	146.6	167.7	190.0
2.1 Equity securities	43.3	63.6	106.5	129.0	150.5	174.8
2.2 Debt securities	13.3	13.0	14.2	17.6	17.2	15.2
3. Other investment	227.1	267.5	315.2	377.8	379.6	450.8
3.1 Trade credit	80.9	106.3	119.6	148.7	129.6	161.7
3.2 Loans	88.0	87.0	98.5	103.3	103.0	111.4
3.3 Currency and deposits	38.1	48.4	59.5	79.1	91.8	103.4
3.4 Other liabilities	20.0	25.7	37.7	46.7	55.2	74.2
Net position/GDP (%)	16.8	18.2	24.3	37.5	33.1	37.1
Assets/GDP (%)	56.3	54.8	64.3	76.3	65.4	70.5

Source: State Administration of Foreign Exchange website (http://www.safe.gov.cn/).

external liabilities, and other information. While to some extent these data demonstrate a country's overall economic strength and international market dependence, they also provide important information on the vulnerability of its financial system.

China's IIP

Table 4.3 shows China's international investment position from 2004 to 2009. As at the end of 2008, China had net international assets of US$1,519 billion. Converting China's GDP into US dollars at the year-end exchange rate, we can see that the ratio of net IIP to GDP continued to rise, reaching 34.47 percent as at the end of 2008, 17.28 percent higher than at the end of 2004. In addition, the ratio of gross assets to GDP increased steadily over that period.

China's net IIP is mainly attributable to the rapid growth in asset items in the IIP table, for which the annual compound growth rate is 33.65 percent. Moreover, China's direct investment in foreign countries has also increased at pace, with the growth rate reaching 46.03 percent in 2008. The liabilities in the IIP table mainly consist of foreign direct investments, which are stable at around 60 percent of total liabilities.

An Analysis of Specific IIP Items

Direct Investment Overseas   As direct investment in foreign countries is a major component of China's "going out" strategy, the foreign exchange management for this is more liberal. Direct investment abroad has grown rapidly since 2007, surpassing US$100 billion for the first time in 2007, and reaching US$185.7 billion and 229.6 billion at the end of 2008 and 2009, respectively. Annual growth rates of direct investment abroad were 40.5 percent, 28.0 percent, 60.1 percent, and 23.6 percent from 2006 to 2009, higher than corresponding annual growth rates of 30.3 percent, 14.5 percent, 30.1 percent, and 8.9 percent in foreign direct investment (FDI) in China in the same period. Despite the higher growth of direct investment abroad since 2006, it is still only 23 percent of FDI in China at the end of 2009.

Securities Investment   Securities investment consists of stocks, mid-to-long-term bonds, money market instruments and other forms of investment. China's foreign-investment portfolio mainly comprises bond investments, while foreign investment in China's securities is mainly in equity instruments, with debt investment making up only 10.67 percent of foreign investment in Chinese securities.

Foreign Exchange Reserves   China's trade surplus has continued to widen in recent years, greatly increasing its foreign exchange reserves, which at the end of 2009 had reached US$2.45 trillion, an increase of 24.7 percent over the previous year. The total foreign reserve at the end of 2009 was almost half of China's GDP in 2009.

Figure 4.1 shows that China's holdings of US government bonds as a proportion of foreign exchange reserves have consistently remained above 30 percent.

Figure 4.2 compares China's US-bond holdings with those of Japan and OPEC over the same period. China's total holdings of US Treasury bonds rose swiftly, reaching US$767.9 billion by March 2009, 13 times the level of March 2000. By contrast, Japan's holdings steadily declined from a peak of US$700 billion in August 2004 before bouncing

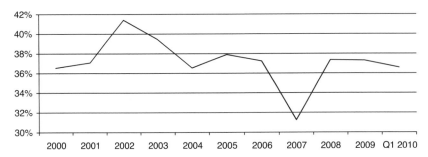

FIGURE 4.1 China's holdings of US government bonds as a percentage of its foreign exchange reserves, 2000–2010
Source: US Treasury Department and SAFE.

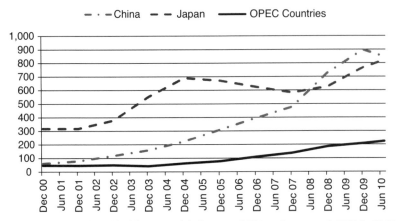

FIGURE 4.2 US government bond holdings (US$ billions) of China, Japan and OPEC, 2000–2009
Source: US Treasury Department.

back after the sub-prime crisis emerged, when US government bonds were regarded as relatively secure reserve assets. OPEC's holding of US treasuries has ranked third or fourth while growing steadily.

Foreign investment in China   Over the past few years, China has been encouraging local governments to attract FDI, offering generous tax benefits. At the same time, China's rapid economic development, huge market potential, and high return on investment, coupled with strong pressure for the CNY to appreciate, pushed FDI up at an annual growth rate of more than 30 percent in 2008; yet it fell to a mere 8.9 percent in 2009. FDI constitutes the most important form of liability in China's IIP.

Table 4.4 describes the distribution of corporate income tax (CIT) between domestic and foreign-invested enterprises from 2000 to 2007. This shows that CIT paid by domestic enterprises accounted for around 80 percent of the total. This imbalance in the tax burden results in unfair competition, and contributes to building a foreign monopoly in the domestic market.

In January 2008, the *Enterprise Income Tax Law* introduced a uniform tax rate of 25 percent for both domestic and foreign firms. This rate is still advantageous compared to those

TABLE 4.4 Distribution of CIT of domestic and foreign-invested enterprises, 2000–07 (CNY billion)

Year	Domestic Companies	Foreign-invested Companies	Total	% of Domestic CIT
2000	144.46	32.61	177.07	81.58
2001	212.19	51.25	263.44	80.55
2002	197.28	61.80	259.08	76.15
2003	234.22	70.54	304.76	76.85
2004	314.17	93.25	407.42	77.11
2005	436.31	114.77	551.08	79.17
2006	554.59	153.48	708.07	78.32
2007	772.37	195.12	967.49	79.83

Source: State Administration of Taxation website (http://www.chinatax.gov.cn).

in effect in many neighboring countries and regions, including Japan (37.5 percent), Thailand (36 percent), South Korea (34 percent), India (30 percent), and Vietnam (28 percent).

In line with China's Eleventh Five-Year Plan, the introduction of foreign investment should have a focus on quality, with the aim being to optimize the distribution of foreign investment in such areas as high-tech industries, emerging sectors, the modern services industry, and in R&D. Foreign investment should also be directed to agriculture, horticulture and aquaculture, where the projects should include the use of high technology to add value and boost farmers' incomes. More international talent should be attracted to enhance China's own R&D capability.

Supervision of foreign investment also needs to be strengthened. While FDI promotes economic development, it also affects economic stability. With lax capital oversight, FDI could easily become a major channel for international speculative capital going in and out of a country. Empirical studies have shown that having a large amount of international hot money that having a large in circulation is a significant factor in increasing economic instability.

Figure 4.3 shows China's actual utilization of foreign investment from January 2000 to March 2009 and reveals that this has declined since the outbreak of the economic crisis.

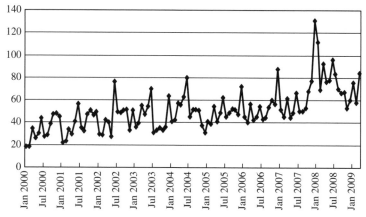

FIGURE 4.3 China's utilization of foreign investment, 2000–09 (US$100 million)
Source: Ministry of Commerce of the PRC website (http://www.mofcom.gov.cn).

In December 2008, foreign investment dropped 54.35 percent year-on-year, with signs of an outflow of foreign capital. During periods of economic downturn, a lack of supervision and an outflow of foreign capital can undoubtedly make things worse for a country's economy.

IIPS COMPARED

The US is the world's largest economy and financial system, but has the world's largest liabilities and is thus not very comparable with China. The UK is a world-class center of foreign exchange and derivative products. Although its international assets account for a high proportion of its GDP, its net assets have been low (and even negative) over the past two years, again causing low comparability with China. As Asia's financial center, Hong Kong's economy relies mainly on transit trade, and it is small compared with other developed countries, so again it is not appropriate to compare it with the mainland.

Germany and Japan are export-oriented economies whose total net international assets have ranked high in the world in recent years, thus bearing strong comparability with China. As at the end of 2008, the respective proportions of international assets to GDP for Germany and Japan were 205.6 percent and 93.7 percent, while China's was only 65.4 percent. As at the end of 2009, the respective proportion of international assets to GDP for Japan was

TABLE 4.5 IIP/GDP ratio for selected countries/regions, 2004–09 (%)

Country/ Region	Ratio Accounts	2009	2008	2007	2006	2005	2004
US	Financial assets	—	138.62	127.76	109.13	96.29	79.93
	Financial liabilities	—	162.80	145.44	126.02	111.79	99.15
	Net position	—	−24.18	−17.68	−16.89	−15.50	−19.21
Japan	Financial assets	105.65	102.30	118.36	110.00	100.89	87.06
	Financial liabilities	54.95	57.86	69.85	67.61	64.87	49.78
	Net position	50.69	44.43	48.51	42.39	36.01	37.28
Canada	Financial assets	—	138.66	126.41	129.42	106.18	100.67
	Financial liabilities	—	134.52	128.11	128.12	115.55	115.96
	Net position	—	4.14	−1.70	1.30	−9.36	−15.30
UK	Financial assets	—	494.86	455.37	393.75	383.76	325.82
	Financial liabilities	—	499.46	476.59	421.80	403.57	344.14
	Net position	—	−4.60	−21.22	−28.04	−19.81	−18.32
Hong Kong	Financial assets	—	1,062.31	1,311.98	987.70	816.69	807.39
	Financial liabilities	—	772.01	1,078.38	722.34	576.64	558.22
	Net position	—	290.30	233.60	265.37	240.05	249.17
Germany	Financial assets	—	205.60	206.54	196.02	182.42	158.34
	Financial liabilities	—	177.90	179.94	168.61	160.90	147.14
	Net position	—	27.70	26.61	27.41	21.52	11.20
China	Financial assets	70.48	65.42	76.32	64.28	54.75	56.33
	Financial liabilities	33.37	32.37	38.79	39.93	36.50	39.57
	Net position	37.11	33.05	37.53	24.34	18.25	16.76

Source: National statistics department and central bank websites of the above countries/regions.

105.65 percent, while China's was only 70.5 percent. This wide gap suggests great potential for future growth in China's international assets.

In recent years, China's commercial banks, policy banks, securities companies, and other enterprises have entered into various cooperation and merger and acquisition agreements with foreign companies and institutions. With the establishment of China Investment Corporation, a Sino–foreign partnership, the pace of equity investment, acquisitions and mergers will accelerate, boosting China's IIP/GDP ratio in the future.

Substantial growth in international assets has laid down professional requirements for corresponding international investment experience and risk management expertise, without which it will be difficult to gain appropriate returns in an increasingly competitive international market and to gauge risks in the international market.

Table 4.5 gives the IIP/GDP ratios for selected countries and regions from 2004 to 2009. This shows that both China's financial asset/GDP ratio and liability/GDP were lower than all other countries and regions in the table, yet China's net position/GDP ratios in 2007 and 2009 were comparable to those of Japan in 2004 and 2005, implying that China's net international position was four to five years behind Japan's.

CONCLUSION

With the opening up of its financial industry and the implementation of international strategies by its financial institutions, China's dependence on international finance will rise rapidly. This calls for an understanding and complete command of all kinds of popular risk management tools in the international market within a relatively short period of time. Domestic institutions and individuals will increasingly need to hedge risks through various exchange-traded and over-the-counter derivatives in the international market, such as products linked to exchange rates, interest rates, stocks, and commodities, and the demand for CNY derivative products will also grow. Therefore, an immediate improvement in the corresponding market liquidity is essential to prevent risk management failures and resultant losses.

In the new international environment, China must, as a matter of urgency, improve its exchange rate formation mechanism, gradually liberalize capital accounts, and build domestic exchange-traded and over-the-counter derivatives markets. At the same time, it needs to strengthen monitoring and oversight, with the aim of controlling market risk and promoting the market's orderly development.

Major Onshore CNY Products and Their Markets

Having introduced the Chinese economy and financial markets in Part I, we now focus on major CNY products in the inter-bank marketplace, the progress made in this area over the past few years, and potential problems to overcome in order for the market grow steadily.

CNY Foreign Exchange Forwards

Foreign exchange forwards are the most fundamental foreign exchange instruments and can be used for both hedging and speculation. Foreign exchange forwards are widely traded in the currency markets of all developed and most developing countries.

A BRIEF HISTORY OF THE CNY FORWARD MARKET

The China Foreign Exchange Trade System (CFETS) began foreign exchange spot trading in the spring of 1994, and set up a trial run of CNY forward transactions a year later. Because the system had been established for less than a year and improvements had yet to be made in this initial stage, the first trial was not successful. However, the People's Bank of China (PBC) recognized the importance of CNY forward transactions, and conducted related research before issuing the *Provisional Measures on CNY Forward Settlement and Foreign Exchange Sale* ("the Measures") in January 1997. The issuance of the Measures cleared away the obstacles to CNY forward transactions and provided the necessary supervisory standards (Ye and Li, 2001).

The Bank of China (BOC), as the only authorized pilot bank, began its CNY forward foreign exchange settlement and sales business in April that year. Although foreign exchange forwards are common even in developing markets, the BOC's CNY forward foreign exchange settlement and sales services marked a milestone in the development of China's foreign exchange derivatives market. The birth of CNY forward transactions made it possible for import and export companies and other entities to hedge their exchange rate risks.

Based on the two expansions of the trial program in 2003 and 2004, the PBC broadened the range of banks permitted to operate forward foreign exchange transactions to include all those qualified to conduct spot foreign exchange and derivatives transactions. These banks can quote prices to customers according to their operating and risk management capabilities, thus enhancing the market's price discovery functions, promoting trade, and providing customers with better services.

AN ILLUSTRATIVE CNY FORWARD TRANSACTION

As the first authorized bank to operate CNY forward transactions, the BOC has maintained its leading position. This section will use the BOC as an example to introduce a typical CNY forward transaction.

BOC's Application Criteria

At present, the BOC can provide CNY forwards for trades classified under current account and certain capital account items, such as loan repayments to the bank, repayment of foreign debts and other cash flows in foreign exchange which have been registered with, or approved by, the State Administration of Foreign Exchange (SAFE).

Currency

The bank now provides forward foreign exchange transactions between CNY and eight foreign currencies as listed below. Table 5.1 lists the durations and opening middle prices of CNY forward products traded on June 15, 2009.

TABLE 5.1   CNY forward foreign exchange quotation of bank of China (middle price), June 15, 2009

Duration	US$	EUR	JPY	HK$	GBP	CHF	AU$	CA$
7 days	683.85	954.80	6.96	88.23	1,119.65	632.29	552.23	610.08
1 month	684.02	954.83	6.96	88.27	1,119.88	632.59	551.41	610.30
3 months	684.21	954.51	6.96	88.34	1,120.00	633.25	549.05	610.71
6 months	683.95	953.63	6.97	88.37	1,119.31	633.93	545.29	610.86
9 months	683.79	953.17	6.99	88.39	1,118.91	635.29	541.83	611.36
12 months	683.69	953.62	7.01	88.41	1,117.93	637.00	538.00	611.84

Note: The quotation is CNY per 100 units in the foreign currency in opening middle price; transaction prices may fluctuate with the market.
Source: BOC website (www.boc.cn).

Business Process

The business process for a typical CNY forward is as follows:

- Application: The customer must open the relevant BOC accounts when applying to conduct forward foreign exchange settlement and sales business.
- Signing of agreement: An "Agreement of Forward Foreign Exchange Settlement and Sale" is signed in duplicate, one for the customer and one for the bank.
- Verification: The customer fills in the form "Power of Attorney for Forward Foreign Exchange Settlement and Sale" and attaches valid certification in accordance with the regulations of foreign exchange settlement and sale; these are then verified by the bank. The amount the client applies for should not exceed the expected amount, and the transaction duration should be consistent with the actual duration.
- Deal: When the BOC confirm the client's power of attorney, the client is required to pay a certain amount of security or reduce the amount of its authorized line of credit. After the deal has been made, the bank sends the client a "Confirmation of Forward Foreign Exchange Settlement and Sale."
- Review and settlement on maturity date: On the maturity dates, the BOC reviews the clients' certification and documents in accordance with the regulations for foreign exchange settlement and sale, before settling with the client.

- Extension: If, where circumstances warrant, the customer cannot complete the deal on time, the customer may apply for an extension.
- Breach of contract: If the customer fails to perform the contract, the bank has the right to liquidate the unperformed positions of the contract on the last settlement day.

CURRENCY COMPOSITION OF CNY FORWARD TRANSACTIONS

Total Transaction Amount

Table 5.2 lists the total turnover of BOC CNY forward transactions and the domestically contracted spot foreign exchange turnover from 1997 to 2004. During the seven years from 1997, the changes in transaction amounts of CNY forwards were much higher than those of spot transactions. Through years of development, the average proportion of the amount of forward foreign exchange in the related spot transaction amount was just less than 1.5 percent in 2005 and 2006, only 1 percent of the corresponding proportion in the international market. This indicates that the forward foreign exchange market was not active in China.

TABLE 5.2 Forward foreign exchange and foreign exchange turnover compared, 1997–2007 (US$ billion)

Year	Forwards Turnover (US$ billion)	Annualized Growth (%)	Spot Market Turnover (US$ billion)	Forwards/ Spot (%)	Forwards/ Trade (%)
1997	0.80	—	70.0	1.10	0.2
1998	2.10	162.5	52.0	4.00	0.6
1999	3.70	76.2	31.5	11.70	1.0
2000	12.08	226.5	42.2	28.60	2.5
2001	9.22	−23.7	75.0	12.30	1.8
2002	3.76	−59.2	97.2	3.90	0.6
2003	8.52	126.7	151.1	5.60	1.0
2004	9.61	12.8	209.0	4.60	0.8
2005	16.39	70.5	401.3	3.90	1.2
2006	29.63	80.8	1,012.8	2.93	1.7
2007	62.40	110.6	1,500.8	4.16	2.8

Note: Data for 1997 to 1999 are from Zhang (2008); the turnover of 2000 to 2005 is from Zhao (2006), and assumes that the BOC market share for 2003 to 2005 was 90 percent, 80 percent, and 70 percent respectively. the turnover of 2006 was estimated on the basis of the data from Zhao for the first five and a half months in 2006 and the full year in 2005, and assumes that the BOC market share in 2006 was 60 percent. The turnover in 2007 was estimated on the basis of the average turnover of CNY products in April 2007 issued by the Bank for International Settlements (BIS).

Currency Composition

The US dollar (with almost 98 percent of the total number of foreign exchange transactions from 2002 to 2004) is the most widely traded currency in the inter-bank market in China, followed by the HK dollar, the Japanese yen and the euro. According to *Chinese Money*

Market magazine, the turnover of forwards between the CNY and these currencies in 2008 was US$16.9 billion, HK$1 billion, ¥300 million, and €200 million, respectively.

FOREIGN EXCHANGE SETTLEMENT AND SALE BEFORE AND AFTER FOREIGN EXCHANGE REFORM

Below, we analyze the changes in the CNY/US$ forward exchange rates before and after the exchange rate reform in 2005. Figure 5.1 lists the daily middle rates of BOC's one-year CNY/US$ forward from 2002 to 2009.

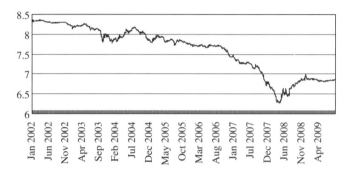

FIGURE 5.1   CNY/US$ forward middle rates, 2002–09
Source: Reuters.

From the beginning of January 2002 to September 2003, the one-year forward exchange rate rose from 8.2152 to 8.3543, indicating that the domestic forward exchange rate market did not respond to the appreciation pressure on the CNY until late September 2003. However, between October 2003 and mid-December 2004, the rate fell to 8.1, and by July 2005, it had fallen to 8.006, a clear sign that the domestic market did respond to the pressure on the currency. On July 23, 2005, the one-year forward exchange rate declined to 7.843 (from 8.006 the previous day), a fall of approximately 0.1665 in the corresponding spot rate. From data for the 10-month period following the reform, the one-year rate continually responded to the pressure for the CNY to appreciate against the US dollar.

Foreign exchange Settlement and Sales Reflect Appreciation Pressure

In a given period of time, the changes in foreign exchange settlement and sales amounts can accurately reflect the extent of currency appreciation or depreciation. If depreciation pressure increases, then the settlement amount will fall, while the sale amount will rise, and vice versa. As shown in Figure 5.2, from January 2000 to March 2001, the foreign exchange settlement amount did not change significantly; rather, the amount of foreign exchange sales rose continuously. This indicates obvious pressure for the CNY to depreciate. From March to October 2001, sales declined to around US$2 million while the settlement amount did not change substantially, which indicates a lessening of the depreciation pressure on the CNY. From October 2001 to March 2004, sales fell to US$0.2 million, while the settlement amount rose from US$1.6 million in March 2003 to US$20 million in September that year, when pressure to appreciate the Chinese currency peaked. Figure 5.2 also shows that in February and November 2004, May and December 2005 and April 2006, the foreign exchange settlement amount exceeded US$10 million, while changes in sales were immaterial, indicating that CNY price appreciation pressure became stronger in these months. This tallies with the results from the overseas CNY non-principal forward market and illustrates how promptly and accurately the domestic forward market reacts to overseas pressure on the CNY. This will be discussed further in following sections.

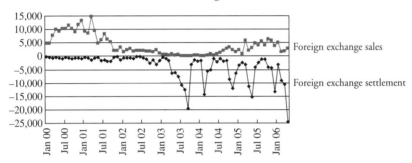

FIGURE 5.2   BOC monthly foreign exchange settlement and sales amounts, January 2000–April 2006 (US$ thousand)
Source: Data derived from Zhao (2006).

Price and Turnover Perspective on CNY Appreciation Pressure

While Tables 5.1 and 5.2 provide the prices and turnover of CNY forward foreign exchange settlements and sales, we cannot accurately estimate the supportiveness of the prices because details of the turnover at a given price level are not available. Figure 5.3 combines the price and turnover of CNY/US$ forward exchange rates to estimate the

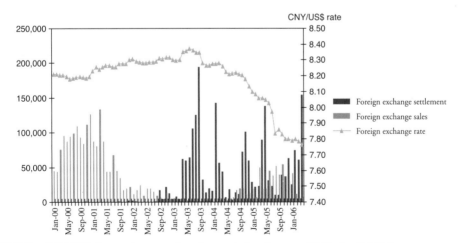

FIGURE 5.3   CNY/US$ forward rate and settlement/sales, January 2000–April 2006
Source: Data derived from Figures 5.1 and 5.2.

appreciation/depreciation pressure on the CNY against the US dollar. From this, it is evident that in September and October 2003, the large settlement amount corresponds with major CNY gains (the exchange rate fell in September and October). This was also the case in November and December 2004, and in May 2005 when settlements surged and the exchange rate dipped, signaling three peaks of CNY appreciation pressure. Figure 5.3 shows no CNY gain peak in February 2004 because there were no major changes in the exchange rate despite substantial settlements. In April 2004, the exchange rate dropped CNY0.038 over the previous month, with a notable increase in settlements, demonstrating another peak (although lower than the previous three) in CNY gains for the period.

STATUS OF CNY FORWARD TRANSACTIONS IN CFETS

The Launch of CNY Forward Trading

The implementation of the PBC's exchange rate reform plan accelerated the pace of innovation in CNY exchange products, such as forwards, swaps, and other derivatives, and in expanding the number of market participants.

In August 2005, the CFETS formally introduced inter-bank foreign exchange forward products, which made it possible for banks to hedge against exchange rate risks. However, at that time, CNY forwards trading was not active. The reasons for this are three-fold: first, the fluctuation of the CNY exchange rate remained minor, so there was little market demand to mitigate exchange rate risks; secondly, the costs were a concern for enterprises or institutions deliberating whether to join the inter-bank forward market; thirdly, given the limited extent of a market-formed interest rate in China, there was no reliable method by which to estimate the forward exchange rate. There is a close relationship between innovation in foreign exchange products and the liberalization of interest rates. China still needs time to improve risk awareness and interest rate liberalization in developing its foreign exchange derivatives market.

Market-makers in the CNY Forward Market

After three years' practice and development, activity in the CNY forward market has increased. The number of participants and the turnover has improved significantly. Table 5.3 shows that up to June 2009, there were 16 market-makers—four domestic banks and 12 foreign banks—in the CFETS.

CNY Forward Members of CFETS

As shown in Table 5.4, as at June 2009 there were 67 members of the CFETS foreign exchange forward market, comprising 20 domestic banks and 47 foreign banks (including one Sino–foreign jointly funded bank, Xiamen International Bank, and all 16 market-makers).

Foreign exchange Forward Turnover

According to figures published in *China Money Market*, the respective total turnover for foreign exchange forward transactions in 2006, 2007, and 2008 was US$14.06 billion, US$20 billion and US$17.4 billion respectively. The respective monthly transactions for the first

TABLE 5.3 Market-makers in inter-bank foreign exchange trade market, June 2009

Serial Number	Institution	Abbreviation	Serial Number	Institution	Abbreviation
1	Industrial and Commercial Bank	ICBC	9	Standard Chartered Bank, Shanghai Branch	SCCN
2	Bank of China	BCHO	10	Calyon Corporate and Investment Bank (London)	CALH
3	China Construction Bank	CCBH	11	Australia and New Zealand Banking Group (Singapore)	ANZA
4	CITIC Bank	CTIB	12	ING (Amsterdam)	INGX
5	HSBC (Hong Kong)	HSBC	13	Deutsche Bank (Singapore)	DBAG
6	BNP PARIBAS (China) Limited	BNPC/BNPP	14	UBS	UBSS
7	Bank of Montreal, Guangzhou Branch	BMCN	15	Bank of Tokyo-Mitsubishi UFJ (China), Ltd	TMSH
8	Citibank (China)	CTSH	16	The Royal Bank of Scotland	RBOS

Source: CFETS.

TABLE 5.4 CNY forward members of CFETS, June 2009

Serial Number	Institution	Abbreviation	Serial Number	Institution	Abbreviation
1	Industrial and Commercial Bank of China	ICBC	16	China Development Bank	CDBB
			17	Bank of Beijing	BOBJ
			18	Bank of Shanghai	BKSH
2	Agricultural Bank of China	ABCI	19	Bank of Ningbo	NBCB
			20	Ping An Bank	SZPA
3	Bank of China	BCHO	21	Bank of East Asia	BEAI
4	China Construction Bank	CCBH	22	First Sino Bank	FSBK
5	Bank of Communications	BCOH	23	Xiamen International Bank	XIBH
6	CITIC Bank	CTIB			
7	China Merchants Bank	CMHO	24	BNP PARIBAS (China) Limited	BNPC/BNPP
8	China Everbright Bank	EBBC			
9	Hua Xia Bank	HXBJ	25	Shanghai Pudong Development Bank	SPDB
10	Shenzhen Development Bank	DESZ			
			26	DBS Bank (China)	DBSC
11	Industrial Bank	IBCN	27	Bank of America, Shanghai Branch	BASH
12	China Minsheng Bank	CMSB			
13	China Zheshang Bank	CZSB	28	HSBC (China)	HKSH
14	China Bohai Bank	BOHC	29	Bank of Montreal, Guangzhou Branch	BMCN
15	Export and Import Bank of China	EIBC			
			30	Citibank (China)	CTSH

(*continued*)

TABLE 5.4   (*Continued*)

Serial Number	Institution	Abbreviation	Serial Number	Institution	Abbreviation
31	Standard Chartered Bank, Shanghai Branch	SCCN	50	Deutsche Bank	DBSH
32	ABN AMRO Bank (China)	ABNA/AASH	51	Westdeutsche Landesbank Ltd., Shanghai Branch	WLBS
33	JPMorgan Chase Bank (China)	JPSH	52	Chiyu Banking Corporation, Xiamen Branch	CYXM
34	Dresdner Bank, Shanghai Branch	DRSH	53	Fortis Bank, Shanghai Branch	FBSH
35	Société Générale	SGSH			
36	Calyon Corporate and Investment Bank (London)	CALS	54	The Bank of Nova Scotia, Guangzhou Branch	BNSG
			55	OCBC Bank (China)	OCBS
37	Sumitomo Mitsui Banking Corporation, Shanghai Branch	SMSH	56	Mizuho Corporate Bank Ltd., Beijing Branch	MHBJ
			57	Mizuho Corporate Bank Ltd., Dalian Branch	MHDL
38	Credit Suisse First Boston Limited, Shanghai Branch	CSSH	58	Mizuho Corporate Bank Ltd.	MHSH
39	Australia and New Zealand Bank, Beijing Branch	ANZB	59	Mizuho Corporate Bank Ltd., Shenzhen Branch	MHSZ
			60	UBS, Beijing Branch	UBSB
40	Australia and New Zealand Bank, Shanghai Branch	ANZC	61	The Royal Bank of Scotland, Shanghai Branch	RBSH
41	Commerzbank, Shanghai Branch	CBSH	62	Handelsbanken, Shanghai Branch	SHSH
42	KBC Bank NV, Shanghai Branch	KBCS	63	The Bank of Tokyo-Mitsubishi UFJ, Ltd. (China)	TMSH
43	Sanpaolo IMI Bank Ltd., Shanghai Branch	ISSB	64	Norddeutsche Landesbank Girozentrale Shanghai Branch	NLSH
44	Hang Seng Bank (China)	HSSH			
45	Rabobank, Shanghai Branch	RNSH			
46	ING Bank, Shanghai Branch	INGS	65	CITIC Ka Wah Bank, Shanghai Branch	KWSH
47	The United Overseas Bank Ltd., Shanghai Branch	UOBS	66	Skandinaviska Enskilda Banken AB(publ), Shanghai Branch	SEBH
48	Platinum Natexis Banques Populaires, Shanghai Branch	NXSH	67	Barclays Bank, Shanghai Branch	BBSH
49	Deutsche Bank, Beijing Branch	DBBJ			

Source: www.chinamoney.com.cn.

four months of 2009 amounted to US$0.93 billion, US$0.3 billion, US$0.524 billion, and US$0.52 billion, which accounted for just 0.5 percent of the total foreign trade. Figure 5.4 gives the quarterly turnover of CNY forward trading in the CFETS from the first quarter of 2006 to the third quarter of 2009. It shows that forward trading grew steadily up to the third quarter of 2008, before dropping dramatically as a result of the financial crisis.

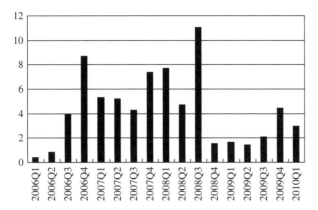

FIGURE 5.4 Quarterly CNY forward turnover of the CFETS, 2006–10 (US$ billion)
Source: Quarterly Implementation Reports of Chinese Monetary Policies, 2007–10, People's Bank of China website (www.pbc.gov.cn).

Using these figures, we calculate that the annual turnover of CNY forwards grew year-on-year by 58.5 percent in 2007 and 12.9 percent in 2008. It then fell from US$ 25.15 billion in 2008 to US$9.8 billion in 2009, decreasing by 61 percent because of the financial crisis. Although data for CNY merchant forward trading are not readily available, trading and liquidity in the CFETS reflects the activities of the market as a whole and this suggests that measures should be taken to accelerate the development of the CNY foreign exchange forward market.

MERCHANT FOREIGN EXCHANGE FORWARD TRADING

Merchant foreign exchange forwards are transacted between banks and their merchant clients, and banks have to hedge their foreign exchange forward positions with other financial institutions. The CFETS provides such a place so that banks can hedge their positions easily. As the merchant forward business is still in the experimental stage after more than 12 years, data for this market have not been released regularly since 1997. Thus we do not really know the scale of the market relative to forward trading in the CFETS. However, as we saw in Chapter 4, the Bank for International Settlements (BIS) triennial report in 2007 showed that the average value of daily forward trading for April 2007 was US$2.82 billion, from which we infer that the annual transactions amounted to around US$705 billion, which accounted for less than one-third of China's total international trade that year. This indicates that less than one-third of China's international trade is hedged with CNY foreign exchange forwards.

From Figure 5.4, we estimate that the total CNY foreign exchange trading value in the CFETS was US$22.38 billion, that is, just 3.2 percent of the total value of CNY foreign exchange forward trading in 2007, indicating that the great majority of the merchant CNY foreign exchange forwards are not hedged in the CFETS market.

PROBLEMS IN THE CNY FORWARD MARKET

Trading amounts have been small since the emergence of CNY forwards, and the correlation between CNY forwards and foreign exchange spot transactions has been low. Following is a list of the problems that currently exist in the CNY forward foreign exchange market.

The Limits on Participation are Too Strict

The regulations issued by the PBC prescribe the "authentic needs" principle for CNY forwards. Under this principle, a participant that has entered into a forward contract with a bank must provide documentary evidence of genuine export and import trade or other hedging activities before the settlement date; otherwise the bank has the right to terminate the contract, with the participant bearing any consequent losses. Because of these limitations, participants have lost enthusiasm for forward products which cannot satisfy their particular needs. In Japan, South Korea, and other countries, the "authentic needs" principle was also put in place in the initial development phase, but was removed when the market matured, thus accelerating the foreign exchange liberalization process. Speculation and investment are essential for any financial products, which are often indistinguishable. In fact, a financial product can barely succeed without speculation. If these limitations are not reduced or abolished, the market will not be able to operate normally.

The Low Fluctuation of the CNY Exchange Rate

Low levels of variation or volatility of the CNY against the US dollar have directly reduced participants' incentive to hedge or to speculate. In the half-year following the reform of the foreign exchange regime the average rate fluctuation was only 0.4 percent. This increased to around 1 percent in 2006, and for the following three years reached 1.80 percent, 2.63 percent, and 0.86 percent, figures which were, respectively, about 30 percent, 19 percent, and 3 percent of the corresponding US$/euro exchange rates. According to some market analysts, only 30 percent of companies actually needed to hedge their exchange rate risks.[1]

Lack of a Market Mechanism

Although interest rate liberalization has improved in the recent years, China still lacks a real market-oriented interest rate system. Without reliable yield curves, pricing foreign exchange forward contracts is difficult.

THE POTENTIAL FOR THE CNY FORWARD MARKET

In China, the spot foreign exchange market is still in its early stages and the forward exchange market has also yet to mature. However, as we saw in Chapter 1, imports and exports have grown rapidly in recent years, ranging between 21.8 percent and 35.7 percent since China's accession to the WTO in 2001. This compares with GDP growth of around 10 percent in the same period. Foreign direct investment has also increased in the past decades, with rising numbers of, and enlarged quotas for, Qualified Foreign Institutional Investors (QFII) and Qualified Domestic Institutional Investors (QDII). These elements have combined to help build demand for spot and forward trades to hedge foreign exchange risk.

Our findings reveal that from 2002, the ratio of foreign exchange spot transactions to total foreign trade was well below 20 percent; at the same time, the ratio of foreign exchange forward amounts to total trade was approximately 3 percent. We believe that, along with the deeper integration of the world economy, international trade will continue to be a major contributor to GDP, and overseas assets will surge as a share of GDP. Accompanying this trend will be more import and export companies, "going-out" enterprises and financial institutions needing to hedge their exchange rate risk. Since March 2009, there has been increasing pressure to appreciate the CNY. The PBC's reforms of the exchange rate regime in 2005 increased the volatility of the CNY against the US dollar and raised the level of awareness of the need to hedge exchange rate risk. In the future, as demand for using the foreign exchange market in investment and speculation rises, the CNY forward market will develop quickly and should have a potential average annual growth rate of around 30 percent from 2010 to 2020.

CONCLUSION

Foreign exchange forwards are an important part of traditional foreign exchange transactions, and are the simplest foreign exchange hedging instruments. Although there have been more than 12 years of successful trials, the scale of forward trade remains relatively low for reasons discussed above. A refinement of the exchange rate regime, together with increased fluctuations in the exchange rate and a gradual phasing out of the existing restrictions, will accelerate the progress of the forward market. In fact, with more banks approved to conduct forward foreign exchange settlements and sales, the inter-bank market has grown continually from 2006 and will progress further in the future.

Measures should be taken to accelerate the development of the CNY foreign exchange forward market. The reform of the exchange rate regime accelerated innovation in CNY products and the moves taken to broaden the range of banks qualified to conduct forward exchange and swap services have played a role in accelerating the development of the CNY forward market. The introduction by the CFETS of inter-bank foreign exchange forward products provided both a venue and the tools for banks to hedge exchange rate risks. Along with interest rate liberalization and raised foreign exchange risk awareness, there will be wider space for the foreign exchange forward market to develop.

ENDNOTE

1. See, for example, Foreign Exchange Reference 5, 1998; and Ye and Li, 2001: 120.

CHAPTER 6

The Foreign Exchange Swap Market

INTRODUCTION

A foreign exchange swap is a contract in which both parties agree to make two currency swaps in opposite directions on two different trading days. In the first swap ("the spot leg"), one party will exchange a foreign currency for a local currency at an agreed rate; in the subsequent swap ("the forward leg"), the same party will again exchange the local currency for an equivalent amount of the earlier-swapped foreign currency at another agreed rate. The difference between the two agreed exchange rates is called the swap point.

LAUNCH OF CNY FOREIGN EXCHANGE SWAPS

China commenced trading in inter-bank CNY foreign exchange swaps in April 2006, marking the launch of the next key product in the domestic inter-bank foreign exchange market. Participating institutions were initially the most active in swap bidding and trading. The first CNY foreign exchange swap deal was completed by the Export-Import Bank of China (EIBC) and the Bank of China (BOC). After three years, the CNY foreign exchange swap market has expanded faster than the CNY forward market.

Figure 6.1 illustrates the cash flow in a one-year US$/CNY swap transaction.

From a customer's point of view, swaps have various advantages over single spot or forward transactions, as we shall see below.

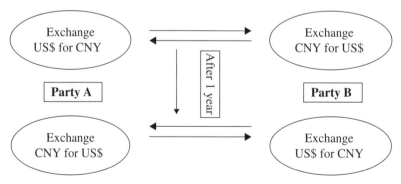

FIGURE 6.1 Cash flow in swap transactions

FUNCTIONS OF FOREIGN EXHANGE SWAPS

Hedging Against Exchange Rate Risk

When a company (especially an import and export business) knows in advance that there will be two foreign exchange transactions in opposite directions at two different points in the future, it can hedge against exchange rate risk through matching foreign exchange swaps with spot transactions.

Lower Transaction Costs

A swap consists of a spot and a forward or two forward transactions with different maturities. Entering into a contract for each transaction would incur higher fees than entering into a swap contract. Furthermore, swap transactions make it easier for banks to manage exposure positions, and swap points will be less than the sum of the premium or discount for two separate transactions, thus in turn reducing the cost of hedging against exchange rate risk.

Lower Financing Costs

Assume the following: a company needs CNY10 million in financing with a choice between the CNY and the Japanese yen (JPY) at one-year lending rates of 7.02 percent and 2.25 percent, respectively. It will need to pay in CNY after financing. The JPY/CNY spot exchange rate is 15.2585:1, while the one-year forward rate is 15.2015:1. The company may borrow JPY loans and, through a swap transaction, change the borrowed JPY into CNY in a spot transaction, and then change the CNY back into JPY through a 12-month forward to repay the loan. Calculating the financing cost, the company would save CNY438,700 in interest expenses as compared to the direct use of CNY loans.

As foreign exchange swaps can help enterprises, banks, and individuals to manage their local and foreign currency cash flow and respective exchange rate risks, they have become an important, well-received foreign exchange product across the world.

CNY foreign exchange swap transactions also bring other benefits. First, they provide additional sources of short- and medium-term foreign exchange funding to effectively maintain foreign exchange liquidity. Secondly, through CNY foreign exchange swaps within a certain period of time, banks can take advantage of differences in local and foreign currencies, which can help to increase the flexibility of their fund raising and management, reduce overall funding costs, and improve operating efficiency. Finally, transactions with emerging markets will help upgrade banks' treasury business and develop domestic CNY derivatives.

DEVELOPMENT OF CNY FOREIGN EXCHANGE SWAP MARKET

Under the guidance of the PBC, CNY forward inquiry transactions commenced in the inter-bank foreign exchange market in August 2005. Members of the forward foreign exchange market who had held the forward transaction qualification for six months were allowed to conduct spot-and-forward and forward-and-forward CNY foreign exchange swaps on the inter-bank market. In April 2006, the BOC and the EIBC completed the first CNY foreign exchange swap on the inter-bank market. The development of the market can be divided into three stages, as follows.

August 2005–July 2006

At this stage, swap transactions were not as active as forward transactions, and were mainly short-term, for two reasons. First, non-market-maker banks managed their overall foreign exchange positions on a cash basis. They included foreign currencies in their overall positions on the settlement day of the customer-driven foreign exchange transactions, transactions for their own account, and inter-bank transactions. In this way, some market participants may create a negative position *vis-à-vis* the US dollar through selling spot or forward dollars on the inter-bank market. With expectations that the CNY would appreciate, this approach would ensure that the banks fulfilled regulatory requirements on their overall foreign exchange positions and also maintained an exposure position of short US dollars and long CNY, placing them in a position to gain upon appreciation of the CNY. This not only increased the pressure for the CNY to revalue, but also led to mostly short-term inter-bank foreign exchange swaps.

Secondly, there were obvious spreads for forward transactions of the US dollar and the CNY settled in and outside mainland China. Profit could be made through risk-free arbitrage across different markets by selling domestic forwards and buying foreign non-deliverable forwards with the same maturities and principal amounts. With a large number of overseas speculators for foreign forwards, fluctuations in exchange rates were greater, leading to frequent volatility in forward/swap rates on the domestic market. For market participants looking to hedge against exchange rate risk, this market was far from attractive. Their reluctance in this respect partly restricted the development of the domestic CNY foreign exchange swap market.

July 2006–May 2007

In June 2006, the State Administration of Foreign Exchange (SAFE) instructed banks to adjust the methodology for managing their overall foreign exchange positions, requesting that they changed to an accrual basis by including positions of customer-driven foreign exchange transactions, transactions for their own account, and inter-bank transactions on trading days. Unlike with the cash basis, the accrual basis prohibited banks from maintaining overnight short US-dollar and long CNY exposures. The basis for risk-free arbitrage for overseas and domestic US$/CNY was removed, and domestic US$/CNY rates started to be based on interest parity.

At this stage, the US$/CNY foreign exchange swaps chiefly reflected movements in the spread between US dollar interest rates and CNY interest rates. Since interest rate volatility was lower than exchange rate volatility, and the influence of overseas non-deliverable forward rates on domestic forward rates was eliminated, the market became more stable. With this enhanced market stability, more participants were willing to trade, greatly increasing the inter-bank forward/swap transactions and narrowing quoted bid-ask spreads. According to the PBC's report on China's monetary policy for the first half of 2007, the notional principal amount of inter-bank foreign exchange forward transactions was equivalent to US$10.7 billion. In addition, the average daily transaction volume was US$90 million, 1.6 times the average daily transaction volume in 2006, while the principal amount for CNY foreign exchange swaps amounted to US$133.4 billion, and the daily average trading volume was US$1.14 billion, 3.8 times the average daily trading volume of the previous year. Taking a one-year swap as an example, the inter-bank market bid-ask spread decreased from 400 basis points at the initial stage to 30 basis points.

May 2007–October 2007

At this stage, the premium for US$/CNY swaps increased significantly, meaning the implied CNY yield included in CNY foreign exchange swaps declined, and even dropped to negative at one point. Liquidity in foreign exchange swaps decreased and market volatility grew, while the bid-ask spread reached 100 to 200 basis points. The major factor affecting the development of the inter-bank foreign exchange swap market was the liquidity shortage in domestic US dollars caused by the SAFE's further opening of the foreign exchange market and sharply reducing short-term overseas debt limits. As early as October 2006, the SAFE issued a circular on designated banks' exposure management of CNY foreign exchange forward and swap transactions. In accordance with the circular, the requirement that affected the inter-bank forward and swap market most was to specify that forward foreign exchange transactions were subject to performance authorization. Banks would be able to operate in accordance with their business needs and risk management decisions to transact with customers. When a forward contract expires, the banks executed foreign exchange with customers who provided appropriate credentials. Before the circular was issued, customers were required to provide banks with relevant documents for approval on the same day as the forward contract was signed.

Since forward foreign exchange transactions are usually subject to considerable uncertainties, the old requirements had turned away a number of customers who needed the business, and the introduction of new regulations has helped customers seeking to hedge against exchange rate risk. Since China is a country with enormous exports and there is an expectation that the CNY will appreciate steadily, the introduction of new regulations has greatly increased customers' demand for forward selling US dollars. Apart from the increased demand, the upgrading of China's export industries has placed new requirements on the maturities of forward transactions and the inter-bank swap market. Shipbuilding, machinery and other industrial exports can last as long as several years, and customers need to hedge against exchange rate risk within one, two, or three years, or even longer. This demand has created the ultra-forward foreign exchange swap market. However, because domestic banks having insufficient risk management capability and liquidity, this is not as active as the one-year and shorter-term foreign exchange swap market. Moreover, the new rules have lessened inspection requirements for parties entering into forward contracts, and created demand for arbitrage over domestic and overseas forwards. As mentioned earlier, when the SAFE revised and unified requirements on overall foreign exchange positions, banks could no longer arbitrage the difference between domestic forward rates and overseas forward rates. Therefore, the difference in respect of one-year forwards domestically and overseas enlarged to as much as 3,000 basis points.

Multinational corporations (MNCs) in China face no regulatory requirements regarding their own foreign exchange positions, and the new regulations have relaxed restrictions on their shorting forward US dollars within China. MNCs can sell forward US dollars to domestic banks, and buy non-deliverable forward US dollars of the same period and principal from foreign banks. When both contracts mature, the overseas contract is settled according to the middle price of the day. For the domestic contract, companies may choose to provide relevant certificates to settle the transaction; if there is no valid certificate, they can choose to cancel the transaction according to the market price. The companies can therefore profit from the results of settling two contracts.

The demand has led to domestic commercial banks accumulating open positions of foreign exchange swaps. The demand for spot long US dollars and forward short US dollars continuously pushed down US$/CNY swap points. In one three-month period, the one-year US$/CNY swap points once dropped from −1,800 to −4,000 basis points.

In theory, if the US$/CNY swap point keeps declining, the implied CNY interest rate will fall, bringing opportunities for arbitrage between People's Bank of China (PBC) bills and other CNY assets. Arbitrage activities should push the swap points back to normal. However, drastic reductions in short-term foreign debts have broken the balance. In March 2007, the SAFE issued a circular designed to strengthen the management of short-term foreign debt by controlling the size of the debt, regulating financial institutions' short-term overseas borrowings, protecting national economic, and financial security, and promoting a balance in international payments (see Table 6.1). The limit for domestic banks to borrow foreign funds was reduced to 30 percent of the 2006 approved level, while the limit for non-bank financial institutions and foreign banks was reduced to 60 percent of that level. Reduced limits on short-term foreign debt meant that domestic financial institutions could no longer borrow unlimited US dollars or other foreign currency assets from overseas. US-dollar interest rates thus soared. At the end of August 2007, the domestic one-year US-dollar lending rate reached Libor +180 points. The shortage of US dollars broke the balance necessary to determine interest parity, and the original arbitrage traders gave up trading to stop-loss as a result of their inability to obtain US dollars. This in turn greatly increased the US$/CNY swap premium.

TABLE 6.1   Reduction in short-term foreign debt indicators

	Domestic Banks
June 30, 2007	Adjust short-term foreign debt balance to within 45% of approved limit in 2006
September 30, 2007	Adjust short-term foreign debt balance to within 40% of approved limit in 2006
December 31, 2007	Adjust short-term foreign debt balance to within 35% of approved limit in 2006
March 31, 2008	Adjust short-term foreign debt balance to within 30% of approved limit in 2006
	Foreign Banks
June 30, 2007	Adjust short-term foreign debt balance to within 85% of approved limit in 2006
September 30, 2007	Adjust short-term foreign debt balance to within 75% of approved limit in 2006
December 31, 2007	Adjust short-term foreign debt balance to within 65% of approved limit in 2006
March 31, 2008	Adjust short-term foreign debt balance to within 60% of approved limit in 2006

Source: SAFE website (www.safe.gov.cn).

TRANSACTION VOLUME, MATURITY PROFILE, PRODUCT MIX, AND CURRENCIES FOR FOREIGN EXCHANGE SWAPS

Turnover and Transaction Volume

The turnover and transaction volume of inter-bank CNY foreign exchange swaps have expanded rapidly since their launch in April 2006. As shown in Figure 6.2, the quarterly turnover of CNY foreign exchange swaps stayed around US$100 billion from the third quarter of 2007 to the first quarter of 2009, before increasing steadily from the second quarter of 2009. The annual trading value of 2009 reached US$801.8 billion, 82.1 percent higher than 2008 and twice the annual growth rate from 2006 to 2007.

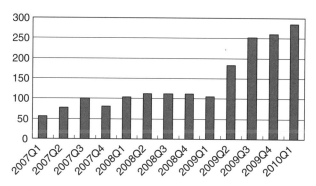

FIGURE 6.2   Historical changes in CNY foreign exchange swaps turnover (US$ billion)
Source: Quarterly Implementation Reports of Chinese Monetary Policies 2007–10, PBC website (www.pbc.gov.cn).

Maturity Profile

Table 6.2 depicts the maturities of CNY foreign exchange swaps in the first half of 2007. Data in the table are arrived at by dividing the turnover of products with different maturities by the overall turnover for the respective periods. Transactions maturing within one month accounted for nearly 70 percent of the total turnover, while transactions maturing within one week accounted for between 50 percent and 70 percent, and those maturing within more than one year had a very low percentage. This demonstrates higher market demand for hedging against short-term exchange rate risk, and caution in addressing long-term exchange rate risks.

Figure 6.3 illustrates the percentages of overnight transactions of CNY foreign exchange swaps from July 2007 to April 2009. Before September 2008, when the international financial crisis broke out, these percentages remained at between 30 and 50 percent, but increased sharply thereafter, reflecting the preference of market participants for overnight transactions to avoid risks amid the financial crisis.

Product Mix

Following the launch of CNY foreign exchange swaps, spot/forward products have always commanded a larger market share than forward/forward products. Figure 6.4 gives the proportions of the turnover of these two products to the overall turnover. For most of

TABLE 6.2   Maturity profile of CNY foreign exchange swaps, January-August 2007 (% of turnover)

Time Period	Contractual Maturity						
	<1w	1w–1m	1m–3m	3m–6m	6m–9m	9m–1y	>1y
January 2007	39.5	23.9	16.0	9.6	5.3	5.6	0.1
February 2007	44.6	22.4	18.4	4.7	2.7	6.7	0.5
March 2007	54.9	16.6	14.6	3.1	2.0	8.5	0.3
April 2007	48.1	28.6	9.0	4.7	2.3	6.6	0.7
May 2007	59.5	10.6	4.6	4.3	5.8	11.7	3.5
June 2007	64.4	12.2	6.1	6.0	3.0	7.6	0.7
July 2007	57.7	8.0	4.6	4.8	3.2	10.9	10.8
August 2007	68.5	6.7	3.7	4.1	1.8	14.1	1.0
Q4 2006	52.9	17.1	14.3	5.4	2.6	7.4	0.3
2006	51.8	18.9	14.1	5.9	2.6	6.4	0.2
Q1 2007	46.6	20.8	16.2	5.8	3.4	7.0	0.3
H1 2007	52.9	18.5	10.6	5.3	3.6	8.0	1.1

Source: www.chinamoney.com.cn; foreign exchange operational reports from *China's Journal of Money* for 2006 and 2007.

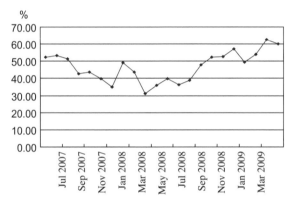

FIGURE 6.3   CNY foreign exchange overnight swap transactions, July 2007–April 2009 (%)
Source: www.chinamoney.com.cn; foreign exchange operational reports from *China's Journal of Money* for 2007, 2008, and 2009.

the time, the spot/forward products had a share of over 95 percent, with a high of 99 percent in March 2007.

Currencies

CNY swaps against the US dollar, the euro, the yen, the HK dollar, and the British pound to be executed in the inter-bank foreign exchange market are permitted. In reality, the US dollar is the principal currency in swap trades. In 2008, swaps with the above-mentioned currencies recorded a turnover of US$439.4 billion, HK$3.8 billion, ¥15.3 billion and €0.2 billion, respectively.

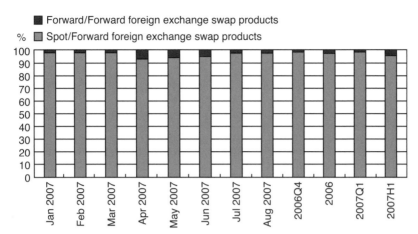

FIGURE 6.4 Changes in CNY foreign exchange swap product mix (by turnover)
Source: www.chinamoney.com.cn; foreign exchange operational reports from *China's Journal of Money* for 2006 and 2007.

MARKET PARTICIPANTS

The PBC rules allow domestic institutions that are members of the inter-bank forward foreign exchange market to conduct CNY foreign exchange swap trades in the inter-bank foreign exchange market, with the SAFE regulating the CNY foreign exchange swap business through filing requirements. According to *China's Journal of Money*, a total of 73 institutions were members of the foreign exchange swap market as at April 2009.

INTERNATIONAL COMPARISONS

Using the BIS triennial data for April 2007, the total average daily trading value of CNY foreign exchange swaps was a mere 0.04 percent of the world average and was equivalent to only 6.6 percent of the Indian-rupee swaps trading value, and much lower than the corresponding CNY foreign exchange forward weight of 30.2 percent discussed in Chapter 5. Bearing in mind that China's GDP was 1.89 times larger than India's for 2007, this implies that the CNY foreign exchange swap market was much less active compared to the Indian foreign exchange forward market, both in absolute terms and in relation to GDP.

MAJOR ISSUES FOR THE SWAP MARKET
Late Development of a Legal Framework

As derivatives, foreign exchange swaps require precise legal definitions of contracting parties' rights and obligations and essential contract elements. After years of development in mature overseas markets, banks have prepared a concise legal document, the *Master Agreement of the International Swaps and Derivatives Association (ISDA),* to govern all parties concerned to reduce risk and lower transaction costs. They have also adopted a series of credit guarantee documents or terms and conditions to prevent swap defaults from affecting counterparties and market stability.

Because of the lack of experience and self-regulatory bodies in the initial development stage of China's over-the-counter derivatives market, market participants could only enter into simple one-to-one contracts. These were either prepared by the parties themselves, or copied from the globally accepted ISDA master agreement.[1] In 2007, the SAFE promulgated the *Master Agreement for CNY/Foreign Exchange Derivatives Trading in China's Inter-bank Foreign Exchange Market* and the PBC produced the *Master Agreement for Financial Derivative Trading in China's Inter-bank Market.* The two agreements overlapped in their application and having two agreements in one market inconvenienced over-the-counter financial derivative trading. As a result, under the guidance of the PBC, the National Association of Financial Market Institutional Investors drew up a unified master agreement, the text of which was released in March 2009. This agreement removed another technical obstacle to the development of China's derivative market. At present, a total of 103 organizations—65 banks, 21 securities companies, 11 insurance companies (including asset management companies), two fund companies, and four non-financial institutions—have signed up to the PBC's *Master Agreement.*

The Lag in Inter-bank Credit Limits

Unlike spot transactions, inter-bank forward foreign exchange transactions and swap transactions involve an exchange of future cash flows, and therefore require appropriate supporting credit limits for counterparties. However, for a number of reasons, this initiative has lagged behind. Firstly, with no offsetting permitted under Chinese law, the same counterparties executing two transactions in opposite directions with the same expiry dates need to obtain credit approval twice. Secondly, the localization of foreign banks has greatly reduced the capital of these banks, leading to credit ratings also falling lower than those of their former branches. This has reduced not only credit limits approved by domestic banks to foreign banks, but also mutual credit limits between foreign banks. Thirdly, it is difficult for a substantial number of domestic small- and medium-sized financial institutions to obtain credit limits from well-established financial institutions, and from foreign-invested financial institutions in particular, despite their needs for forwards and swaps. This has therefore blocked their entry to the CNY foreign exchange forward and swap market. However, we believe that it will take time to develop the market and build up trust and understanding among all parties concerned. As China's foreign exchange market continues to grow, these issues will be resolved.

The Need to Build the Short-term CNY Interest Rate Curve/Domestic Short-term US-dollar Interest Rate Curve

In mature markets overseas, the development of foreign exchange swaps is closely linked to the formation of the local currency interest rate curve, and the short-term interest rate curve in particular. As mentioned earlier, the swap points arrived at are, in theory, the differences in the interest rates of two currencies. From another perspective, foreign exchange swaps can help the market identify and build up a short-term interest rate curve. Regarding the US dollar in the domestic market, the short-term interest rate curve is distorted by the limits on foreign debts, but it still truly reflects the fundamentals of the domestic US-dollar lending market.

Regarding the CNY, as the majority of funds are controlled by state-owned banks, inter-bank lending is mostly short-term: overnight, one week or one month. The lack of money market data on interest rates for longer maturities of six months and one year might affect the pricing of CNY foreign exchange swaps with similar maturities. To address this issue, China's interest rate control has to be further liberalized to allow the market to decide currency prices. Currently, the PBC has launched Shibor, which is similar to Libor, the overseas short-term US-dollar interest rate curve. This move represents a good start for China to further liberalize its interest rate.

CONCLUSION

Foreign exhange swaps are the most important part of traditional foreign exchange transactions, occupying more than half of the total foreign exchange trading value in the world since the beginning of this century. Despite their relatively late introduction into China, the annual trading value of the foreign exchange swap market surpassed US$800 billion in 2009 and is expected to exceed US$1 trillion in 2010. The average annual growth rate of 150.7 percent from 2006 to 2009 was significant. While the annual growth rate is significant, the scale of the swap market is extremely limited, not only by international standards (55.6 percent of total foreign exchange trading value in April 2007) but also by domestic standards (a mere 7.4 percent of China's total foreign exchange trading value for April 2007). There is clearly significant growth potential for this market, a subject we will explore further in Chapter 20.

ENDNOTE

1. See Qiu He, *First Financial Daily*, March 17, 2009.

CHAPTER 7

CNY Bond Forwards

INTRODUCTION

From December 1992 to May 1995, China had implemented a trial program of government bond futures, which proved, ultimately, to be unsuccessful. The underlying reason for this was the underdevelopment of the government bonds spot market and limited transaction types, which resulted in manipulation and forced liquidation. In addition, the supervision system adopted was the same as that for the spot market. Inadequate disclosure of information and a lack of regulation, together with primitive market interest rates and a lack of risk avoidance tools, caused pricing distortions.

In May 2005, the People's Bank of China (PBC) issued its *Provisions Governing the Forward Transactions of Bonds in the National Inter-bank Bond Market* (the "Provisions") announcing that bond forward transactions were to be reintroduced to the inter-bank bond market from June 15 that year. Bond forward transactions as mentioned in the Provisions refer to the acts by which both parties to a transaction agree, on a certain date in the future, to buy and sell the underlying bonds in accordance with a stipulated price and amount. The types of underlying bonds that could be used for forward transactions included central government bonds, central bank bonds, financial bonds and other types of bonds issued with the approval of the PBC that had been traded in the inter-bank bond market.

Once the PBC had specified the Provisions as the policy framework, the National Inter-bank Lending Center and the China Government Securities Depository Trust & Clearing Co., Ltd (CDC) individually established related dealing and settlement rules in accordance with the Provisions. These two bodies, in conjunction with market participants, then jointly drafted and signed a master agreement by which the industry was to abide. The PBC was responsible for formulating information disclosures regarding transactions.

The Provisions specified the requirements governing the terms and scale of trading of the forward transactions, establishing a maximum time limit of 365 days from the trade date to the settlement date (including the former and excluding the latter). At maturity, the funds and the bonds are settled. The total purchase or selling balance of the forward transactions of a single bond by any market participant must not exceed 20 percent of the turnover of the bond, and the total balance of the sales must not exceed 200 percent of the total balance of the market participant's own bonds. The total balance of net purchases by a single fund must not exceed 100 percent of its net asset value; the total balance of net purchases by a China-based branch of a foreign financial institution may not exceed 100 percent of its CNY operating capital. For any other institution participating in forward transactions, the total balance of net purchases must not exceed 100 percent of its paid-in capital or net assets.[1]

On June 15, 2005, the initial bond forward transaction completed by the Industrial and Commercial Bank of China (ICBC) and the Industrial Bank re-opened bond forward transactions in the inter-bank bond market. The first transaction was a bond issued in March 2005 with remaining maturity of 4.86 years, a term of two months, and a forward yield of 3.3908 percent. On that day, 13 deals were completed, with the total value of these transactions amounting to CNY500 million (US$60 million). The inter-bank bond market showed great interest in bond forward transactions. To prepare for the initial deal, the transaction system opened early and by the official opening time of 9:00 a.m. two public quotations and 13 confirmed quotations had been finalized, including the initial public quotation from the ICBC. Eight types of bonds were used: half were short-term government bonds and the other half were bills issued by the PBC within the previous 12 months. Institutional behavior was tentative on that first day. The terms of the forward transactions were relatively short: eight of the 13 transactions were seven-day bonds, and two were two-month bonds. At the same time, from the structure of the bond term, three-quarters of the bonds were within one year and only two short- and medium-term bonds were longer than one year.[2]

THE SIGNIFICANCE OF BOND FORWARDS

The launch of bond forwards has been of great importance in the enhancement of the China's bond market and its whole financial market.

Strengthening Market Structures

The introduction of bond forwards enhanced the function of the bond market, further improving indirect control capabilities, including monetary policy. Bond forwards have facilitated the discovery of bond prices in the bond market, helped form sound yield curves, and provided a reliable basis for the formulation and implementation of the central bank's monetary policy. At the same time, the introduction of such transactions provided the central bank with a new operational tool to achieve indirect control through open market operations using an appropriate mix of spot trades, repurchases, and forward transactions to achieve its macro-monetary objectives.

Promoting Interest Rate Reform

The introduction of bond forward transactions has assisted in accelerating the market-oriented reform of interest rates. These transactions have improved the price discovery function of the bond market and promoted the formation of benchmark yield curves. They have been conducive to interest rate pricing for financial institutions, and provide a good market environment for interest rate liberalization. Bond forward transactions have made it possible for the majority of institutional investors to set up risk management mechanisms, which will in turn help speed up market-oriented reform of interest rates. In addition, the forward interest rates implied by the bond forward transactions represent the market expectation of future interest rates, an expectation determined by supply and demand, unlike official interest rates. The forward interest rates are thus an important component of interest rate liberalization.

Improving Risk Management

Bond forwards, which are themselves risk management tools, and other financial derivatives facilitate internal control and risk management mechanisms for financial institutions. The rich product offering in the financial market plays a role in optimizing profitability and upgrading operations, thus contributing to the transformation of financial enterprises into micro-economic entities that meet the requirements of the market economy.

The introduction of bond forwards has been conducive to safeguarding financial stability. Compared to the traditional means of managing risk, they provide greater accuracy and timeliness. At present, China's banking system has accumulated substantial risk exposures, which could undermine financial stability. Commercial banks are the principal investors in the bond market; they can use bond forwards to mitigate exposures arising from their huge bond portfolios as well as from asset/liability mismatches. Bond forwards can also provide hedging tools for institutions that do not hold debt securities.

Supporting Development of the Financial Market

The introduction of bond forwards supports a well-coordinated and highly efficient financial market, and greatly promotes the development of the bond market. Firstly, the increase in product variety in the market has attracted new investors, which helps boost spot trading and enhance liquidity. Secondly, bond forwards have introduced short selling to the market in order to reduce market volatility and to avoid unilateral market movements. They have also served to back the market's price discovery function, and play an important role in upgrading market efficiency. The introduction of bond forwards lays the foundation for the future introduction of bond futures and other derivative products, and is of great significance for the long-term development of the financial derivatives market.

Encouraging Diversification of Operations

Bond forwards provide a diversified operating tool for the market. They can be used as either a hedging tool or a new speculative tool, and also to enrich the arbitrage model. In addition, the long or short two-way trading mechanism makes it possible to avoid having funds lying idle when prices fall, effectively reducing transaction costs.

They have paved the way for the introduction of other derivatives, and play an increasingly important role in improving China's financial market system.[3]

THE CURRENT POSITION

Since the introduction of bond forward transactions in 2005, the market has been increasingly active, as shown in Table 7.1.

TABLE 7.1 Transactions in bond forward markets, 2005–10

Year	Number of Transactions	Transaction Amount (CNY billion)	Transaction Amount (US$ billion)	Annual Growth (%)
2005	108	17.8	2.2	
2006	398	66.4	8.3	282.1
2007	1,238	251.8	33.1	297.6
2008	1,327	550.6	79.3	139.3
2009	1,599	655.6	96.0	21.1
2010Q1	552	195.1	28.6	114.0

Source: "Report on the Implementation of China's Monetary Policy" from 2005 to 2009, and Q1, 2010, PBC.

For the first two years of trading, the market achieved an average annual growth rate of 231.3 percent. In 2009, the transaction amount recorded 21.1 percent, significantly lower than previous annual growth rates; the total annual transaction amount reached US$655.6 billion in 2009. Even though the financial crisis hit the market significantly from the fourth quarter of 2008 and the first quarter of 2009, the general increasing trend continued from the second quarter of 2009. Despite the steady growth of the market, it was still rather thin compared to the spot bond market, which had a daily average transaction amount of about CNY500 billion (US$73 billion).

UNDERLYING BOND TYPES

Table 7.2 shows the types of bonds traded in the forward market. The most important of these were bills issued by the PBC and debt securities issued by policy banks, which accounted for 58 percent and 24.9 percent, respectively, of total transactions by book value. Bond forward transactions on underlying government bonds and short-term financing bills reached 7 percent and 7.5 percent of the total.

However, there have been changes in the respective importance of the underlying bond types. At the outset, government bonds were the most important, reaching 73.8 percent in 2005 and 48.2 percent in 2006. However, the proportion has become markedly less significant, to the point where, in 2009, it was recorded at just 0.5 percent. The status of short-term financing bills has gone through a similar decline, with its proportion falling from 24.8 percent in 2006 to 1.67 percent in 2009. By contrast, bills issued by the PBC and debt securities issued by policy banks showed a steady rising trend. PBC bills increased from 3.8 percent in 2005 to 65.7 percent in 2008. Debt securities issued by policy banks increased from 8.4 percent in 2005 to 31.5 percent in 2009.

TABLE 7.2 Underlying bonds in the forward market, 2005–09

Type of Bond	Average Forward Term (Days)	Number of Transactions	Capital Amount (CNY million)	Book Value (CNY million)	%	Average Book Value Per Transaction (CNY million)
Total	16.1	3,294	921,863.93	920,887.23	100	279.57
1 Government bonds	107.1	272	64,650.61	64,074.82	7	235.57
1.1 Normal bonds	107.1	272	64,650.61	64,074.82	7	235.57
1.2 Local government bonds	—	—	—	—	—	—
2 Bills issued by the PBC	8.9	971	532,282.11	534,409.60	58	550.37
3 Financial institution bonds	9.7	879	236,603.39	234,221.81	25.4	266.46
3.1 Debt securities issued by policy banks	9.7	837	231,222.72	228,905.81	24.9	273.48
3.1.1 China Development Bank	9.7	590	164,788.96	163,071.81	17.7	276.39
3.1.2 The Export-Import Bank of China	7.4	82	18,590.00	18,330.00	2	223.54
3.1.3 Agricultural Development Bank of China	10.8	165	47,843.76	47,504.00	5.2	287.90
3.2 Commercial bank bonds	8.9	39	4,753.62	4,696.00	0.5	120.41
3.3 Non-financial institution bonds	6.0	2	524.79	520.00	0.1	260.00
3.4 Security company bonds	5.0	1	102.26	100.00	0	100.00
3.5 Short-term financing bills of securities companies	—	—	—	—	—	—
4 Corporate bonds	17.3	109	10,523.59	10,562.00	1.1	96.90
4.1 Central corporate bonds	18.0	65	6,822.12	6,758.00	0.7	103.97
4.2 Local corporate bonds	16.0	44	3,701.47	3,804.00	0.4	86.46
5 Short-term financing bills	10.2	1,028	69,410.29	69,437.00	7.5	67.55
6 Asset-backed securities	—	—	—	—	—	—
7 Notes	8.1	35	8,393.94	8,182.00	0.9	233.77
8 Others	—	—	—	—	—	—

Source: China Government Securities Depository Trust & Clearing Co., Ltd.

TERMS OF BOND FORWARDS

Table 7.3 shows bond forward transactions by bond terms from 2005. In the years since the introduction of bond forwards, short-term bonds with terms of less than one month have taken the dominant position, accounting for 96.4 percent of the total. The fact that transactions have gradually concentrated on such bonds indicates that China's inter-bank bond market participants appear to be conservative forwarding their transactions, and appropriate hedging tools have yet to be provided in the market. China's bond forward market is therefore still to develop and mature.

INSTITUTIONAL PLAYERS

Table 7.4 shows the types of investors in the bond forward market from 2005 to the first quarter of 2009. Among institutional players, joint stock banks and city commercial banks showed the greatest enthusiasm for bond forwards and maintain the largest

TABLE 7.3   Terms of bond forwards, 2005–09

Term	Internal Term (Days to Expiry)	Number of Transactions	Capital Amount (CNY million)	Book Value (CNY million)	%	Average Book Value Per Transaction (CNY million)
Total	15.3	3,559	1,063,011.99	1,059,395.23	100.0	297.67
7 days	5.4	2,300	724,460.55	722,922.23	68.2	314.31
14 days	10.8	692	176,509.58	174,582.00	16.5	252.29
21 days	18.3	234	43,804.01	43,716.00	4.1	186.82
1 month	27.5	203	79,290.32	79,747.00	7.5	392.84
2 months	33.6	56	15,312.58	15,000.00	1.4	267.86
3 months	79.3	17	1,907.36	1,900.00	0.2	111.77
4 months	102.1	17	1,974.41	1,940.00	0.2	114.12
5 months	133.0	6	971.02	940.00	0.1	156.67
7 months	181.0	1	542.07	500.00	0.0	500.00
9 months	245.0	2	609.12	600.00	0.1	300.00
11 months	309.5	4	355.18	340.00	0.0	85.00
1 year	352.9	27	17,275.79	17,208.00	1.6	637.33

Source: China Government Securities Depository Trust & Clearing Co., Ltd.

TABLE 7.4   Investor types in the bond forward market, 2005–09

	Average Forward Terms (Days)	Number of Transactions	Capital Amount (CNY million)	Book Value (CNY million)	%	Average Book Value Per Transaction (CNY million)
Total	15.3	7,118	2,126,023.98	2,118,790.46	100.0	297.67
1. Special settlement accounts	4.1	2	90.78	90.00	0.0	45.00
2. Commercial banks	12.6	5,768	1,969,234.88	1,963,113.64	92.7	340.35
2.1 State-owned banks	7.2	1,135	409,374.40	409,871.00	19.3	361.12
2.2 Joint stock banks	17.1	1,841	901,787.69	898,264.73	42.4	487.92
2.3 Foreign banks	7.7	134	45,353.43	45,455.00	2.1	339.22
2.4 City banks	10.0	2,649	611,464.04	608,272.91	28.7	229.62
2.5 Rural banks	43.0	1	195.82	190.00	-	190.00
2.6 Others	15.1	8	1,059.50	1,060.00	0.1	132.50
3. Credit unions	57.2	87	10,098.10	10,143.00	0.5	116.59
4. Non-bank financial institutions	165.2	57	35,562.80	35,372.00	1.7	620.56
5. Securities companies	10.3	1,176	101,683.95	100,826.82	4.8	85.74
6. Insurance companies	10.6	18	8,726.45	8,615.00	0.4	478.61
7. Funds	8.2	10	627.01	630.00	0.0	63.00
8. Non-financial institutions	—	—	—	—	—	—
9. Others	—	—	—	—	—	—

Source: China Government Securities Depository Trust & Clearing Co., Ltd.

transaction volumes, with their respective deals accounting for 42.4 percent and 28.7 percent of the total. State-owned commercial banks and securities companies were also actively involved. Other institutions had low levels of participation. The conclusion to be drawn from this is that bond forwards have not yet fully satisfied the hedging demands of all market participants.

CONCLUSION

The first derivative product introduced to the inter-bank bond market since the 1995 suspension of the government bonds trial program, the CNY bond forward started trading in June 2005. As the market has developed, transactions have become more active and the transaction amounts have increased rapidly. Despite significant drops in trading activity in the fourth quarter of 2008 and the first quarter of 2009 with declines in hedging demand, the volume of trade has returned to an increasing trend from the second quarter of 2009.

With increased transaction activity, bond forwards will become more important tools for market participants in managing risks, and be of greater significance in promoting effective price discovery and forming a complete set of yield curves. Bond forward products are expected to lay a solid foundation for the introduction of other derivatives to China's financial markets and to promote healthy and rapid market development.

Though China's bond forward market has grown by leaps and bounds, the liquidity of the market is far from adequate. The main reason for this is the relatively low levels of liquidity in the secondary bond market. Moreover, China's bond forward market has a utilitarian atmosphere; that is, many forward transactions are not undertaken for hedging or asset allocation reasons. There is still great potential for the market to grow further.

ENDNOTES

1. *China Securities News*, "Issuance of 'Provisions Governing the Forward Transactions of Bonds in the National Inter-bank Bond Market,'" May 17, 2005.
2. See "Bond Forwards Kick Off with Eagerness," *Shanghai Securities News*, June 16, 2005.
3. See *Financial News*, June 30, 2005.

CHAPTER 8

CNY Interest Rate Swaps

Interest rate swaps have been the most important derivative products in the international over-the-counter (OTC) marketplace, with amounts outstanding accounting for more than 70 percent of the total amounts of OTC derivatives since 2000 because of the important role they play in managing interest rate risk. Thus, the introduction of the CNY interest rate swaps in 2006 was of great importance for the development of China's financial market.

The People's Bank of China (PBC) introduced the swaps to the domestic market in February 2006. Commercial banks authorized to conduct financial derivative business were allowed to engage in interest rate swaps with their clients (depositors or borrowers) and other commercial banks were authorized to provide swap-related services on behalf of their clients. Other market investors can only engage in interest rate swaps with permitted commercial banks with which they maintain deposit/lending account relations for hedging purposes.

IMPORTANCE IN THE GLOBAL OTC MARKET

Interest rate swaps have been the most important OTC derivative products for decades because interest risk has been the most important risk in the global financial market. Figure 8.1 gives the weights of interest rate swap notional amounts outstanding over total OTC derivatives notional amounts outstanding from 1998 to 2009. It shows that these weights have moved from around 70 percent in the late 1990s to a peak of around 80 percent in the first half of 2009, indicating the great importance of interest rate swaps in the global OTC derivatives market. Their significance is reinforced by a consideration of the total notional amount outstanding by the end of 2008: this figure of US$309.8 trillion was 5.2 times higher than the corresponding world GDP for that year.

Because of the large amounts of interest rate swaps outstanding and the OTC nature of interest rate swap contracts, the interest risk has to be hedged with interest rate futures and interest options. Figure 8.2 shows the significant contribution of interest rate futures to the total value of all futures traded in all exchanges in the world, together with that of interest rate options to the total annual trading value of all options for the years from 1994 to 2009.

The total trading values of both interest rate futures and options from 2006 to 2008 were 33.5, 36.5, and 32.3 times the corresponding world GDP figures, indicating the tremendous significance of interest rate derivatives in the organized global marketplace.

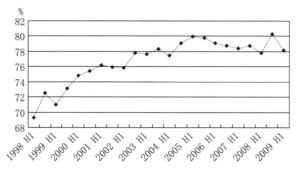

FIGURE 8.1   Weights of interest rate swap notional amounts outstanding over total OTC derivatives notional amounts outstanding, 1998–2009
Source: Bank for International Settlements website (www.bis.org)

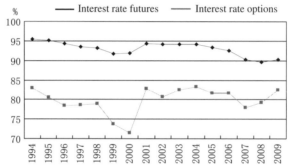

FIGURE 8.2   Interest rate futures and options as a proportion of total world futures and options trading, 1994–2009
Source: Bank for International Settlements website (www.bis.org)

KEY CONCEPTS

An interest rate swap is a derivative in which one party exchanges a stream of interest payments for another party's stream of cash flows on agreed dates. Interest payments to be exchanged are calculated on the agreed principal amount, known as the notional principal amount, and the exchanged payment is equal to the agreed interest rates multiplied by the notional principal amount. The amount exchanged is limited to the interest payments only, excluding the notional principal amount. In the most common type of interest rate swap, one party (the fixed interest payer) pays a fixed rate to another party (the floating interest payer), while receiving a floating rate from the other party (usually pegged to a reference rate).

Interest rate swaps have the following characteristics: (i) the counterparties have equal rights and obligations as they are both creditor and debtor to one another. The objects of exchange are different types of interest rates, including swaps of the fixed and floating interest rate, or floating interest rates swaps with reference to a different basis interest rate, and both interest income and payments can be swapped; (ii) in the interest rate swap agreement, the agreed principal amount is generally not exchanged between counterparties, but is used only for calculating the interest; hence, it is called the nominal principal amount; (iii) for each of the counterparties to the swap, the swap transaction and the actual lending practices are independent of each other. In lending activities, lenders are not concerned about whether their borrowers engage in swap transactions. In a swap, each counterparty bears the risk that the other may not pay the interest on schedule. The defaulting party also bears the risk that the counterparty may not pay the exchanged amount in the case of default. However, the exchange does not allow the counterparties to avoid their obligation to pay the principal and interest to their respective lenders as scheduled.

Interest rate swaps started in 1980s and were initially aimed at reducing the financing costs of counterparties through comparative advantages in fixed rate and floating rate markets. As more investors began to use the swaps to manage interest rate risk or match assets and liabilities, the swaps market developed rapidly and has become one of the world's largest financial markets. The market helps to reduce financing costs, hedge interest rate risk, offset the exposures of different financial instruments, increase financing channels, and boost the effectiveness of asset–liability management.

The "comparative advantage" theory of international trade was raised by the renowned British economist David Ricardo. In his view, if two countries can both produce two different products with one country doing so at a lower cost than the other, both countries can benefit from specialization and international trade if the former country specializes in the production of the product with greater advantage and the latter country specializes in the less disadvantageous product. Interest rate swaps best illustrate this theory in the financial sector. Under this theory, a swap can create value if the following two conditions are met: each party is in need of the other's assets or liabilities and has comparative advantage in two types of assets or liabilities.

The CNY interest rate swap is an agreement in which two parties exchange their cash flows arising from the agreed principal over a specific period of time. The cash flows of one party are calculated at a floating rate, while the cash flows of the other party are calculated at a fixed rate.

TYPES OF CNY SWAPS

The three main types of interest rate swaps are coupon swaps, basis swaps, and cross-currency interest rate swaps.

A coupon swap, the most basic type, is the exchange of a fixed rate for a floating rate in the same currency in which one party pays the fixed rate interest in exchange for the floating rate interest from the other. The other party pays the floating rate interest in exchange for the fixed rate interest.

A basis swap is a swap agreement involving the exchange of two floating rate interests in the same currency, one pegged to one reference rate and the other tied to a second reference rate. In such a transaction, the counterparties pay or receive interest at different floating rates respectively. The amount of interest is calculated on the same notional principal amount.

A cross-currency interest rate swap is the exchange of different interest rates in different currencies: an exchange of a fixed rate in one currency for a floating rate in another. In other words, it is a swap of different currencies and different interest rates.

When the PBC introduced interest rate swaps in February 2006, cross-currency swaps were not included. These did not come into play in China until August the following year, when CNY swaps with the US dollar, the euro, the Hong Kong dollar, the British pound and the Japanese yen were introduced.

A CNY–foreign currency swap was defined as an agreement in which the counterparties exchange the interest of two different currencies periodically and the agreed notional principal amount of CNY and the other currency within a specified period of time. The two parties exchange the principals of CNY and foreign currency at the agreed exchange rate on the effective date of the agreement and reverse the exchange at the same rate and amount on the expiry date. Other methods set out by the PBC and the State Administration of Foreign Exchange (SAFE) may also be used. The exchanged interest is interest paid to the counterparty periodically, which is calculated on the currency swapped in; the interest rates can be fixed or floating.

HISTORY AND DEVELOPMENT

Interest rate swaps may be conducted either through the trading system of the National Inter-bank Funding Center or by other means such as telephone and facsimile communications between the two parties. Market investors involved in interest rate swaps are required to file details of newly completed transactions with the Inter-bank Center (except for swaps conducted through the Center's own trading system). The Center is obliged to disclose relevant information to the market in a timely fashion in accordance with the PBC rules and authorization.

CNY interest rate swaps developed rapidly to become the most important derivatives market in China. Initially, there were two types of swap reference rates for the floating leg: the secured repurchase rate in the inter-bank bond market, which mainly refers to the basis rate of repurchase agreement within seven days (FR007); and the deposit interest rate of the one-year time deposit set by the PBC. In January 2007, the Shibor—offering three-month, one-week and overnight rates—was launched and became one of the reference rates of the floating leg.

As mentioned earlier, in August 2007, the PBC launched foreign currency swaps for domestic institutions with membership of the inter-bank foreign currency forward market. It also specified that the reference rates in the transaction should be the money market interest rates announced by the Inter-bank Funding Center and authorized by the PBC, or the basis deposit and lending interest rates set by the PBC. The foreign currency reference rate in the swap is determined by the counterparties.

The early market-makers of CNY interest rate swaps were the China Development Bank (CDB), which started to provide CNY interest rate swap FR007 bilateral quotations on Bloomberg in May 2006, and the Bank of China (BOC), which offered bilateral quotations in the inter-bank bond market from early July. In early September 2006, two foreign banks, Citibank and Standard Chartered Bank, also joined the bidding, followed by a third domestic bank, the Industrial Bank, and the foreign banks HSBC and JP Morgan Chase. As at the end of June 2007, a total of seven banks provided bilateral quotations on Bloomberg: CDB, BOC, and Industrial Bank, and four foreign banks—Citigroup Bank, Standard Chartered Bank, HSBC, and JP Morgan Chase.

Shortly after the central bank launched Shibor in January 2007, the Industrial Bank and Citibank agreed the first Shibor-based swaps.[1] Prior to this, swaps could only refer to the seven-day repurchase rate and the one-year time deposit rate. In international practice, the payment cycle of interest rate swaps is generally three or six months, so pricing distortions may occur if it is based on the seven-day or one-year rates. Moreover, the seven-day repurchase rate mainly reflects short-term capital market conditions, which are sensitive to short-term capital fluctuations and unable to reflect market changes and trends. It is therefore not an appropriate reference for hedging interest rate risks. One-year time deposit interest rates cannot fluctuate with the market and are therefore not ideal for the purposes of hedging interest.[2]

The key to designing a swap contract is the reference floating rate, which should ideally satisfy three basic conditions:

- Dealers should be able to lend or borrow in the money market based on this rate.
- The rate should be determined by an authorized institution, with transparent methodology and free from manipulation by the parties to the transaction.
- There should be a large number of floating rate instruments in the capital market, such as bonds and loans linked to that interest rate.

There were high expectations that Shibor would meet these requirements and develop as a suitable reference for floating rate bonds, and that interest rate swaps and options that could match the assets and liabilities of issuers or investors, with relatively simple pricing and good prospects.

In July 2007 a quotation information interface for bill discounting, repurchases and interest rate swaps linked to Shibor was launched on www.shibor.org, where institutions could offer prices for standard products every day, providing benchmarks for the market. The first batch of banks to quote for interest rate swaps included the Agricultural Bank of China, Bank of China, China Construction Bank, Bank of Communications, China Merchants Bank, CITIC Bank, Industrial Bank, Beijing Bank, Shanghai Bank and HSBC.

CONTRACT HIGHLIGHTS

CNY interest rate swap contracts lay out the terms and conditions controlling such things as counterparties; transaction, value, expiry, and payment dates; fixed and floating interest payments; calculation methods; and so on.

The two most critical factors are the fixed and floating interest rates, because the fundamental purpose of the swaps is to exchange the future cash flows of the two groups of interest. In this exchange, the price of the swaps, which is the fixed interest rate, is of great importance to the counterparties. To facilitate calculation and comparison, these two streams of cash flow are generally converted to their present value. In the conversion, the discount rate can be derived from bond prices, but the cash flows of floating rate interest are unknown. If the fixed rate is known, the present value of relative cash flows is easier to calculate, but it is important to get the exact fixed rate. This calculation seems to be an "infinite loop." However, at the same point in time and in a fully effective and competitive bond market, the preference to get income from the floating rate bonds and fixed rate bonds with the same risk factors and term structure is the same, implying that the time value of money should be consistent; otherwise there will be arbitrage. These two streams of interest cash flow should be equivalent in absolute terms, so we can conclude that any streams of floating rate cash flow can be matched (on a time structure) by a stream of fixed rate cash flow, and the unknown fixed rate can be derived from the other known bond yields in the bond market. This is the basic methodology for calculating interest rate swap quotations.

As mentioned above, the floating rate in CNY interest rate swaps refers to FR007, the one-year time deposit rate or Shibor. It should be noted that different reference floating rates vary widely in resetting interest rates, which is determined by the nature of each floating rate.

USE AND SIGNIFICANCE OF CNY SWAPS

The two basic applications for fixed and floating rate swaps are to reduce financing costs, and to realize the exchange of fixed interest assets and liabilities with floating interest assets and liabilities. Reducing financing costs is based on the theory of comparative advantage which, as we saw earlier, comes into play when a company has a comparative advantage in the fixed rate market but needs floating rate finance, while another company has a comparative advantage in the floating rate market but needs fixed rate finance. The two companies can acquire the financing to meet their respective needs and then sign a swap agreement to reduce their respective financing costs. Because of the default risk and the difficulty of finding counterparties, banks and other financial institutions have become intermediaries in this business, meaning that companies only need to enter swaps with banks without having to find another company as the counterparty. As interest rate swaps have become more widely traded, they have been used more in the exchange of floating rate and fixed rate assets or liabilities. If a company has floating rate assets and is not willing to take the risk of changes in cash flow, it can exchange these assets for fixed rate assets by means of interest rate swaps.

China's interest rate swaps market has been in existence for a relatively short time but, as we have seen, it now offers three options: swaps based on the one-year time deposit rate, the seven-day repurchase interest rate (FR007), and Shibor (mainly three-month). Accordingly, an investor's fixed rate bond can be exchanged for a floating rate bond by buying interest rate swaps (the exchange of floating rate to fixed interest rate, which is equivalent to a price to pay fixed interest rates). If the interest rate goes up, the investors will gain from the long position of the interest rate swaps which offsets all or part of the loss of the fixed rate bond; if investors have a floating rate bond, this can be synthesized into a fixed rate bond through selling interest rate swaps (receiving fixed interest and paying floating interest). If the yield is higher than that of a fixed rate bond with the same period, considering the risk of reference rates (the reference rates of floating rate bonds and interest rate swaps are not exactly the same), then it may be better to invest in a synthesized fixed rate bond than an ordinary fixed rate bond.

In addition to hedging interest rate risk, interest rate swaps are a good speculative tool for interest rates. Since interest rate swaps are derivatives based on reference interest rates, investors can bet on increases or decreases in the reference interest rate through trading in interest rate swaps: if the reference rate is expected to rise, the investors buy; if the rate is expected to decline, they sell. As they require no principal, have good liquidity in mature markets, and are more convenient than bonds, the swap rate has become a signpost of interest rate trends, effectively helping to determine interest rate prices.

Interest rate swaps have improved the pricing of floating rate and fixed rate bonds for the entire market. For instance, by comparing a synthesized fixed rate bond (floating rate bond and floating to fixed interest rate swaps) with a fixed rate bond with the same term structure, we can amend pricing errors in the floating- or fixed rate bonds to develop more accurate pricing. Interest rate swaps also increase the liquidity of such bonds, as demand for floating rate bonds increases because of the existence of interest rate swaps and deals on fixed rate bonds also go up for speculative purposes.

As a result of all this, China's swaps market has developed rapidly. The total notional principal of transactions in 2008 reached CNY412.15 billion (US$59.3 billion), 11.6 times that of 2006, the year the swaps were launched. In 2009, as a result of the sudden release of liquidity into the money market, the inter-bank market yield curve decreased sharply. Despite interest rates not being expected to rise in the short term, the total notional principal of interest rate swaps still reached CNY80.1 billion (US$11.5 billion) in the first quarter of 2009, showing that participants in the inter-bank market had begun to attach importance to the use of interest rate swaps for asset allocation or risk management purposes.

TURNOVER AND FUTURE DEVELOPMENT

Figure 8.3 shows the total notional principal of CNY interest rate swaps from 2007 to the third quarter of 2009. Not surprisingly, the first-year turnover was insignificant compared to subsequent years, with a total notional principal of just CNY35.57 billion (US$4.46 billion). In the following two years, however, this jumped to CNY218.69 billion (US$28.77 billion) and CNY412.15 billion (US$59.34 billion), respectively. The turnover in 2008 was more than 10 times the level of 2006. The relatively low turnover figures in the fourth quarter of 2008 and the first quarter of 2009 may be attributable to the impact of the financial crisis (as we saw with the CNY forwards market in Chapter 7) or simply the result of seasonal adjustments. Despite the relatively low growth in 2009 of 13.9 percent—much lower than the three-digit growth rates in previous years—the annual average compound growth rate of turnover was 147.5 percent for the three years from 2006 to 2009, which is as significant as the CNY foreign exchange swaps and CNY bond forward markets introduced in earlier chapters. It is remarkable that the quarterly growth rate reached 162.3 percent in the first quarter of 2010 compared to the same period in 2009, and much higher than any other quarterly growth rate from the first quarter of 2008.

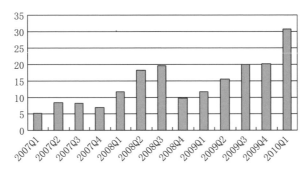

FIGURE 8.3 Turnover of CNY interest rate swaps, 2007–10 (US$ billion)
Source: "Report on the Implementation of China's Monetary Policy" from 2007 to 2009, and Q1 2010, PBC.

This growth is mainly attributable to the growing enthusiasm of inter-bank market participants and continuously enriched product varieties, to which three-month Shibor-based interest rate swaps have made a major contribution.

Despite its comparatively late launch, Shibor has unparalleled advantages over the one-year time deposit rate. As a consequence, CNY interest rate swaps linked to Shibor have become the leading choice in the Chinese market.

As Table 8.1 shows, the one-year time deposit rate, which was the most important reference rate before CNY interest rate swaps were introduced, had almost disappeared by 2009. By contrast, the market share of the interest rate swaps referred to the seven-day repurchase rate and Shibor had increased to more 95 percent since 2007. Although Shibor has from the outset been recognized as a potential reference rate for the interest rate swaps market, its market share is much lower than the swaps referring to the seven-day repurchase interest rate. Despite the fact that Shibor has undoubted advantages as a reference rate, it has not been able to dislodge the seven-day repurchase rate as the first-choice reference because market participants tend to favor short-term varieties. Moreover, historical data show higher fluctuations in the seven-day repurchase rate, which also seems to match investors' hedging needs more closely than Shibor. It should also be noted that Shibor is not based on real market transactions but is quoted by a dozen banks, making it hard for it to be universally accepted by market participants.

TABLE 8.1   Reference rates and market share (%)

Reference Rate	Initial Transaction Date	1H 2006	2H 2006	1H 2007	2H 2007	1H 2008	2H 2008	1Q 2009
FR007	February 2006	38	72	95	66	75	72	79
One-year time deposit	February 2006	62	19	4	10	5	3	1
One-year time deposit + interest spread	November 2006	0	9	0	0	0	0	0
Shibor	January 2007	0	0	1	24	19	26	20
Six-month time deposit	January 2007	0	0	0	0	0	0	0
Three-year lending rate	February 2007	0	0	0	0	0	0	0
Total	—	100	100	100	100	100	100	100

Source: Data based on statistics from chinamoney.com.cn.

Based on the enormous demand for hedging interest rate risks in the domestic market, the CNY interest rate swaps business will continue its rapid development over the next few years. FR007 will continue to be the most important reference rate for some time, but Shibor's importance is expected to rise and Shibor-based swaps are likely to become a mainstream variety in the near future.

INTERNATIONAL COMPARISONS

The Bank for International Settlements (BIS) triennial data released in 2007 showed that the world average daily trading value of all interest rate swaps in April 2007 was US$1.21

trillion. Extrapolating from this, the annual trading value was around US$302.5 trillion. The trading value of CNY interest rate swaps for 2007 was US$28.77 billion, that is, a mere 0.01 percent of the world value (lower even than the value of CNY foreign exchange swaps for that year) and 3.84 percent of the trading value of India's interest rate swaps market.

CONCLUSION

Since their launch in 2006, CNY interest rate swaps have developed rapidly to become one of the most important derivatives in China. The most fundamental reason for this is that financial institutions, enterprises, and other market players have an overwhelming need to hedge against CNY interest rate risk.

The key to CNY swaps is the design of reference rates for the floating leg and the pricing of the fixed rate, as well as revaluation and risk control. Initially, there were two swap reference rates of the floating leg: the secured repurchase rate in the inter-bank bond market, which mainly refers to the basis rate of repurchase agreements within seven days (FR007); and the deposit interest rate of one-year time deposits set by the PBC. In 2007, these were joined by Shibor which, unlike the others, has no inherent term-mismatch defects. Shibor is expected to become the most widely used reference rate in the future.

The PBC's launch of foreign currency swaps in August 2007 marked an important milestone in the maturity and improvement of the CNY interest rate swap market. Such transactions enable market participants to exchange CNY principal with an equivalent amount of a designated foreign currency to meet their specific needs.

As interest rate risk is the most significant market risk, interest rate swaps have become the most important of all OTC derivatives. With the pace of CNY interest rate liberalization continuing to gather, domestic institutions, enterprises and individuals will face higher interest rate risks. In this environment, the use of CNY interest rate swaps to hedge against these risks, to manage assets and liabilities, or to speculate has immeasurable development prospects in China. Despite the rapid growth of the market, annual turnover has still been lower than that in the CNY foreign exchange swaps and CNY bond-forward markets in recent years, a position we expect to see rectified in coming years.

ENDNOTES

1. See *Economic Observer News*, January 23, 2007.
2. See Chen Shiyong, "Possible Ways to Expand Monetary Policy," *Shanghai Securities News*, 2007.

CHAPTER 9

Forward Rate Agreements

INTRODUCTION

A forward rate agreement (FRA) is a financial contract between two counterparties who agree to exchange interest for an agreed period, calculated on the contract interest rate and reference interest rate, and a specified notional amount. The buyer of the FRA pays interest based on the contract interest rate while the seller pays interest based on the reference rate.

An FRA is a derivative product with an interest rate as its direct underlying asset. It has the following unique features:

- The underlying asset of an FRA is not a physical asset, but a reference rate, which is often a widely recognized floating rate in the market, such as Libor, or Shibor in China.
- Cash, rather than a physical asset, is used in settling an FRA.
- Every FRA has two maturities: the forward term and the contract term. The forward term is the number of days between the transaction day and the settlement day. The contract term is the number of days between the settlement day and the maturity day.

The maturity of an FRA is usually expressed as $n \times m$. The m and n represent the period to maturity and the forward term, respectively. The contract term is equal to $m - n$.

FRAs were launched in China in November 2007. The first transaction was executed by China CITIC Bank, with the three-month Shibor as the reference rate, a nominal principal of CNY200 million, and maturities of three months and six months.

REGULATIONS

The PBC's *Administrative Provisions on Forward Rate Agreement Business* announced in September 2007 clearly defined the concept of FRA transactions (as outlined above) between banks in the PRC.

The provisions also define three levels of traders for FRAs:

- Financial institutions with market-maker or settlement agency qualifications that can enter into FRAs with all other market participants.

- Other financial institutions that can trade with all other financial institutions.
- Non-financial institutions that can only trade in FRAs for hedging purposes with market-makers or financial institutions that have clearing agency qualifications.

Under the provisions, before entering into FRAs, financial institutions should report their internal operation measures and risk management systems for FRAs to dealers' associations and trading centers. The management systems should cover, at a minimum, risk measurement and monitoring, internal authorized credit, information monitoring and management, risk reporting, and internal audit. FRAs can be reached through the trading systems of trading centers or by telephone or fax. In respect of transactions not made through trading systems, financial institutions should record FRA trading status in the trading centers on the next working day after making a deal.

IMPLICATIONS OF MARKETING CNY FRA TRANSACTIONS

There are significant implications for launching CNY FRAs as typical interest rate derivatives.

First, they help investors improve their management of interest rate risk. With the further reform of China's financial system, interest rates are more market-oriented. Investors are subject to a greater risk of interest rate volatility. FRAs enable investors to fix the interest rate from a future date to manage the short-term interest rate risk effectively.

Second, they are conducive to market stability and increased market efficiency. They transfer and disperse risk by fixing the interest rate level in the future, which can improve market stability. They can also lower investors' trading costs and enhance market efficiency.

Third, the interest rates agreed in FRAs represent demand for hedging, arbitrage, speculation and other needs, reflecting all kinds of market information and future expectations. This in turn helps the market develop its price discovery functions, and price changes can provide the PBC with important reference for its monetary policies.

Finally, FRAs are conducive to the coordinated development of the financial derivatives market. China's financial derivatives market emerged a short time ago when there were only forward bonds and interest rate swaps. The subsequent introduction of FRAs has not only widened the choice of derivative products, giving investors more flexibility to choose risk management tools, but also provided an effective tool for hedging existing interest products.

Current Market Development

Since the first CNY FRA deal in November 2007, the FRA market has not been very active, as Figure 9.1 shows. Although trading values grew to a peak of US$600 million in the fourth quarter of 2008, they have fallen dramatically since then and, in the third quarter of 2009, were below the point at which they started in 2007. That the dramatic fall from the second quarter of 2009 coincided with the significant growth reported in CNY foreign exchange, bond-forward, and interest rate swaps indicates that there are problems in the market mechanism.

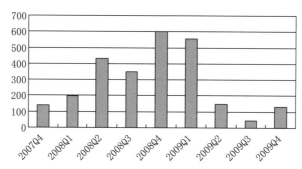

FIGURE 9.1   CNY FRA trading values, 2007–09 (US$ million)
Source: "Report on the Implementation of China's Monetary Policy" from 2007 to 2009, PBC.

MATURITY STRUCTURE

As mentioned earlier, FRAs have two maturities. The contract term usually has the same maturity as the reference rate, which for FRAs in China is the three-month Shibor, at 98.72 percent. The seven-day Shibor was first used as the reference rate in 2009. Table 9.1 shows the structure of forward terms of FRAs.

TABLE 9.1   Term structure of CNY FRAs, 2007–09

Forward Term	Notional Principal Amount [CNY (US$) thousand]	Proportion (%)
7-day	200,000 (29,338)	1.3
1-month	2,500,000 (366,730)	16.0
2-month	890,000 (130,556)	5.7
3-month	6,150,000 (902,156)	39.3
4-month	100,000 (14,669)	0.6
6-month	4,480,000 (657,181)	28.6
9-month	1,230,000 (189,431)	7.9
10-month	30,000 (4,401)	0.2
12-month	80,000 (11,735)	0.5

Source: www.chinamoney.com.cn.

From the launch of FRAs to the first quarter of 2009, products with maturities of three months, six months and one month dominated the market, with a combined total notional principal of CNY13.13 billion (US$1.93 billion).

Table 9.2 shows the quarterly changes in forward term structures over the same period.

While there was no significant trend in the changes in the maturity structure, the changes for some products were very significant. For example, trading in products with a one-month maturity, which had commanded an almost-50 percent market share in the third quarter of 2008, came to an abrupt halt. This inactivity has greatly affected the maturity structure of each transaction, making it difficult to comprehend fully. The only trend that could be

TABLE 9.2 Quarterly changes in forward term structures, 2007–09 (%)

	4Q 2007	1Q 2008	2Q 2008	3Q 2008	4Q 2008	1Q 2009
7-day						5.3
1-month	19.0	14.7	33.9	45.8		
2-month		7.4	1.7	29.2	1.0	
3-month	59.0	15.4	23.7	12.5	56.6	52.6
4-month				4.2		
6-month	9.5	26.5	23.7	8.3	39.5	39.5
9-month	9.5	30.1	16.9		2.9	2.6
10-month		2.2				
12-month	2.9	3.7				

Source: www.chinamoney.com.cn.

extrapolated from these changes could be that FRA transactions have increasingly focused on products with specific maturities.

CONCLUSION

FRAs have not become a major derivative product in China's inter-bank market, nor have they attained a significant market standing. This is because they were not linked directly to underlying assets such as bonds, and institutions have approached them with caution given the volatile nature of these non-deliverable instruments. Moreover, interest rate swaps could combine with floating rate bonds to create hedged portfolios, which was the major rationale of institutions for trading interest rate swaps. With their short-term and single settlement features and failure to directly combine with underlying assets to form hedged portfolios, FRAs failed to compete against interest rate swaps.

With the increased liberalization of the interest rate regime and the emergence of sophisticated financial markets in China, the CNY FRAs will become more flexible and effective in interest rate risk management, which will in turn generate more FRA transactions.

CHAPTER 10

Wealth Management Products in China

Wealth management products are developed by commercial banks to provide customers with integrated and personalized banking products. They incorporate client-relationship, capital and portfolio management services. Wealth management products are barometers of the capital market and their launch indicates the shift of commercial banks from traditional business to mixed operations.

With liberalization, China's banking industry is facing fierce competition from foreign banks, which provide wealth management services as part of their core business. On the one hand, there is an internal force driving the banking sector to restructure; on the other hand, there is a growing number of affluent residents and high net worth individuals who are increasing the demand for wealth management. Combined, these forces, internal and external, are driving high-speed growth in the banking and financial markets.

DEVELOPMENT OF WEALTH MANAGEMENT PRODUCTS

As shown in Table 10.1, since the introduction of wealth management products into the Chinese banking sector in 2004, the business has become increasingly active in both the number of products and the contributions made by CNY products. In fact, by 2008, CNY products had come to dominate the market.

TABLE 10.1 Issuance of wealth management products in China

Year	No. of Products	No. of CNY Products	No. of Foreign Currency Products	CNY Contribution (%)
2005	684	118	566	17.3
2006	1,048	287	761	27.4
2007	3,062	1,302	1,760	42.5
2008	7,799	5,774	2,025	74.0

Source: Evaluation Report on Banking Wealth Management Products, Chinese Academy of Social Sciences.

After five years of development, the amount invested in CNY products is significantly higher than that invested in foreign currency products, with more being invested in products linked to stock or mixed underlying assets than in any other product. Chinese banks outperform their foreign counterparts in this regard. However, though Chinese banks have issued more products, the emphasis within foreign banks on product design and sound marketing gives them an advantage in their product returns and risk indicators.

Market Deficiencies

Despite the rapid growth of the market in China, there are some clear deficiencies.

Most products provided by domestic banks are fairly basic and lack diversity. At present, the products provided by commercial banks are highly homogeneous and few of them have been genuinely designed for wealth management purposes. Chinese commercial banks are still slow at gauging the market, and have yet to set up professional teams to thoroughly analyze the entire capital market and customer demand for products. Few differentiated products with competitive advantages have been developed. Chinese banks rely heavily on their network and marketing channels, as well as favorable policies and serve merely as a sales channel, adding little value further down the wealth management business chain. The partners seize most of the benefits and domestic banks only receive negligible agency fees.

Given the short time span of liberalized operations in the domestic banking industry, and the shortage of financial instruments available in domestic markets, commercial banks have a very limited capacity to conduct hedging transactions for complex financial products. When selling their own financial products, many banks fail to split the products into basic units or to operate independently in the financial markets to obtain maximum profit. Instead, they package their own deposits and structured products to transact with foreign banks. As a result, whatever financial products the banks launch, they act as retail terminals for foreign banks. In effect, therefore, Chinese commercial banks are not directly involved in the wealth management market, have limited capacity to manage derivative products portfolios, and are therefore forced to accept the products offered by foreign banks.

Wealth management products suffer from the asymmetric provision of information to customers and insufficient risk descriptions. While banks may disclose possible risks in detailed product descriptions, many fail to place risk notices prominently in their branches to warn investors about related risks. Some emphasize the returns without mentioning the risks, a practice that has triggered numerous disputes and damaged reputations. In addition, the information disclosure and post-sales service of many commercial banks remain inadequate. Banks are unable to maintain sound communication with customers to provide them with timely and professional analysis. Therefore, when products generate lower returns than the after-tax interest income from savings deposits, investor complaints are common. For that reason, when China encourages banks to design innovative products, it should also educate investors in risk awareness. Investors should be able to make a rational choice of products in accordance with their own risk preferences.

Ordinary products rather than structured products have dominated the CNY wealth management market, both in quantity of products and the amount of funds raised. In 2008, for example, ordinary products raised CNY2,054 billion (US$301 billion), or 97 percent of the total funds raised.

As Table 10.2 shows, the underlying assets or rates of structured products have changed considerably, with the top three products in 2007—equities, credit, and funds—being replaced by foreign exchange rates, commodities, and credit in 2008. These changes clearly show the trend of chasing after high-yield assets and avoiding risk.

TABLE 10.2 Underlying assets or rates of CNY wealth management products (by funds raised), 2007–08 (%)

Underlying Asset or Rate	2007	2008
Equity	39	9
Commodity	6	25
Credit	33	19
Funds	15	3
Foreign exchange rate	1	26
Interest rate	4	10
Others	2	8
Total	100	100

Source: Evaluation Report on the Operations of Chinese Banking Wealth Management Products 2008.

An analysis of the returns of CNY wealth management products shows that most products (some 70 percent) do not guarantee the principal (see Table 10.3), even in 2008 when wealth management products recorded negative returns. At that time, the substitute effect of fixed income products and "floating return but-guaranteed principal" products was obvious. This indicates that Chinese investors lack a true sense of risk awareness, and that there is an urgent need for education in this regard.

TABLE 10.3 Returns of CNY wealth management products (by funds raised), 2007–08 (%)

Type of Return	2007	2008
Guaranteed returns	4	12
Floating returns with principal guaranteed	4	18
Floating returns with principal not guaranteed	72	70
Total	100	100

Source: Evaluation Report on Operation of Chinese Banking Wealth Management Products 2008.

Targeting Higher-yield Assets

CNY wealth management products primarily invest in IPO applications, transferred loans, bonds, trust loans, inter-bank lending, bills, and bank deposits. They have limited investment channels, which is one reason for their relative homogeneity. As with the changes in linked targets of structured products, they tend to invest in assets that currently have a high yield. In 2007, the most favored type was new share applications; this gradually shifted to bonds in 2008, as shown in Table 10.4.

Such choices proved to lack foresight, since a number of wealth management products recorded negative returns in 2008. As of the end of 2009, 98 commercial banks had launched a total of 5,728 wealth management products, with a total book balance of CNY974.4 billion (US$143 billion).[1]

TABLE 10.4 CNY wealth management investment channels (by funds raised), 2007–08 (%)

Investment Channel	2007	2008
IPO application	52	25
Transferred loans	13	7
Bonds	10	22
Trust loans	7	15
Inter-bank lending	0	1
Bills	1	18
Others	17	12

Source: Evaluation Report on the Operations of Chinese Banking Wealth Management Products 2008.

Domestic Banks Dominate

Although domestic banks still lag behind foreign banks in developing and operating wealth management products, they account for much of the funds raised, as shown in Table 10.5. The large number of financial products issued by domestic banks has enriched their business types and profit patterns, as well as their experience in the design of wealth management products. As China's financial market continues to develop, domestic banks will become more competitive in this area.

TABLE 10.5 Market share of CNY wealth management products (by funds raised), 2007–08 (%)

Bank	2007	2008
State-owned banks	40%	63%
Listed joint stock banks	56%	33%
Other Chinese commercial banks	2%	3%
Foreign banks	2%	1%

Source: Evaluation Report on the Operations of Chinese Banking Wealth Management Products 2008.

Short-term in Nature

An analysis of the maturity terms of China's CNY wealth management products shows that they are mainly short-term varieties. As Table 10.6 shows, in 2007 and 2008, products maturing within one year accounted for up to 80 percent and 72 percent of the respective totals of CNY products. Such a structure cannot reduce the fluctuations in returns from capital markets. Furthermore, it limits long-term investment choices, causing the returns of the products and the funds raised to fluctuate significantly. This can hinder the sustained and stable development of the wealth management market. Therefore, the lack of diversity of maturity terms is a major issue.

TABLE 10.6 Maturity terms of CNY wealth management products (by funds raised), 2007–08 (%)

Maturity Term	2007	2008
1–6 months	27	58
6–12 months	53	14
12–24 months	9	27
24–36 months	3	1
Over 36 months	8	0

Source: Evaluation Report on the Operations of Chinese Banking Wealth Management Products 2008.

DEVELOPMENT OF FOREIGN CURRENCY PRODUCTS IN CHINA

When wealth management business was first introduced in China, the bulk of the market was made up by foreign currency products. While such products no longer dominate, they remain an important category nevertheless. Since foreign banks have deeper knowledge of wealth management products, a broader range of more complex and sophisticated foreign currency derivatives is available.

Structured Products Linked to Interest Rates

Structured products outweigh ordinary products and dominate the foreign currency wealth management market. In 2008, structured products accounted for 59 percent of the total funds raised by foreign currency products.

Structured products are mainly linked to interest rates, represented by Libor, which accounted for 50 percent and 65 percent, respectively, in 2007 and 2008 (see Table 10.7). At the same time, equity-linked products also play an important role. The assets or rates underlying these products are relatively stable and do not blindly follow the market, reflecting both their relative sophistication and the difficulty the Chinese banking sector faces in participating in the international financial market.

TABLE 10.7 Underlying assets or rates of foreign currency structured products (by funds raised), 2007–08 (%)

Underlying Asset or Rate	2007	2008
Interest rate	50	65
Equity	24	12
Funds	4	2
Commodity	7	4
Foreign exchange rate	10	3
Others	5	14

Source: Evaluation Report on the Operations of Chinese Banking Wealth Management Products 2008.

Products with a floating return but a guaranteed principal dominate the market, accounting for 70 percent of the market in 2008. This reflects the cautious attitude adopted by banks in launching products as well as investors' need for safe foreign currency products. This market is becoming more rational, cautious, and sound.

State-owned banks have maintained more than half (56 percent in 2007 and 2008) the market share of foreign currency wealth management products. Competition in the market comes primarily from listed joint stock banks and foreign-invested banks, each with a 22 percent share in 2008.

Foreign currency wealth management products are more short-term in nature than their CNY counterparts. As Table 10.8 indicates, products with a maturity of less than one year accounted for 90 percent and 75 percent of the respective totals in 2007 and 2008. This is consistent with the cautious approach adopted by investors, particularly during the financial crisis and its attendant difficulties in estimating exchange rate risk. Short-term products are a good choice for maintaining reasonable investment returns.

TABLE 10.8 Maturity terms of foreign currency wealth management products (by funds raised), 2007–08 (%)

Maturity Term	2007	2008
1–6 months	78	24
6–12 months	12	51
12–24 months	5	16
24–36 months	3	2
Over 36 months	2	7

Source: Evaluation Report on the Operations of Chinese Banking Wealth Management Products 2008.

RISKS ATTENDING WEALTH MANAGEMENT PRODUCTS IN CHINA

During a visit to Shenzhen in February 2005, Liu Mingkang, chairman of the China Banking Regulatory Commission (CBRC), required the Chinese banking sector to "enhance brand awareness, strengthen strategies and reinforce risk management." In his speech, Liu pointed out that risk management was to be the focus of banking supervision that year, with top priority being given to the management of innovative financial products such as wealth management products. Earlier that year, Liu had expressed the need for regulation "to supervise legal entities, risks and internal controls and improve transparency." It was clear from this that the focus of development and regulation of the fast-growing wealth management market was to shift from product development to regulating operations and improving risk management. This section focuses on the risks and major problems associated with wealth management products.

Liquidity Risk

The vast majority of foreign currency wealth management products can only be redeemed upon maturity (the early-termination option rests only with the banks). Therefore, when investing in medium- and long-term products, customers have to be sure that they do not need the funds during the potentially long period of the life of the product. Otherwise, if they wish to redeem the products early, they will often be asked to pay a high default fee, thus reducing their principal.

Interest Rate Risk

Interest rate-linked products command a large share of the amount invested in wealth management products. For individual investors, the movement of interest rates is difficult to predict, especially in the long run. Once the actual movements depart from expectations, losses in the form of opportunity cost increase, even if the principal remains intact. Libor-linked products, which are particularly difficult for domestic investors to manage, bring higher interest rate risks.

Foreign Exchange Risk

Changes in the linked foreign exchange rates affect the returns of customers and banks. The risks associated with the international market have risen significantly since 2007, amid escalating credit risks triggered by the sub-prime debt crisis in the United States. As a result, the risk of such products has also increased.

Option Risk

Many products with floating returns have embedded options, the asymmetrical payment feature which exposes sellers to risks. When developing products with embedded options, banks usually set a ceiling for the maximum interest payment or reserve the right to terminate contracts early. Therefore, banks need to design an appropriate structure and be able to judge interest rate movements accurately to keep risks within a certain range. Particularly important is the timing of the early-termination option, which involves the judgment of future movements of long- and medium-term financial parameters, as well as the management of bank funds. Banks also incur losses if they are unable to take early-termination options as a result of liquidity risk and are forced to accept high interest rates. When taking on the role of option sellers, banks should design a reasonable structure to avoid option risks and, at the same time, use hedging instruments to reduce the risks. A typical example of such a product is the Bank of China's "Qiquanbao." In addition, other products with embedded options also bear higher risks, such as Standard Chartered Bank's "Premium Currency Deposit." Since banks have the option to choose the settlement currency, when exchange rates fluctuate substantially, the principal may still be guaranteed when measured in one currency while incurring huge losses in another. In such circumstances, banks usually choose to repay customers with the depreciating currency, resulting in the risk of customers losing on the principal.

REGULATION AND FUTURE DEVELOPMENTS

The wealth management business has become a major area of financial innovation for China's banking sector. Despite its rapid growth, the variety and flexibility of its products remain at a preliminary stage. As we have seen, the business has considerable risks and its future development will require careful regulation.

Regulation

Since 2005, the CBRC has put in place a number of regulations and risk management measures designed to strengthen and improve the wealth management business conducted by commercial banks. These regulations were drafted with reference to international experience, taking into account the current status of the wealth management business in China, and existing financial laws and regulations. They include specific measures to ensure that commercial banks do not bundle savings deposits into their personal wealth management services. The measures clearly define the categories of wealth management products in the market, and regulate such activities as asset segregation and accounting treatment to standardize and stabilize the development of CNY products.

In November 2005, the CBRC introduced measures and guidelines[2] to allow commercial banks to provide guaranteed-returns products. The guidelines stipulate a minimum investment amount of CNY50,000 (US$6,049) for CNY guaranteed-returns products or US$5,000 for their foreign currency counterparts. The minimum investment amount for other wealth management plans and products is not to be less than that of guaranteed-returns products. However, to prevent banks from exploiting deposits with them, the measures specify that commercial banks must not make unconditional commitments to guaranteed returns higher than the interest rates of savings deposits given in the same period of time.

The various measures specify the basic requirements for commercial banks to conduct wealth management business and the basic principles to manage related risks. They clarify the regulatory framework for the business and stipulate the legal liabilities and penalties for breaching laws and regulations governing wealth management issues.

Through enacting these measures and guidelines, the CBRC's aim is to promote the sound and stable development of wealth management business of the commercial banks.

Future Developments

At present, Chinese banks can only bring in sophisticated but straightforward products from overseas, and they have yet to design any products which cater specifically for local economic and financial conditions. While learning from mature products overseas is a necessary process for Chinese banks to develop their own innovative financial products, it is vital that they launch CNY products appropriate for the Chinese economic and financial environment if they are to interest investors. For example, China's consumer price index (CPI) has stayed at around 2 to 3 percent since 2004. If banks were to launch CPI-linked savings products, they could reduce the pressure from dwindling savings while investors could increase their returns. Such products could be designed as follows: the interest rate of one-year fixed-term savings could be set at 0.20 percent above the benchmark rate if the CPI was above 5 percent, at 0.3 percent if inflation stayed above 5 percent for two consecutive months, at 0.40% if inflation stayed above that level for three consecutive months, and so on. While this would increase the banks' costs (since high inflation rates presage upward interest rate adjustments which would further increase their expenses), these products could be able to absorb savings and reduce the inflation risk of savers, which could assure their success. The future for China's wealth management business lies in developing innovative CNY products suitable for the current economic and financial conditions and for investors' needs.

CONCLUSION

With financial liberalization and internationalization, Chinese commercial banks have accelerated financial innovation. Providing consumers with integrated and personalized financial services has gradually become the focus and an inevitable trend. The wealth management business benefits both customers and banks, providing consumers with a greater range of investment products and helping commercial banks to become more competitive. Although this business has developed rapidly in recent years, especially in joint stock banks, China's wealth management products are still at a preliminary stage since most of them are simple, traditional products. As the liberalization of China's interest rate and CNY exchange rate progresses further, interest rate and foreign exchange rate risks will also increase. Products linked to interest rates or foreign exchange rates will have an extensive potential market, and innovative products catering for China's specific economic and financial environment will emerge.

On the strength of their experience in product innovation, foreign banks have begun to launch a variety of wealth management products and this will expedite the development of China's wealth management business and other CNY derivatives. With the improvement of China's financial markets, Chinese banks will achieve faster and greater progress in the wealth management market.

ENDNOTES

1. *CBRC Annual Report 2009.*
2. See, for example, "Provisional Measures for the Administration of Personal Wealth Management Business of Commercial Banks" and the "Guidelines on Commercial Banks' Risk Management of Personal Wealth Management Business," at the PBC website www.pbc.gov.cn.

CHAPTER 11

Other CNY Products

The new domestic financial products mentioned in previous chapters are mainly traded in the inter-bank market. In recent years, China's exchanges have also made relentless efforts in product innovation, with notable achievements in the areas of warrants and convertible bonds.

China started to develop warrants during the reform of the split share structure in 2005. A subscription warrant is a single stock option introduced by financial institutions and was the first exchange-traded financial derivative in China. Warrant transactions not only provide investors with a tool to mitigate risks, but also provide banks with reliable and useful market parameters that can be used to manage market risk. The prices and transaction volume of warrants also provide important information that the stock market cannot provide investors in analyzing the underlying listed shares.

Convertible bonds were developed much earlier than warrants, the first being issued in December 1992. Combining the features of both debt and equity, they have injected new vitality into financial markets, providing effective low-cost financing for Chinese enterprises and a diversified investment instrument for investors.

DEVELOPMENT OF THE GLOBAL WARRANTS MARKETS

A warrant is, in fact, an option and has the characteristics of either a call option or a put option, and either an American option or a European option. A subscription warrant with shares as its underlying asset is essentially a type of stock option. The differences between exchange-traded subscription warrants and stock options are as follows:

- Duration: The duration of a warrant (that is, the length of time between the issuance and maturity dates) is generally over one year, whereas for stock options this is usually within one year.
- Standardization: Warrants are usually non-standardized, so that issuers can decide the issue volume, exercise prices, issuance dates and duration. In contrast, exchange-traded stock options are standardized contracts.
- Quantity in circulation: Generally, short selling is not allowed in warrants transactions. Even if it is allowed, short selling can only be carried out after physical warrants are borrowed in advance. Other than through new issues and the maturing of existing warrants, the number of warrants in circulation is fixed. For stock options, investors are free

to short sell, and can open or close positions. The net position of options in the market varies with the opening and closing of positions.

■ Credit risk: Subscription warrants are settled between issuers and holders, while stock options are settled by professional institutions independent of buyers and sellers. Therefore, the credit risk of stock option trading is slightly lower than for subscription warrants.

■ Market-maker: Whether or not officially designated by an exchange, issuers generally automatically take up the market-making obligation to create a liquid market for their own subscription warrants. In contrast, market-makers of stock options have to be duly authorized by exchanges.

Warrants can be divided into two categories: equity warrants and derivative warrants. Derivative warrants, a term used in the Hong Kong Stock Exchange (HKEx), are also called covered warrants, synthetic warrants, or third-party warrants in the international market.

Equity warrants are issued by listed companies or any of their subsidiaries. Equity warrants have to be settled by physical shares, that is, issuers of warrants have to deliver the shares after holders pay the exercise price in full, thus increasing the number of outstanding shares in listed companies. The exercise of equity warrants has the effect of diluting the equity of existing shareholders.

In general, issuers of derivative warrants are investment banks, third parties that are independent of the issuers of the underlying securities or any of their subsidiaries. The underlying assets can be stock, bonds, stock indices, currencies, commodities or a basket of securities. Derivative warrants can be settled by physical objects or cash. Furthermore, as the underlying assets of derivative warrants are securities that are already in circulation, their exercise does not dilute the equity held by shareholders, unlike equity warrants.

Because derivative warrants are more flexible and have a wider applicability, they far surpass equity warrants in number and trading volume in global markets.

Development of Global Warrants Markets

According to statistics provided by the World Federation of Exchanges (WFE) (see Table 11.1), in its 51 member exchanges (including all major global stock exchanges), the number of warrants listed at the end of 2008 reached almost 490,000—more than 10 times the number of listed companies at that time—with an annual growth rate of more than 54 percent. Yet the growth slowed down significantly from 2008 to 2009, with a corresponding annual growth of just 3.1 percent during that period. At the same time, despite the continued growth in the number of warrants in issue from 2007 to 2009, turnover actually fell during this period. The two-digit drops of turnover from 2007 to 2009 are largely the result of the global financial crisis, particularly from 2007 to 2008. Another important observation that can be made from Table 11.1 is that the declining rate of warrant turnover, 1.1 percent, was much lower than the corresponding decline, 29.2 percent, in shares from 2008 to 2009.

Table 11.2 shows the geographical distribution and turnover of listed warrants for 2008 and 2009. Europe had the world's greatest number of warrants in those two years, with

TABLE 11.1 Number and trading volume of listed warrants, 2007–09

Year	2009	2008	2007	Annual Growth Rate 2008–09 (%)	Annual Growth Rate 2007–09 (%)
Number of listed warrants at year-end	504,275.0	489,315.0	317,286	3.1	54.2
Turnover of warrants (US$ million)	817,152.7	1,041,982.0	1,449,129	−21.6	−28.1
Number of listed companies	45,358.0	45,846.0	46,492	−1.1	−1.4
Turnover of shares (US$ million)	80,827,344.3	114,146,673.5	112,968,380	−29.2	1.0

Note: The statistics exclude the China warrants market.
Source: WFE website (www.world-exchanges.org).

Germany accounting for 84.9 percent of that total. However, in turnover terms, the Asia Pacific markets were the most active, accounting for nearly two-thirds of the total in 2008 and more than three-quarters in 2009, with the number of listed warrants accounting for around 3 percent. The Hong Kong market itself accounted for more than half, while Germany's turnover accounted for only 15.8 percent of the total in 2008.

TABLE 11.2 Geographical distribution of global warrants markets, 2008 and 2009

2009/Region	Number of Listed Warrants		Turnover	
	Number	% of Global Market	US$ million	% of Global Market
Europe, Africa, and Middle East	488,222	96.82	201,584.40	24.67
Asia Pacific	15,897	3.15	614,802.40	75.24
US	156	0.03	765.9	0.10
Total	504,275	100.00	817,152.70	100.00

2008/Region	Number of Listed Warrants		Turnover	
	Number	% of Global Market	US$ million	% of Global Market
Europe, Africa, and Middle East	476,284	97.34	349,774.40	33.57
Asia Pacific	12,892	2.63	691,119.80	66.33
US	139	0.03	1,087.80	0.10
Total	489,315	100.00	1,041,982.00	100.00

Note: The statistics exclude the China warrants market.
Source: WFE website (www.world-exchanges.org).

Although the United States has the world's most developed securities markets, its warrants market is not well developed. This is because it has a well-developed market for stock options and stock index options, and stock options are good substitutes for warrants.

We mentioned earlier that the number and trading volume of derivative warrants far surpass equity warrants, a point illustrated in Table 11.3, which shows a breakdown of the warrant transactions on the Main Board of the HKEx in 2008 and 2009. From a total of more than 3,000 warrants only 34 were equity warrants and the market value and turnover of derivative warrants accounted for almost the entire market. The trading of derivative warrants, too, was vastly superior. Table 11.3 also shows that, although the number of listed warrants increased by 11.4 percent, from 3,045 in 2008 to 3,392 in 2009, market value and turnover decreased by 19.1 percent and 51.8 percent, respectively, from 2008 to 2009.

TABLE 11.3 Number and volume of warrant transactions on HKEx Main Board, 2008–09

2009/Type	Number of Listed Warrants		Market Value		Turnover		Turnover Rate
	Number	Market Share (%)	HK$ million	Market Share (%)	HK$ million	Market Share (%)	Current Turnover/ Market Value (%)
Equity warrants	25	0.7	1,103.4	0.8	524.1	0.0	47.5
Derivative warrants	3,367	99.3	136,441.3	99.2	1,654,894.8	100.0	1,212.9
Total	3,392	100.0	137,544.7	100.0	1,655,418.8	100.0	1,203.6
2008/Type	Number	Market Share (%)	HK$ million	Market Share (%)	HK$ million	Market Share (%)	Current Turnover/ Market Value (%)
Equity warrants	34	1.1	948.5	0.6	1,130.3	0.0	119.2
Derivative warrants	3,011	98.9	169,573.6	99.7	3,433,736.3	100.0	2,024.9
Total	3,045	100.0	170,122.1	100.0	3,434,866.6	100.0	2,019.1

Source: Hong Kong Exchanges and Clearing Ltd website (www.hkex.com.hk).

DEVELOPMENT OF THE WARRANTS MARKET IN CHINA

In the early days of China's securities markets, the Shanghai Stock Exchange (SSE) and the Shenzhen Stock Exchange (SZSE) launched several warrants. However, the lack of self-restraint from market players and inadequate laws and regulations led to excessive speculation in the warrants market that greatly damaged the interests of ordinary investors. In 1996, four years after being launched, the market closed and warrants gradually faded out for 10 years.[1]

In 2005, as part of the split share structure reform, warrants began to reappear in the A-share markets. Since the Baogang warrants in the SSE in August and the issuance of

Wuhan Iron and Steel warrants in late November that year, the trading of warrants in China has been very active, attracting extensive attention. In 2006, China's A-share markets had only 20-plus subscription warrants; however, their turnover hit CNY1,989.956 billion (US$249.605 billion). As a result, China overtook Hong Kong as the world's second-largest warrants market. The following year, the market went one better with a turnover of CNY7,587.2 billion (US$951.5 billion), placing it first in the world rankings, a position it was able to retain in 2008 despite the declining worldwide turnover. The relaunch of warrants not only provides investors with a tool to avoid risks, but also presents banks with reliable and useful parameters to manage market risk.

Trading Volume and Amount

Table 11.4 provides an overview of warrant trading in the period 2005 to 2009. The number of warrants issued peaked at 27 at the end of June 2006. With some warrants maturing, the number of subscription warrants in A-share markets gradually decreased from 2007 onward. A total of 41 warrants (matured or outstanding) were traded in the two exchanges, including 23 call warrants, 18 put warrants, 28 derivative warrants, and 13 equity warrants. While the number of warrants issued in the A-share markets cannot compare with the tens of thousands issued in the markets in Germany and Hong Kong, their level of activity and turnover are in no way inferior to these markets. On the contrary, they outperform the others.

TABLE 11.4   Warrants trading in A-share markets, 2005–09

	Year	Annual Transaction (thousand)	Annual Volume (billion unit)	Annual Turnover (CNY billion)	Annual Turnover (US$ billion)	Annual Growth Rate (%)
Shanghai Stock Exchange	2005	12,685.5	127.5	176.3	21.6	
	2006	81,572.5	1,418.3	1,494.1	187.4	767.4
	2007	165,033.5	2,767.4	4,793.8	630.6	236.6
	2008	222,128.0	4,377.0	5,962.1	858.5	36.1
	2009	153,401.0	1,782.1	4,900.7	717.4	−16.4
Shenzhen Stock Exchange	2005	3,300.9	42.3	42.6	5.2	
	2006	30,045.3	454.0	495.9	62.2	1092.8
	2007	88,608.9	628.3	2,793.4	367.5	490.9
	2008	37,300.9	242.1	1,006.4	144.9	−60.6
	2009	16,148.9	58.3	463.9	67.9	−53.1
Total	2005	15,986.4	169.8	218.9	26.8	
	2006	111,617.8	1,872.2	1,990.0	249.6	830.6
	2007	253,642.4	3,395.7	7,587.2	998.1	299.9
	2008	259,428.9	4,619.1	6,968.5	1,003.4	0.5
	2009	169,550.3	1,840.4	5,364.6	785.3	−21.7

Source: Shanghai Stock Exchange website (www.sse.com.cn) and Shenzhen Stock Exchange website (www.szse.cn).

The table shows that following the relaunch of warrants in China's securities markets, both the volume and total turnover grew rapidly in the first two years, particularly in the SZSE, yet they fell more rapidly in the SZSE from 2007 to 2009. In 2008, while the number of listed warrants fell, the turnover remained very active, yet turnover fell significantly from 2008 to 2009.

Problems in the Market

The high levels of activity in the warrants market cannot disguise the fact that it faces some serious problems. First of all, in the first four years of trading only 41 warrants were listed and only 13 were still trading in the two exchanges at the end of 2009. While turnover remained high, it lagged a long way behind developed markets in Germany and Hong Kong in the number of warrants issued. Developed markets are generally dominated by derivative warrants and have few equity warrants. In China, securities-issuing companies dominate the issuance of warrants, among which there is a low proportion of derivative warrants. There is a big gap between securities-issuing companies and issuers of derivative warrants in risk management and financial technology.

Second, excessive speculation related to the small number of listed warrants in the market has caused great losses to many investors, especially on put warrants. Given their relatively low exercise prices, the intrinsic value of put warrants has stayed at nearly zero, making the actual prices relatively cheap and an easy target for speculation. The creation mechanism introduced by the SSE and the introduction of a 30-minute halt in trading by the SZSE have inhibited speculation somewhat. However, for the warrants market to develop rationally, the fundamental solutions are to increase the supply of warrant products, especially derivative warrants; set up adequate arbitrage mechanisms; and have market-makers who can maintain warrant prices at reasonable levels.

Third, warrants are complex financial products. Because small- and medium-sized investors were not properly educated in the workings of warrants, many of them suffered heavy losses in speculative activities prior to maturity. Increasing investor education, particularly in relation to the distinction between warrants and stocks, is extremely important for the healthy development of China's warrants market.

Finally, warrant pricing theories have to be revised to suit domestic markets. Most of the assumptions used in the classical models currently adopted in financial markets, such as the Black-Scholes model and the Binary Tree model, are better suited to mature or relatively mature capital markets and regulatory environments. However, China's capital market is currently laboring under many institutional constraints. In particular, it lacks a short-selling mechanism, and thus cannot meet the most important condition of option pricing theory. The domestic capital market cannot be improved overnight and the issuance of warrant and option products cannot wait until the markets are mature. Revising the classical theories in such a way that they can be applied to domestic capital markets is a major topic in the development of financial innovation and risk management in China.

Significance of the Development of China's Warrants Market

The volume and implied volatility of trading in the warrants market provides important information that is unavailable in the stock market and crucial for the risk management of banks. In addition, as a result of the similarity between stock warrants and stock options, the development of stock warrants prepares for the launch of exchange-traded or over-the-counter stock index options, stock options, foreign exchange options, commodity futures options, and interest rate options in domestic markets in the future. Options are essential for risk management and embedded components for other products, such as asset-linked financial products. With the launch of stock index futures in domestic markets, such options, which are actively traded internationally, will be introduced gradually in domestic markets. The development of the warrants market will provide a solid foundation for the development of China's financial markets and product innovation, and will speed up the maturity of financial institutions.

CONVERTIBLE BONDS

A convertible bond is a special corporate bond that can be converted into ordinary shares at a specified time in accordance with specified conditions.

Convertible bonds have the features of both debt and equity. Like other bonds, the interest rates and terms are specified. Investors can choose to hold to maturity and collect the principal and interest. But they are also equity. Before conversion, they are purely bonds. After conversion into shares, the original bondholders become the issuing company's shareholders and have rights to participate in decision-making and dividend distribution. This affects the issuing company's capital structure to a certain extent.

Holders of these bonds can convert them into shares in accordance with stipulated conditions, an option that is not enjoyed by other bondholders. Those who do not want to convert can hold to maturity and collect the principal and interest, or sell the bonds in a liquid market. If bondholders are optimistic about the growth potential of the issuing company's shares, they can exercise the conversion rights after the grace period at predetermined conversion prices and the issuer cannot refuse. Because they are convertible, their interest rates are generally lower than those of other corporate bonds. The issuance of convertible bonds can reduce an enterprise's financing costs.

Because these bonds are both convertible and redeemable, investors have the option to convert but they need to bear the opportunity cost of lower interest rates, while issuers have the right to execute redemption clauses but they need to pay higher interest rates than bonds without redemption clauses. Enabling these dual options allows both investors and issuers to control risk and income within a certain range, and this feature can be used to hedge risk on shares to obtain a more certain income.

Convertible bonds appeal strongly to both issuers and investors. Their features enable enterprises to rapidly obtain funds at low financing cost and avoid undue financial pressure when the bonds mature. However, the equity of the issuing company's original shareholders will be diluted on conversion. While investors can only receive low interest income from convertible bonds compared with investment in other corporate bonds, they may receive substantial proceeds on conversion.

DEVELOPMENT OF CHINA'S MARKET

Current Status

Convertible bonds were first introduced in the United States in 1843 and have since become an important financing tool in all international capital markets. By the end of 2004, the year before China started to issue convertible bonds, the global market capitalization of convertible bonds was close to US$610 billion.

China's convertible bond market lags behind the markets of Western countries. Convertible bonds were first introduced into China in 1991, when Hainan New Energy introduced one as part of a trial even before the regulatory authorities had issued any formal documents pertaining to this form of financing. A few enterprises in need of financing began to issue convertible bonds and raised some funds from international capital markets. However, with the failure of the first formal issue—that of Shenzhen Bao'an, in December 1992—the market came to a standstill until the promulgation of the *Interim Measures for the Administration of Convertible Corporation Bonds* in March 1997. The market was then revitalized after three non-listed companies, Nanning Chemical Industry, Wujiang Silk, and Maoming Petrochemica, issued convertible bonds.

Late in April 2001, the China Securities Regulatory Commission (CSRC) issued a number of measures governing the implementation of convertible bonds, which marked a new phase in the development of the market. Such has been the growth since then that, in May 2009, a total of 40 convertible bonds, amounting to a total financing of more than CNY40 billion (US$5.86 billion), were listed on exchanges.

In 2006, a new product was launched. A detachable bond is a listed company-issued corporate bond with a warrant attached. By nature, they are convertible bonds, but are different in the sense that the transaction of the warrants is separate from that of bonds. In November 2006, the first detachable convertible bond—the 06 Magang bond—was traded simultaneously with the Magang CWB1 (Magang warrant) on the SSE, providing investors with a new trading product.

By the end of 2009, a total of 13 convertible bonds were trading—10 on the SSE and three on the SZSE. However, both trading volume and turnover have not been very active, as Table 11.5 clearly demonstrates. The annual turnover in the two exchanges amounts to just CNY63.6 billion (US$9.3 billion). Compared with the vigorous warrants market, the trading of convertible bonds is insignificant. One reason for this is the inactive bond market. To investors, convertible bonds are just corporate bonds and cannot arouse their interest.

Characteristics of the Convertible Bond Market

Compared with mature convertible bond markets in developed countries, the small, low-level market in China is still in its infancy. It also lags behind China's stock markets, accounting for just 0.32 percent of the total market value. By contrast, the corresponding figures for the United States, Japan, and Indonesia are 1.15 percent, 8.15 percent, and 2.59 percent, respectively.

The 14 convertible bonds currently in issue are mainly concentrated in traditional industries, such as iron and steel, energy, petrochemical, and medical. In developed countries, the issuers of convertible bonds are concentrated in high-growth and high-risk industries (for example, IT and life sciences), capital-intensive industries (telecommunications and healthcare), as well as industries with high capital costs (finance and consumer products). This shows that convertible bonds have not played a positive role in the development of specific industries in China.

TABLE 11.5 Trading of convertible bonds, 2005–09

Exchange	Year	Total Transaction (thousand)	Total Volume (million lot)	Total Turnover (CNY billion)	Total Turnover (US$ billion)	Annual Growth Rate of Total Turnover (%)
Shanghai	2005	308.6	30.0	32.2	3.9	
Stock	2006	185.9	15.0	16.9	2.1	−46.2
Exchange	2007	315.1	13.0	21.2	2.8	31.5
	2008	565.5	26.0	30.2	4.3	55.9
	2009	473.1	31.0	41.8	6.1	41.0
Shenzhen	2005	199.4	18.0	19.2	2.3	
Stock	2006	136.3	9.0	10.6	1.3	−43.7
Exchange	2007	176.1	11.0	19.7	2.6	96.3
	2008	235.8	12.0	14.1	2.0	−22.1
	2009	216.7	168.5	21.8	3.2	57.8
Total	2005	508.0	48.0	51.4	6.3	
	2006	322.2	24.0	27.5	3.4	−45.3
	2007	491.2	24.0	40.9	5.4	56.4
	2008	801.3	38.0	44.2	6.4	18.3
	2009	689.8	199.5	63.6	9.3	46.4

Source: Shanghai Stock Exchange website (www.sse.com.cn) and Shenzhen Stock Exchange website (www.szse.cn).

Most issuers of convertible bonds are listed companies because the regulatory authorities have set strict examination and approval conditions for such issues, with detailed requirements on their profitability, continuing operations, and assets and liabilities. This, in effect, restricts convertible bond issues by non-listed or non-profit enterprises. The exceedingly stringent requirements on issuing companies suppress the development of the market and the expansion of trading.

The vast majority of China's convertible bonds also set harsh redemption conditions. Investors can only sell convertible bonds back to issuing companies after meeting certain conditions. Otherwise, they have to convert bonds into shares. This approach reduces the pressure on issuing companies to repay the principal and interest in cash, and supports the financing and reform of state-owned enterprises.

SIGNIFICANCE OF THE DEVELOPMENT OF CHINA'S CONVERTIBLE BOND MARKET

The development of the convertible bond market has the potential to enrich the product structure of China's financial markets and bring many benefits to investors and financiers.

Significance to Financiers

A key reason why companies choose to issue convertible bonds is the restrictions on the size of share placements and additional offering conditions. Large-scale financing plans can only be realized through the issuance of convertible bonds, which is classified as delayed equity financing for listed companies. This has the following advantages:

- **Lower financing costs:** In accordance with the rules, nominal interest rates for convertible bonds cannot exceed the interest rates on bank deposits for the same period. Unconverted, such bonds are in fact long-term bonds bearing low interest rates. The experience of past issues shows that the coupon interest rate of one-year convertible bonds is about 1 percent.
- **Large-scale financing:** The conversion price is generally higher than the average market price of the shares over a period of time prior to the bond issue. When the bonds are converted, the issuer in effect issues shares at above the market price. Given the same conditions of capital expansion, the issuer can raise more funds through a convertible bond than an additional issue and share placement.
- **Less pressure on financial performance:** An investment project often has a cycle of three to five years, with little or no return in the short term. When financed by an additional issue or share placement, the new shares and the funds raised are included in the total share capital and the net assets. As a result, two key indicators—earnings per share and return on equity—are diluted immediately, putting great pressure on the company's financial performance. However, when financed through convertible bonds, the bonds will not be converted into shares until at least six months later, giving at least a six-month grace period for increasing share capital. Even after entering into the conversion period, listed companies can modulate conversion frequency in the issuance notice to prevent equity from being diluted too quickly. Equity can increase when the project gradually yields a return; as such share capital will not be diluted quickly. This avoids rapid expansion of the company's share capital in a short period. Furthermore, the financial pressure on the issuing company to pay the principal and interest decreases when investors convert the bonds. Therefore, financing through issuing convertible bonds is more flexible than additional issuance and share placement.

Significance to Investors

As a key investment product in the securities markets, convertible bonds have attracted increasing numbers of moderate investors. The reasons for this are as follows:

- *Secured income:* Investors can take full advantage of the distinctive features of convertible bonds and achieve higher returns on their investment. They can receive fixed income by holding the bonds, convert these to shares and enjoy profit growth when the issuing company reports good results, or sell the bonds and pocket the gains when the bond price increases with the rising share price. On the other hand, if the share price slumps, the fall of the bond price will be limited to the level of ordinary bonds with similar interest rates. While prices of convertible bonds have no ceiling, the downside risk is limited to the value of ordinary bonds.
- *Attractive terms:* Most convertible bonds have redemption terms to further ensure the safety of the bondholder's principal and interest. Some convertible bonds offer additional interest to holders at maturity to increase their incentive to hold to maturity. In addition, convertible bonds set terms to amend conversion prices to provide that, when the share price falls to 80–95 percent of the conversion price, the issuing company has to, or has the right to, amend the conversion price to safeguard investors' interests.

■ *Circumvention of policy restrictions:* In general, convertible bonds are classified as bonds. Institutional investors with a limit on equity investment can indirectly expand the proportion of equity investment and the scope of their investment portfolio through investing in convertible bonds.

CONCLUSION

Over the past two years, the trading of warrants in the domestic stock markets has been very active and has developed rapidly. There are, however, few domestic warrants and speculation is excessive. Traditional pricing theories are inadequate for the task. If the domestic warrant market is to develop further, a number of issues will require urgent attention. These include controlling transaction risk, regulating trading practices, enriching the variety of warrants issued (in particular, the number of derivative warrants), and improving pricing mechanisms.

At present, China's convertible bond market is still inactive. Promoting the development and making full use of convertible bonds will be very beneficial to China's financial markets, financiers, and investors.

ENDNOTE

1. See Li Hao *et al.*, 2007.

Three

Offshore CNY Derivatives Products

So far, we have examined the major CNY derivatives products in mainland China. Because the domestic product innovation process has been somewhat slow, the offshore market has played an important role for the entire CNY marketplace. As the following chapters show, there is a corresponding non-deliverable product in the Hong Kong SAR for most onshore CNY products. For example, for the CNY foreign exchange forward, the corresponding offshore product is the CNY non-deliverable foreign exchange forward; for the CNY foreign exchange swap, there is the CNY non-deliverable foreign exchange swap; the corresponding offshore product for the CNY interest rate swap (IRS) is the CNY non-deliverable IRS.

In Part III, we will introduce the major offshore non-deliverable CNY products.

CHAPTER 12

CNY Non-deliverable Forwards

As long as a local currency is not fully freely convertible or free-floating, non-deliverable foreign exchange forwards will have a role to play in offshore markets. Offshore non-deliverable forward markets have sprung up in emerging markets despite there already being domestic foreign exchange forward markets. This is chiefly because of the remaining liquidity problems in domestic forward markets. Before China reformed its exchange rate policy, the CNY was managed through movements within a narrow range, and international participants were not able to enter the Chinese foreign exchange market. This spurred the development of a thriving offshore CNY non-deliverable forward market. From late September 2002 to August 2008, the CNY was under pressure to revalue and, from then until March 2009, to depreciate. Since late March 2009, it has been under pressure again to revalue. Currently, the non-deliverable forward market is seeing more active trading than when it was in its infancy from 1996 to 2000.

CNY non-deliverable forwards (CNY NDFs) are the most active offshore CNY derivative products. Since the end of 2002, they have been increasingly under the spotlight in global markets.

DEVELOPMENT HISTORY

Since the mid-1990s, China has witnessed increasing foreign direct investment (FDI). FDI reached US$132.8 billion in 1995 and US$174.5 billion in 1996. Some multinational companies felt the need to protect the value of their investments in China. With the onset of the Mexican economic crisis in 1994, these entities became worried about devaluation and sought solutions to preserve the value of the CNY. Financial institutions in Hong Kong and Singapore launched CNY NDFs to meet this demand, leading to growth in local markets. Initially, the markets expanded slowly, with the longest forward contract term being only six months, and the trading volume was low. It normally took several hours, or even days, to make a deal. In the summer of 1997, the CNY came under great pressure to devalue at the onset of the Asian financial crisis. With the subsequent recovery of the world economy and China's accession to the WTO, China's trade surplus and foreign currency reserves rose. This in turn boosted pressure to revalue the CNY. However, Chinese foreign exchange policy remained stable, and speculation led to steady increases in transactions of CNY NDFs and a variety of CNY derivative products. Currently, the maturity periods for CNY NDFs are as long as three years, and those with a contract term of less than one year are more actively traded.

The launch of non-deliverable forwards in a country usually indicates the need to liberalize foreign exchange policy, and is thus considered to be a criticism of government policy in that area. Non-deliverable forwards are a reflection of the market view of what constitute appropriate foreign exchange rates. Since most global central banks reject offshore derivative products such as non-deliverable forwards, most business entities are unwilling to disclose related information to the public.[1]

REVALUATION/DEVALUATION PRESSURE ON THE CNY AND THE NDF MARKET

In recent years, few currencies have endured the same drastic changes in appreciation/devaluation pressure as the CNY. As with other Asian currencies, the CNY was subject to significant devaluation pressure during and after the Asian financial crisis. However, from the end of 2002 to August 2008, it then suffered more than five years of opposite pressure, that is, to appreciate.

From Devaluation to Revaluation

Reuters data indicate that from early 1999 to the end of 2001, the 12-month CNY NDF rate was between 8.4 to 9.5, implying that the CNY was under significant pressure to depreciate because of the continuing impact of the Asian financial crisis. Figure 12.1 shows the one-year CNY/US$ non-deliverable forward daily rates from January 2002 to May 2010. The implied exchange rates of offshore 12-month CNY NDFs fluctuated between 8.30 and 8.36 from the end of 2001 to mid-June 2002, implying that the CNY was still under moderate pressure. From mid-June to early November that year, the 12-month CNY NDF was between 8.28 and 8.30, implying that the CNY was under only slight pressure to depreciate. However, the rate fell significantly from early November and stayed significantly below 8.2765, the official CNY/US$ exchange rate at that time, implying revaluation pressure on the CNY.

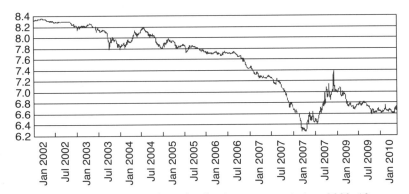

FIGURE 12.1 One-year CNY NDF rates from devaluation to appreciation, 2002–10
Source: Reuters.

Appreciation Pressure

As shown in Figure 12.1, CNY NDF rates hovered around 8.277 in the summer of 2002 and started to shift downward from November, having reached their peak in October. It was clear that the one-year CNY NDF rate was below 8.277, the official spot CNY/US$ exchange rate after November 2002, implying that the CNY was under pressure to appreciate from late 2002. After the change in China's foreign exchange policy in July 2005, one-year CNY NDF rates continued to drop, with the decline gathering momentum from the end of March 2008. In November 2007, the exchange rates dropped even further, reflecting the continued pressure for CNY appreciation. The CNY NDF rate did not stop falling until early April 2008, when it still reflected one-year CNY appreciation of 11.7 percent after a cumulative 17.9 percent realized revaluation of the CNY by early April.

The revaluation continued after the peak in early April 2008 until mid-September 2008 when the financial crisis hit. Thus, the CNY revaluation pressure lasted for four years and 10 months from November 2002 to September 2008.

Return to Appreciation Pressure

Figure 12.1 shows that the CNY was under significant pressure to depreciate as the 12-month CNY NDF was significantly higher than the then spot rate of 6.83. While this pressure reached the highest point of 7.2 percent on December 4, 2008, the depreciation lasted for about six months, to end in late March 2009, shortly after the US Federal Reserve Bank (FED) announced that it would purchase long-term US Treasury bonds through additional money supply. Since late March 2009, the CNY has been under revaluation pressure again. The revaluation and depreciation pressure changes are illustrated in Figure 12.2.

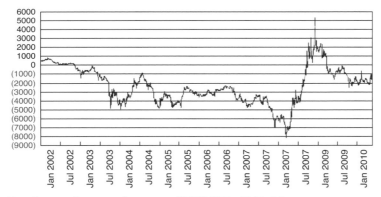

FIGURE 12.2 Premium or discount of one-year CNY NDFs, 2002–10
Source: Calculated using data from Figure 12.1 and spot CNY/US$ rates from the State Administration of Foreign Exchange (SAFE) website (www.safe.gov.cn)

Revaluation/Depreciation Measures

As both the spot and forward-exchange rates change slightly from day to day, banks normally use the product of 10,000 times the difference between forward rates and the corresponding spot rates to measure the underlying currency's revaluation/devaluation range. For example, if the implied rate of offshore 12-month CNY NDFs was 6.9450 and the corresponding CNY/US$ spot rate was 7.4710 on October 31, 2007, the current forward premium or discount should be $10,000 \times (6.9450 - 7.4710) = -5,260$ points.

A negative figure would indicate the US dollar coming under pressure to devalue, or pressure for the CNY to appreciate. Here, the US dollar is at a forward discount of 5,260, or the CNY is at a premium of 5,260. If the figure were positive, the opposite would hold true.

Figure 12.2 illustrates the premiums or discounts of one-year CNY NDFs from December 31, 2001 to December 31, 2009 when the CNY experienced drastic shifts between pressure to devalue and pressure to appreciate. It shows that the CNY was at discounts from the end of 2001 to early November 2002, at premiums from early November 2002 to late September 2008, at discounts again from late September 2008 to late March 2009, and at premiums again from late March 2009, and remained around 1,700 points late in December 2009.

Table 12.1 lists the five stages of CNY appreciation pressure before the foreign exchange policy reforms of July 2005 and two stages after the regime change. The CNY premium range was close to 5,000 in early 2005 and mid-May 2005, implying that the pressure for CNY appreciation was at its greatest before the regime change, and the CNY premium was at the highest point on March 13, 2008 with 8,195 points.

TABLE 12.1 Seven stages of CNY revaluation pressure before April 2008

Stage	Time Interval	Premium Range (Closing Price)	Implied Appreciation Range (%)
1st	November 2002–late April 2003	25–1,450	0.03–1.75
2nd	Late April 2003–late September 2003	90–3,625	0.11–4.37
3rd	Late September 2003–late April 2004	2,300–5,150	2.78–6.22
4th	Late April 2004–early November 2004	910–4,450	1.09–5.37
5th	Early November 2004–late July 2005	2,820–4,950	3.41–5.98
6th	Late July 2005–late December 2007	2,400–6,933	3.14–10.32
7th	Late December 2007–mid-March 2008	5,550–8,195	8.35–13.05

Source: Reuters.

Depreciation Pressure During the Financial Crisis

On March 13, 2008, when Bear Stearns collapsed and the sub-prime mortgage crisis was breaking out, the premium of one-year CNY NDFs stood at a record high of –8,195. The pressure for CNY appreciation disappeared rapidly over the ensuing half-year, with its premium narrowing to zero late in September shortly after the financial crisis broke out. The depreciation pressure mounted quickly from late September 2008 and reached a high point of 5,298 pips on December 4, implying that the one-year CNY depreciated 7.18 percent. During the financial crisis, China's economy—especially its export sector—suffered significantly, with a decrease in FDI and an exodus of capital prompting pressure to devalue the

CNY. By contrast, the US dollar, the most important international reserve currency, maintained its key strategic role and comparatively strong position.

However, the depreciation pressure did not last very long. The US conducted an aggressive currency policy, releasing a huge amount of US dollars, which diluted the US dollar, and the depreciation pressure on the CNY and other currencies dissipated. The pressure on the CNY shifted towards revaluation again shortly after the FED's announcement in March 2009 that it would buy US$300 billion worth of long-term government bonds. The pressure increased rapidly after late September 2009 following the G20, G7, and other international summits. After reaching the highest premium of 2,503 on October 20, 2009, it remained at around 1,700 pips in late December 2009.

MAJOR TERMS OF CNY NON-DELIVERABLE FORWARDS

The model contract used in CNY NDF trading came into effect in December 2004 and was accepted by the Singapore Foreign Exchange Market Committee (SFEMC), the Emerging Markets Trade Association (EMTA), and the Foreign Exchange Committee (FEC).

The underlying currency used in the contract is the CNY and the settlement currency is the US dollar. The official settlement exchange rate—obtainable from the Reuters terminal page CNY SAEC (CNY01)—is released daily at 5:00 p.m. by China's SAFE. The valuation day is generally one working day before the maturity date. In any situation where the valuation day is adjusted because of a holiday, the settlement day is deemed to be the earliest day after the valuation day and cannot be two working days later than the valuation day. The valuation day is determined in Beijing and the settlement day in New York.

Apart from the major clauses specified above, the contract also defines pricing issues, resultant delays, and applicable solutions.

Maturities

Currently, inter-bank CNY NDFs have maturities of one week, two weeks, three weeks, one month, two months, three months, four months, five months, six months, nine months, one year, two years, three years, four years, and five years. However, contracts with maturities of two weeks, three weeks, four months, five months, two years, three years, four years, and fives years are illiquid without price information, while those with maturities of one week, one month, two months, three months, six months and one year are more liquid. Those with maturities of nine months are of moderate liquidity.

Market Participants

Most international banks provide CNY NDFs to their customers. Table 12.2 lists the six most active, as recorded by *Asia Risk* magazine.

The top three banks are HSBC, Citibank, and Standard Chartered Bank. Hong Kong is a major market for CNY NDFs. As an established British bank, HSBC is very active in Hong Kong's derivative market. In 2002, HSBC was named the largest CNY trader by *Euromoney* (Kuramitsu 2003).

TABLE 12.2 Banks involved in the CNY NDF business

Banks	% (2005)	Ranking 2005	Scores 2005	Ranking 2004
HSBC	32.10	1	80	1
Citibank	18.10	2	45	4
Standard Chartered Bank	9.20	3	23	2
Barclays	6.40	4	16	–
ABN AMRO	3.20	5	8	–
Bank of China	3.20	5	8	–

Broker: Prebon Yamane
Source: Asia Risk, June 2005

Trading Volume

As most over-ther-counter derivatives lack transparency, it is hard to find sources that indicate the actual trading volume of CNY NDF markets. Market investigations by the Hong Kong Monetary Authority (HKMA) in June 2003 and February 2004 showed that, in 2002, the daily average trading volume of global CNY NDFs was between US$100–200 million; in the first half of 2003 it was around US$300 million, and in the second half of 2003, it was US$1 billion due to increased market volatility. Based on the HKMA's 2003 findings, we can estimate the upper and lower limits of the four-quarter daily average trading volumes and the total trading volume in 2003, as shown in Table 12.3.

TABLE 12.3 Estimation of CNY NDF trading volume (US$ billion)

Quarter	Daily Trading Volume (Lower)	Quarterly Trading Volume (Lower)	Daily Trading Volume (Higher)	Quarterly Trading Volume (Higher)
1st Quarter, 2003	0.2	12.8	0.30	18.2
2nd Quarter, 2003	0.3	18.2	0.39	25.0
3rd Quarter, 2003	0.75	48.0	0.95	60.8
4th Quarter, 2003	1.00	64.0	1.30	83.2
2003	—	144.0	—	188.2
2003 (Average)	166.1			

Source: Based on an average of 62 trading days quarterly and the HKMA's daily trading volume figures.

According to a subsequent study by the HKMA,[2] the CNY NDF market went quieter during the period immediately following the reform of CNY exchange rate regime in July 2005 as participants generally did not expect another revaluation in the near future. In 2006, the NDF market resumed its growth, with the average daily trading volume reaching around US$1 billion between February and early October 2006. However, when the State Administration of Foreign Exchange (SAFE) issued a guideline restricting the participation of mainland entities, trading activity in the non-deliverable forwards market was reported to have declined noticeably.

FACTORS AFFECTING THE CNY NDF MARKET

Political Factors

The most significant contributions to pressure being applied for a revaluation of the CNY come from political factors. Given the number and complexity of major controversies and events that might cause CNY NDF volatility, it is difficult to list them all. However, it is possible to divide the major political events which have occurred from the end of 2002 up until the appreciation of the CNY into a timeline of five phases:

Phase I: November 2002—Late April 2003   In a research paper entitled "China: Say No to CNY Appreciation," in November 2002, the Morgan Stanley (Hong Kong) economist Andy Xie expressed concerns that CNY appreciation would aggravate deflation and curb domestic demand in China.

In testimony before the Japanese Congress in early December 2002, Japanese Finance Minister Masajuro Shiokawa said that, based on purchasing power parity (PPP), the CNY was greatly undervalued. He promised to call on the Chinese government to unfasten its controls on CNY exchange rates, with a view to allowing the currency to float freely. He said that adjustments to the CNY exchange rate were indispensable for any coordinated and effective plans to restore the world economy and to reverse global deflation. In the G7 finance ministers' meeting in February 2003, Shiokawa proposed that they demand CNY appreciation. Though the proposal was ultimately abandoned, this was the strongest global move in that direction to date.

Phase II: Late April 2003—Late September 2003   In another research report ("Reform Required for the CNY Exchange Rate System"), in June 2003, Goldman Sachs (Asia) director, general manager, and chief economist Fred Hu wrote that it was wiser and more practical for China to change the current exchange system by substituting a more flexible floating exchange rate system for the current fixed rate system. China might realize that it would be in its best interests to do so, even though this would mean a possible appreciation of the CNY at the outset.

In that same month, the then US Treasury Secretary John Snow stated that Washington welcomed China's monetary policy reforms, revealing the US government's desire to solve its large trade deficits by way of a weak US dollar.[3] Snow advised Beijing to allow the CNY to appreciate that week, saying he would be happy to see this happen.

In an Asia–Europe Finance Ministers' Meeting held in early July, the European countries unanimously agreed that the CNY exchange rate failed to reflect China's real economic power against the backdrop of an influx of cheap Chinese goods into their countries.[4] On July 5, European finance ministers put pressure on Asian governments to release their exchange rate controls and to allow their currencies to appreciate against the US dollar, hoping that this would prevent potential damage to European economies from further appreciation of the euro.

On July 17, the then US Federal Reserve Chairman Alan Greenspan made comments in the US Senate Committee on Banking about China's exchange rate policy, saying that China's fixed rate policy would end up hurting China's own economy.[5] After this, the one-year CNY NDF premium increased by 135 points, from –1,535 points, as at July 16, to –1,670 points, as at July 17, 2003.

On September 3, in a meeting with the US Treasury Secretary, Chinese Premier Wen Jiabao emphasized China's position that it would maintain the current CNY exchange rate, while actively studying and exploring a new market-driven exchange rate mechanism.

Phase III: Late September 2003–late April 2004   The G7 meeting of heads of government on September 20, 2003 called for a greater flexibility in exchange rates to maintain the balance of the world economy. This message was directed specifically at Japan, China and other Asian countries. The meeting also proposed an appreciation of the CNY, emphasizing that big countries or economies needed to implement more flexible exchange rates to strengthen the stability and large-scale adjustments of the market-based international financial system. Following this, on September 22, the one-year CNY NDF premium increased by 1,450 points.

US legislators put increased pressure on President Bush in late September, believing that the value of the CNY was being manipulated by China's intervention in foreign exchange markets, and that the Bush government had not done enough about it.

On October 22, US Senators Sue Myrick and John Spratt proposed that if China refused to allow the CNY to float freely in the open market, goods imported from China would be subject to an additional 27.5 percent customs duty.[6]

The G7 meetings held in February 2004 had a major impact on the CNY NDF market. They called for a more flexible monetary policy, targeting all Asian countries without naming specific countries.

Following a speech by Alan Greenspan at the Stanford Institute for Economic Policy Research on February 27, 2004, in which he acknowledged that "We are not aware of the extent to which the CNY is undervalued (if indeed it is), nor are we aware of what will happen in the future after its appreciation," the one-year CNY NDF premium fell 499 points, from −4,178 points to −3,679 points on the following trading day.

US Treasury Secretary John Snow discussed CNY exchange rate issues with the visiting president of the People's Bank of China (PBC) and confirmed that, by the end of March, the US Treasury Department would send a senior-ranking envoy to Beijing to start work on this that summer. Elaborating on this, Snow said he believed that since China had agreed to adopt a flexible exchange rate, the US was making progress. He stated that the best approach was to keep making diplomatic contacts with China and to provide technical assistance in shifting towards floating mechanisms for the CNY. The CNY NDF premium dropped by 101 points, to −3,494 points.

Phase IV: Late April 2004–Early November 2004   On April 28, US Trade Representative Robert Zoellick, the then Secretary of Commerce Don Evans, and Treasury Secretary John Snow stated the position of the Bush government on the Sino–US trade relationship during a joint interview[7] as follows: Unless it met the six standards under US law (the bottom line for the US being market forces), including labor standards and free conversion of currencies with a bearing on the direction of the economy, China would remain a non-market economy. The CNY NDF premium increased by 175 points, to −2,502 points, signaling increasing pressures for CNY appreciation.

On August 4, PBC Governor Zhou Xiaochuan stated that China would maintain a stable CNY exchange rate for the time being, while improving the exchange rate mechanism. This was the second official comment from Chinese authorities on such issues since the end of the previous year. The CNY NDF premium fell by 180 points.

On October 1, China's then Minister of Finance, Jin Renqing, and Zhou Xiaochuan attended meetings in Washington at the invitation of the G7 ministers of finance and central bank governors, the highest-level meetings ever held between China and the G7. Unlike on previous occasions, these meetings did not touch on CNY issues, with a joint statement acknowledging only an exchange of views on oil prices, fiscal and monetary policies, the Asian economic outlook, and exchange rate flexibility. A strong market response to the meetings brought an increase of 300 points to the CNY NDF premium.

Phase V: Early November 2004—July 21, 2005   On November 5, 2004, the International Monetary Fund (IMF) called for an expansion of the floating band of CNY exchange rates. International financial markets reacted immediately, while some overseas media increased the pressure by saying that the CNY should appreciate by 3 percent in the following quarter. The CNY NDF premium then increased by 701 points, signaling further pressure for CNY appreciation.

On November 8, the PBC commented on the IMF report, saying that its recommendations were based on economic data prior to June, and that some of its analysis and judgments needed updating. The market reacted strongly, with a fall in the one-year CNY NDF premium by 937 points.

On February 5 and 6, 2005, Jin Renqing and Zhou Xiaochuan attended the G7 meetings in London. Zhou said that the CNY exchange rate had not been substantially undervalued, and that China would reform and develop its exchange rate mechanism in accordance with its own circumstances. The offshore one-year CNY NDF premium fell by 350 points, to − 3,300 on February 7.

On April 15 and 16, the G7 Finance Ministers held meetings in Washington, focusing on global price hikes for crude oil and the declining US dollar exchange rate. Jin and Zhou decided not to attend, sending their deputies instead. Although the G7 meetings did not publicly discuss CNY appreciation, key member states still talked about the damage they were suffering as a consequence of the CNY being undervalued, reiterating their hopes that China would adopt a more flexible exchange rate mechanism. On April 18, the offshore one-year CNY NDF premium decreased by 520 points.

Chinese Premier Wen Jiabao's comments on CNY exchange rate issues at the Asia–Europe Finance Ministers' meeting on June 26 drew a great deal of attention. He emphasized that exchange rate reform must be controllable and incremental, and conducted on China's own initiative. He added that China would act responsibly in pushing reform forward. On June 27, the one-year CNY NDF premium decreased by 150 points, easing CNY appreciation pressure.[8]

According to a PBC circular, China was set to implement a managed floating exchange rate system based on market supply and demand with reference to a basket of currencies. As the CNY exchange rate would no longer be pegged to the US dollar, this would create a more flexible CNY exchange rate mechanism. At 9:00 p.m. on June 21, the CNY/US$ exchange rate was adjusted to 8.11:1. The one-year CNY NDF reacted strongly the following day, with its premium increasing by 675 points, to −5,765 points.

Domestic Economic and Financial Factors

Although by no means as influential as the political factors involved, the impact of economic and financial factors (such as trade, foreign exchange reserves, GDP, interest rate adjustments, and employment) on CNY NDF cannot be ignored. These factors have also become the market fundamentals which are used to forecast CNY appreciation. Analysis (see Table 12.4) has indicated that foreign exchange reserves are the most important factor influencing the CNY NDF market, with a regression effectiveness of 93.1 percent. This is followed by considerations of GDP and monthly trade surplus data. This shows that the international market focuses on China's foreign exchange reserves and economic growth. As foreign exchange reserves have gradually increased with the trade surplus, the latter's influence has also increased. China's inflation data is not particularly reflected in the CNY NDF market.

TABLE 12.4   The impact of key economic parameters on the CNY NDF market

	Regression Coefficient	Regression Correlation (R^2)	F Statistics	Regression Sum of Squares	Residual Sum of Squares
Foreign exchange reserves	0.00001	0.931	902.181	7.227	0.008011
Trade surplus	−0.00029	0.73	193.751	6.326	0.03443
GDP growth rate	0.106	0.713	52.166	2.063	0.03954
Consumer price index (CPI)	−0.236	0.403	45.967	3.564	0.07753

Note: Computed with linear regression from related economic parameters and the one-year CNY NDF exchange rate for the period January 2002 to October 2007.

Along with gradual improvements in the market-oriented interest rate market and the reform of the CNY exchange rate mechanism, we can expect the influence of these fundamental factors over CNY NDF to be more systematic, lasting, and complete.

US Economic and Financial Factors

As the US dollar is the settlement currency of CNY NDF, we have performed a similar analysis of the impact of US economic and financial factors (such as monthly trade deficits, fiscal deficits, GDP, inflation, interest rates, and the unemployment rate) on CNY/ US$ non-deliverable forward exchange rates (see Table 12.5). The results indicate that

TABLE 12.5   The impact of US economic parameters on the CNY NDF market

	Regression Coefficient	Regression Correlation (R^2)	F Statistics	Regression Sum of Squares	Residual Sum of Squares
Trade deficit	0.002	0.52	73.684	4.51	0.061
Fiscal deficit	0	0.002	0.152	0.019	0.128
CPI	−0.129	0.088	6.525	0.764	0.117
Interest rate	−0.164	0.557	23.86	1.033	0.043
Unemployment rate	0.513	0.687	149.178	5.779	0.039
GDP growth rate	−0.088	0.798	83.688	1.209	0.014

Note: Computed with linear regression from related US economic parameters and the one-year CNY NDF exchange rates for the period January 2002 to October 2007.

US GDP is the most important factor affecting CNY NDF exchange rates, while US fiscal deficits have a limited impact. At the same time, US trade deficits, interest rates, and unemployment rates are also key factors influencing the CNY NDF exchange rate. However, questions remain regarding the impact of US GDP, interest rate, and unemployment rate data in that it appears to contradict traditional economic theory. This means that CNY NDF markets have not properly reflected US interest rate and unemployment data. This issue will be discussed in the next section.

Speculative Factors

The factors outlined above have been used to back calls for CNY appreciation in global markets. However, the markets have not significantly reflected other fundamental Chinese and US data (for example, fiscal deficit, interest rates, and unemployment rates), or have reflected them in a way that contradicts economic theory. These anomalies indicate that CNY NDF markets remain immature while operating under the expectations of CNY appreciation in recent years. Since market participants also have a clear understanding of the political factors affecting pressure for CNY appreciation, their expectations of CNY appreciation have remained unchanged, despite the fundamental data not supporting these expectations. Leading foreign financial institutions have joined the US government in urging CNY appreciation. Because of both political and fundamental factors, market participants have created several waves of CNY appreciation over the past three years. The CNY NDF premium has continued, even after the release of negative data.

MARKET ISSUES

Although CNY NDF business has been transacted in the offshore market for nearly a decade, it did not become significantly active until 2003. The lack of transparency in CNY NDF trade continues to create issues.

It is hard to value CNY NDFs using existing valuation theories. Theoretically, the spot and forward rates should meet the interest rate parity. However, parity cannot be used to price US$/CNY NDFs because the implementation of a fully market-oriented interest rate mechanism is not yet complete. Moreover, as capital projects are restricted, it is hard to borrow in the CNY spot market and invest in offshore markets. Therefore, the CNY NDF exchange rate mainly depends on buyer/seller expectations of CNY appreciation.

The markets also suffer from inadequate liquidity. Although HKMA research indicated that the average daily trading volume of CNY NDF increased from US$100–200 million in 2002, to US$300 million in the first half of 2003, and to US$1 billion in the second half of 2003, inadequate liquidity remains a problem for the CNY NDF market, especially when volatility is relatively low.

Furthermore, the CNY NDF market is highly speculative. In mature markets, data on the macroeconomy, trade, foreign exchange reserves, interest rates and other fundamentals are key factors in determining exchange rates. These factors could be crucial in the CNY NDF market; however, in reality, the extent of their impact compared with political factors is limited. This shows that the current CNY NDF market is highly speculative because the fundamentals have not played a key role in deciding CNY NDF exchange rates.

CONCLUSION

To hedgers and speculators expecting CNY appreciation, the offshore CNY NDF is without doubt the most popular product. Originally, this product was used to hedge against CNY depreciation, and from its introduction before the Asian financial crisis to the end of 2002, when trading volume remained relatively low, this was its primary purpose. After the end of 2002, market sentiment changed from expecting depreciation to expecting appreciation. Since then, CNY NDFs have become major instruments for betting on CNY appreciation. Originally, the CNY NDF exchange rate movements should have been governed by information on trade, the economy, and capital markets. However, they have been influenced more by speeches from government officials in China and the US, as well as other countries and major global organizations. With Chinese enterprises increasingly involved in the global economy, as well as there being a more open domestic capital market environment and expanding FDIs, the CNY NDF market looks set to become more important to both international and domestic investors.

ENDNOTES

1. However, CNY NDF information can be obtained from a Reuters terminal by entering the code "RMBNDF=PREA."
2. "Renminbi Derivatives: Recent Development and Issues," Wensheng Peng, Chang Shu and Raymond Yip, HKMA, *China Economic Issues* Number 5/06.
3. See the Special Report "CNY Policy: Controversies over China's Exchange Rates," *Washington Post*, June 18, 2003.
4. See *Japan Times*, July 31, 2003.
5. See Special Report, op. cit.
6. See *Business Journal*, October 22, 2003.
7. See www.news.sina.com.cn.
8. See finance.sina.com.cn, June 27, 2005.

CHAPTER 13

CNY Non-deliverable Options

Having introduced and analyzed CNY NDFs in the preceding chapter, we will now focus on CNY non-deliverable options (CNY NDOs), another major CNY derivative in the offshore market. At present, research on CNY NDOs lags behind that on CNY non-deliverable forwards (CNY NDFs). It is difficult to find related information in the media, or even in academic journals. Given the lack of information and data for direct use, we are forced to rely on limited information and data to explore the characteristics and functions of the CNY NDO market.

FOREIGN EXCHANGE OPTIONS: BASIC CONCEPTS

Options

An option represents the right for its holder to exercise or to buy or sell an underlying asset at a pre-specified price to make a profit. Specifically, an option is a financial contract that entitles its buyer or holder to exercise it within a specified time span or at a specified time. If the holder can make a profit, he/she will exercise the option; otherwise he/she will leave the option to expire worthless.

Call and Put Options

A call option gives its holder the right, but not the obligation, to benefit from increases in the price of the underlying asset. A put option, on the other hand, gives its holder the right, but not the obligation, to benefit from decreases in the price of the underlying asset.

As a financial contract, a call option entitles its buyer or holder to buy an underlying asset at a designated price within a specified time span. A put option entitles its buyer to sell an underlying asset at a designated price within a specified time span. The designated price is known as the "exercise price" or "strike price," and the end of the specified time span is known as the "expiration date." If the option can only be exercised on the expiration date, it is called a European(-style) option; where the option can be exercised at any time before the expiration date, it is called an American(-style) option. In an option contract, the buyer takes the long position and the seller takes the short position.

Figure 13.1 shows the payoff of China Mobile's call and put options traded at an exercise price of HK$15 on the Hong Kong Stock Exchange (HKEx), expiring on March 15, 2005. The payoff is shown on the Y-axis, while the X-axis represents the price of China Mobile stock. If China Mobile's stock price is above the exercise price on the expiration

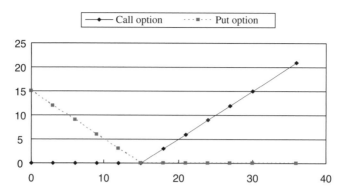

FIGURE 13.1 Payoff of China Mobile's call and put options

date, the return on its put options will be zero, as the return on its call options will be the difference between its market price and exercise price. If the stock price is below the exercise price on the expiration date, the value of its call options will be zero, as the value of its put options will be the difference between its exercise price and market price.

Option Pricing

The buyer or holder of an option has the right to profit from potential movements of its underlying asset; however, this right is obtained by paying a price, or option premium. This is different from a forward or futures contract as no cash is necessary besides the margin requirement. Thus, option pricing is very important for option trading. At present, popular option pricing models include the Black–Scholes model, the Binary Tree model, Monte Carlo simulations, and numerical methods. The principle of option pricing is the same as that for forwards and futures. Basically, the "no arbitrage" or "no free lunch" principle is applicable to the pricing of all kinds of derivatives.[1]

Option Deltas

There are five or six parameters in the option-pricing formula, each affecting prices to varying degrees. Mastering how option prices will change against these parameters is the key to successful trading. The sensitivity of options prices to different parameters is often referred to as options' risk parameters. For example, "Delta" describes the relationship between asset prices and option prices; "Vega" measures the sensitivity of option prices to changes in the volatility of returns on an underlying asset; "Rho" measures the sensitivity of option prices to changes in risk-free interest rates; and "Theta" measures the sensitivity of option prices to the passage of time.

Delta measures the sensitivity of option prices to changes in the spot price of the underlying asset (or changes in futures prices of futures options), that is, the changes in options prices for a one-unit change in the spot prices of the underlying security. The formulae are as follows:

$$\text{Delta of call options} = e^{-r_f \tau} N(d_1),$$

and

$$\text{Delta of put options} = -e^{-r_f \tau} N(-d_1).$$

According to the Black–Scholes model, the possibilities of exercising call options and put options are $N(d_2)$ and $N(-d_2)$ respectively. Compared with the Delta formula, these two expressions are missing the discount factor $e^{-r\tau}$. The discount factor is very close to 1 because the interest rate is generally several percentage points, and the maturities of most of exchange-traded options are less than three months. Consequently, the Deltas shown in the above formulae are usually referred to as the possibilities of options being exercised.

Market statistics show that the vast majority of options have relatively low Deltas. The possibility of the options being exercised is far less than 50 percent of the average Delta, while the prices of these options are far lower than those of at-the-money options.

Volatility of Options

The most important factor affecting option trading is volatility, or the degree of uncertainty of its underlying asset price. Mastering and predicting volatility is key to a thorough understanding of options.

Volatility includes historical volatility and implied volatility. Historical volatility, or the standard deviation of returns other than prices, is computed using historical asset prices. The first step in computing historical volatility is to select a time span, from which the historical price information is then extracted. The underlying assumption of this approach is that historical price movements will repeat in the future. However, though history may repeat itself, it will not do so identically. In fact, the volatility in the option-pricing model is not historical volatility but the volatility from the present to the expiration date. Therefore, the use of historical volatility in options pricing has great limitations.

In order to overcome the limitations of historical volatility, participants in the options market began to adopt the concept of implied volatility shortly after the publication of the Black–Scholes model in 1973. In fact, the implied volatility is the volatility implied in the market quotation or derived from the option price trading in the market. Compared with historical volatility, implied volatility has many advantages, the most obvious of which is that it contains all the information about an underlying asset during the period from the present to the expiration date. In other words, implied volatility is forward-looking because it embodies market expectations for the underlying asset, whereas historical volatility is retrospective.

FUNDAMENTALS OF THE CNY NDO

Development

CNY NDOs came into being shortly after CNY NDFs in Hong Kong and were subsequently also traded in Singapore. Initially, the trading volume was very thin, but it began to increase after the Asian financial crisis in 1997.

Market Participants

In general, options transactions are more complicated than forward transactions, and participants in the option market are not the same as those in the futures market. However, CNY NDO market participants are much the same as those in the CNY NDF market, because the majority of participants use CNY NDOs to hedge their CNY NDF positions. Initially, participants in the CNY NDO market were mostly multinational corporations investing and trading in China. In this respect, they were exposed to the risk of CNY devaluation. This in turn prompted their demand for products to hedge against fluctuations in CNY exchange rates.

Since 2002, and in particular since September 2003, amid a growing global pressure to revalue the CNY, participants in the CNY NDF market have been quite different from those before the Asian financial crisis. As described in Chapter 12, many institutions and individuals have been involved in the CNY NDF and CNY NDO markets not to hedge the risk of CNY devaluation but, rather, to bet on CNY revaluation.

Table 13.1 shows the average daily trading volumes of CNY options according to the Bank for International Settlements (BIS) statistics reports on foreign exchange and over-the-counter derivatives issued in April 2004 and 2007. As can be seen from the table, most CNY option transactions were cross-border transactions. For example, cross-border transactions of reporting institutions accounted for 92.16 percent and 91.94 percent respectively of the total buying and selling volumes in 2004. These proportions were even higher in 2007, reflecting that the development of local options markets lagged far behind cross-border transactions. Although the BIS data did not distinguish between non-deliverable options in the offshore market and traditional options in the onshore market, we have inferred that the bulk of options trading was carried out in the offshore market due to the extremely limited trading volume in the onshore market. We can also see that non-financial institutions were also actively involved in the domestic market. In 2004 and, particularly, in 2007, non-financial institutions commanded 74.1 percent and 80.6 percent of the market shares for offshore CNY options, with average daily trading volumes of US$26 million and US$29 million respectively.

TABLE 13.1 Average daily trading volumes of CNY and other foreign exchange options, April 2004 and 2007 (US$ million)

	Reporting Institutions			Other Financial Institutions			Non-Financial Institutions			
	Local	Cross-border	Sub-total	Local	Cross-border	Sub-total	Local	Cross-border	Sub-total	Total
2004										
Selling options	5	57	62	4	1	5	0	2	2	80
Buying options	3	47	51	5	8	13	0	38	39	112
2007										
Selling options	6	84	90	1	36	36	29	14	43	179
Buying options	4	85	89	3	12	15	20	11	32	154

Source: BIS statistics reports on foreign exchange and over-the-counter derivatives issued in April 2007.

Trading Volume

As with CNY NDFs, it is difficult to estimate trading volumes of CNY NDOs in the absence of statistics. CNY NDO trading volumes have been generally a quarter of those for CNY NDFs.

As analyzed above, all the data in Table 13.1 are related to CNY NDOs. Assuming an average daily trading volume of CNY options in April 2004 of US$171 million, their annual trading volume would be US$42,750 million (1.71 × 250). In April 2007, the annual trading volume is estimated to have been US$76,250 million, with an average daily trading volume of US$305 million.

CNY NDO CONTRACTS

The notional amount of CNY NDO contracts, which are settled in US dollars, ranges from US$10 million to US$30 million, with an average amount of US$20 million. As with CNY NDFs, the settlement exchange rate is the CNY/US$ exchange rate quoted by the State Administration of Foreign Exchange (SAFE) for settlement within two working days after the SAFE quotation.

Most CNY NDOs are European-style options in that they can only be exercised on the maturity date. As with CNY NDF contracts, there are 11 standard maturities in the market. Although they may have maturities of three years or above, contracts with maturities of over one year have lower liquidity than those with maturities below one year.

HISTORICAL VOLATILITY OF CNY FOREIGN EXCHANGE RATES

Volatility is the most important parameter determining options prices. Lower volatility means lower fluctuations in exchange rates, which in turn leads to lower demand for options and lower option prices, and vice versa. Therefore, the secret to options trading lies entirely in accurately estimating the future volatility fluctuations of the underlying asset.

Historical Volatility of CNY/US$ Rates

The most common methods used to estimate volatility are historical data-based models, including the standard deviation of returns, the EMWA model, and the GARCH model. Volatility based on these models is also known as real volatility or historical volatility, which enables us to understand an underlying asset's volatility or uncertainty range and its historical changes, as well as how market information influences its volatility. However, these models, which assume that historical price movements will repeat in the future, are inherently limited because history does not repeat itself identically. Another limitation is the lack of accuracy arising from the fact that estimations are influenced by the time span selected. For example, if we calculate volatility using the previous one week's, two weeks', one month's, or three months' historical data respectively, we will usually arrive at different estimations.

Figure 13.2 illustrates the annualized volatility under the 10-day moving standard mean square deviation of CNY/US$ exchange rates from January 3, 2000 to July 20, 2005, before China embarked on a reform of its CNY exchange rate formation mechanism. The annualized volatility is calculated by multiplying the deviation by the square root of 250. The volatility of CNY/US$ exchange rates before the reform was the highest in mid- to late-February 2001, at only 0.14 percent. It fell to below 0.05 percent after July 2001. The average volatility between February 14, 2002 and June 2005 was only 0.04 percent. This low volatility was mainly attributable to the People's Bank of China (PBC) policy of limiting daily exchange rate fluctuations to within 0.30 percent.

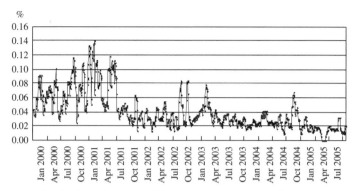

FIGURE 13.2 Historical volatility of CNY/US$ before exchange rate reform
Source: Calculated using data from the China Foreign Exchange Trade Center website.

Figure 13.3 illustrates the annualized volatility under the 10-day moving standard mean square deviation of CNY/US$ exchange rates from July 1, 2005 to August 31, 2005 (within two months before and after China's exchange rate reform). Volatility surged to 10.27 percent between July 22 and August 4 (within 10 trading days of the enforcement of the reform). It fell gradually to 0.5 percent from August 5. The higher volatility in this period was a result of the one-time 2.05 percent appreciation of the CNY against the US dollar on July 21, 2005, which inflated the figure for that period.

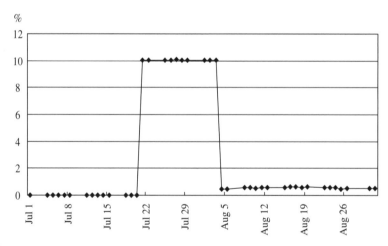

FIGURE 13.3 Historical volatility of CNY/US$ within two months before and after exchange rate reform, July-August 2005
Source: Calculated using data from the China Foreign Exchange Trade Center website.

Figure 13.4 illustrates the annualized volatility under the 10-day moving standard mean square deviation of CNY/US$ exchange rates from August 2005 to April 2010. The volatility remained around 0.5 percent from August 2005 to March 2006, fluctuated between 1.0 percent and 1.5 percent from March 2006 to May 2007, rose gradually to as high as 4.0 percent from May 2007 to December 2008, and narrowed afterwards. Since September 2009, it has been falling below the level of late 2005.

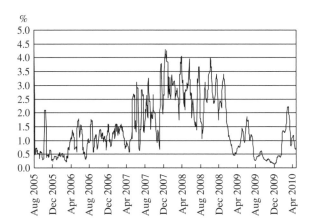

FIGURE 13.4 Historical volatility of CNY/US$ after exchange rate reform, August 2005–April 2010
Source: Calculated using data from the China Foreign Exchange Trade Center website.

According to the above analysis for the three periods, the CNY/US$ volatility was relatively low (around 0.04 percent) in the few years before China launched its exchange rate reform. Ten days after the reform, the volatility surged to 10 percent. Half a year later, volatility rose to a new level of between 0.3 percent and 0.5 percent, more than 10 times higher than that before the reform. It reached 1 percent from March 2006 to May 2007. Volatility rose above 4 percent for a short period of time, and fell significantly from September 2009 to December 2009. Although it rose to above 2 percent in the first nine working days of March 2010, it fell again around 1 percent in late April.

Historical Volatility of Other CNY Exchange Rates

Figure 13.5 illustrates the annualized volatility under the 10-day moving standard mean square deviation of CNY/JPY exchange rates from August 2005 to December 2009. It shows that volatility was around 5 percent in the first two years after the CNY regime change, increased to around 14 percent from August 2007 to August 2008, before increasing further to around 35 percent from August 2008 to December 2009. Volatility has been significantly higher than CNY/US$ volatility, resulting from large daily fluctuation ranges for the CNY against the JPY.

Historical volatilities of the CNY against the euro and the British pound are similar to that shown in Figure 13.5 because daily fluctuation ranges are not as narrow as that for the CNY/US$. However, CNY/HK$ volatility is much lower (from 0.13 percent to 5.23 percent) than those of the CNY exchange rates against the major international currencies, because the Hong Kong SAR has adopted a fixed exchange rate system, pegging the HK dollar to the US dollar. Shortly after the regime change, CNY/HK$ volatility remained at about 10 percent as a result of a one-time adjustment of the CNY/US$

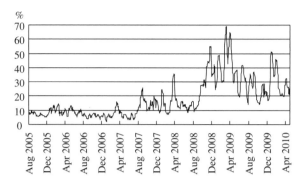

FIGURE 13.5 Historical volatility of CNY/JPY, August 2005–April 2010
Source: Calculated using data from China Foreign Exchange Trade Center website.

exchange rate from 8.2765 to 8.11 as with other currencies. The volatility rapidly adjusted to a normal level of about 1 percent, much higher than that before the reform. As the CNY exchange rate mechanism became increasingly market-oriented, CNY/HK$ volatility stood above 5 percent in December 2008. As the market had stabilized despite the impact of the financial crisis, volatility again fell below 1 percent.

IMPLIED VOLATILITY OF CNY/US$

Concepts of Implied Volatility

Historical volatilities are estimated with historical data, and then used to calculate options prices with pricing models such as the Black–Sholes. The option pricing model is believed to give the true value of the option. If the calculated price is lower than the market price, the option trader can "write," "short," or sell the option to make a profit; if the calculated price is higher than the market price, the trader can "long" or buy the option to make a profit. Though it may sound easy to trade options, it is not, because historical volatility may not repeat itself, and what makes things difficult is that the different time spans used often yield different volatilities.

In the early stages of the options market in the early 1970s, market players worked out a practical method to overcome the shortcomings of historical volatility—the implied volatility. As its name implies, it is derived from existing option prices in the market. Specifically, if we believe that the theoretical option price or true value of an option price is the same as its market price, we can derive the corresponding volatility using the option premium and pricing model because there is a one-to-one relationship between option price and volatility. Thus, the volatility derived from option price is that implied in the option price.

Implied volatility is extremely useful because it contains information of the underlying asset in the future until the option's expiration, or it contains forward-looking information rather than historical data. Thus, implied volatilities are used by option traders and market researchers to forecast future fluctuations of the underlying asset.

Implied Volatilities of CNY/US$ Trading

Figure 13.6 illustrates the implied volatilities of three-month, six-month and 12-month CNY/US$ options, from January 2002 to January 2009. It shows that implied volatilities are generally higher for options with longer maturities.

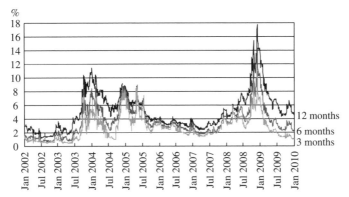

FIGURE 13.6 Implied volatilities from CNY/US$ options, January 2002–January 2010
Source: Reuters.

The figure indicates that implied volatilities were generally low, at around 2 percent, for all CNY options from early 2002 to the summer of 2003 when revaluation pressure was not significant. However, they jumped to historical highs from late September 2003 to early 2004, with implied volatilities of one-year options above 10 percent, and six-month options above 8 percent. This pressure for a revaluation of the CNY resulted from the G7's call for a more flexible CNY exchange rate. In light of this pressure, many international investors speculated in the CNY NDO market, hoping to profit from CNY appreciation. After that, expectations of CNY revaluation became very strong. Despite moderate declines from early 2004 to July 2005 before the CNY regime change, the implied volatilities still remained significantly high, implying continued revaluation pressure.

The regime change in July 2005 released some of this pressure as the implied volatilities dropped significantly shortly afterwards and remained between 2 percent and 4 percent for most of 2006 and 2007. However, they began to increase continuously from the summer of 2007 to December 2008 to create historical highs, with implied volatilities for one-year and six-month options above 17 percent and 14 percent, respectively. Since then, however, there has been a general declining trend.

Implied Appreciation/Depreciation from NDFs and NDOs

As discussed earlier, lower CNY NDF rates imply higher pressure for CNY revaluation. The same can be said for implied volatilities: the higher they are, the more pressure there is for CNY revaluation because it is more expensive to buy CNY options when the revaluation pressure is high. While it is useful to analyze the CNY NDF and NDO markets separately, if we combine the two we get more useful information. Figure 13.7 gives the implied CNY revaluation or depreciation from the one-year CNY NDF market and the implied volatilities from the one-year CNY option market from early January 2002 to January 2010.

FIGURE 13.7   One-year CNY NDF and implied volatilities, January 2002–January 2010
Source: Reuters.

It shows that the implied CNY revaluation rates moved mostly with implied volatilities from November 2002 to July 2005 when the CNY revaluation pressure was strong before the CNY regime change. They then moved largely in the same direction from July 2005 to March 2008. However, from April 2008 to early June 2009, they moved for the most part in opposite directions. From June 2009 to January 2010, they were moving in similar directions. All of this seems to imply that revaluation pressure on the CNY is significant when the two move largely in the same direction and is weak (or there may even be depreciation pressure) when they move in opposite directions.

FACTORS INFLUENCING IMPLIED VOLATILITIES

In Chapter 12, we discussed factors that influence the CNY NDFs. The implied volatilities of CNY options and the implied revaluation/depreciation rates from CNY NDF rates are largely similar from late 2002 to the end of 2009. This similarity is no coincidence, because they are both influenced by the same political, economic, and financial information.

The high correlation between the CNY NDF and the CNY NDO markets confirms that they are influenced by the same information and events. The farther the CNY NDF rates deviate from the effective rates, the higher the option prices and the implied volatility. Of course, different factors may affect forward and option prices to varying degrees, but a further discussion of these does not fall within our current remit.

NECESSITY OF ONSHORE CNY FOREIGN EXCHANGE OPTIONS

Options can be used as insurance contracts. Specifically, put options are essentially insurance contracts for the long positions of the underlying assets because the potential losses of the underlying assets can be completely compensated for by the potential gains of corresponding put options with downward movements of the underlying asset prices. By the same token, call options are insurance contracts for the short positions of the underlying assets because the potential losses of the underlying assets can be completely compensated for by the potential gains of the call options with upward movements of the underlying asset prices. These insurance features are often used for hedging the underlying assets or forwards/futures directly.

Options can also be used for investment or speculative purposes. With good estimation of the movement of the underlying asset, option traders can buy options, often at very low prices with low Deltas compared to underlying asset prices, to achieve higher returns. However, all investment could be lost without any return if options are not exercised, yet the total losses of options investment are the money paid to buy the options. Thus, the risk is limited.

Besides the insurance (hedging) and investment purposes, information from the options markets is extremely useful because implied volatilities from the markets provide us with useful information as to how the underlying asset would fluctuate in the future before the options expire. This forward-looking information from implied volatilities can be obtained neither in the spot nor the forward/futures markets. Implied volatilities are essential inputs, not only for pricing various financial products including wealth management products but also for implementing risk management models. Therefore, it is highly necessary for onshore CNY options to be introduced in the foreign exchange, interest rate, stock, commodity, and other markets.

CONCLUSION

In this chapter we have discussed the features, pricing, and trading strategies of CNY NDOs. Options, having more unique and flexible functions than forwards and futures, play a pivotal role in mature markets. At present, only CNY forwards are traded in China's CNY derivatives market, while the forward market is still being operated on a trial basis. However, the CNY offshore market has developed quickly over recent years, when the CNY has faced strong appreciation pressure. Offshore CNY option trading has set an example for product innovation in the mainland market, and the implied volatility has also provided important information for risk management in China's booming CNY wealth management and other related businesses. Moreover, different implied volatility structures (in maturities and Deltas) of CNY options offer an important approach to analyzing CNY appreciation/depreciation pressure. The offshore CNY NDO and forward markets will remain for the foreseeable future because China needs to take time to launch and improve its CNY exchange rate formation mechanism. China has enjoyed sustained economic growth, with a greater share of foreign trade in its economy and increasing foreign direct investment. With further opening-up of China's capital markets, foreign investors and speculators will focus more on the CNY and its related products. These developments will, in turn, become conducive to the growth of the offshore CNY options market.

ENDNOTE

1. Given the complexity involved in deriving options pricing formulae based on the above principles, we will not dwell on their details. Interested readers may refer to Chapter 2 of Zhang (1998).

CHAPTER 14

CNY Non-deliverable Swaps

In the same way that foreign exchange swaps are a natural extension of foreign exchange forwards, non-deliverable swaps are an extension of non-deliverable forwards. In Chapter 12, we discussed CNY non-deliverable forward (CNY NDF) contracts, including their market participants, annual turnover, and factors affecting them and their applications. In this chapter, we will focus on another CNY derivative: the CNY non-deliverable swap (CNY NDS).

CROSS-CURRENCY SWAPS

A cross-currency swap is an agreement between counterparties to swap interest income arising from different currencies during a specified period at an agreed frequency (such as quarterly, semi-annually, or annually) and to swap the principal at an agreed exchange rate at maturity.

Cross-currency swaps involve principals in two different currencies. Normally, the exchange rate of the principal swap of a postponed transaction is determined based on the spot exchange rate, while counterparties may designate the forward rate as the swap rate. The agreement to exchange the principal at maturity forms the basis of non-deliverable cross-currency swaps.

All foreign currency forwards may be regarded as cross-currency swaps with agreements to swap cash flows in two different currencies (one cash flow for each foreign currency forward). Many banks manage long-term foreign exchange forwards as part of cross-currency swaps. As with all foreign exchange forwards, users of cross-currency swaps need to bear exchange risk. As the main users of cross-currency swaps, bond issuers can sell the "cheap" currency and translate the exchange rate risks they face into the currency they expect to obtain. Moreover, currency swaps enable business entities to make better use of the global capital market.

NON-DELIVERABLE SWAPS

In content, non-deliverable swap (NDS) contracts are almost identical to cross-currency swaps. The only difference is that there is no need to swap currencies because NDSs are settled in US dollars or other similarly highly liquid currencies.

NDSs are conceptually similar to cross-currency swaps and are characterized by a non-deliverable exchange of principal and interest. To be non-deliverable means that the payable named in a maturing, controlled currency will be converted into a major currency (for example, US dollars) at the spot exchange rate. The net settlement amount is valued in a major currency on each interest payment day and at maturity.

At the beginning of a transaction, the principal in a controlled currency is converted into a major currency at the spot exchange rate. The most common practice is that the interest paid for the controlled currency is fixed while the interest rate for the major currency is fixed or floating. The two currencies swap interest on each payment date (for non-deliverables).

For example, on an interest payment day, a customer is due to pay CNY20 million and the relevant bank is due to pay US$2.6 million. The US$/CNY spot rate is fixed on the working day immediately before the due date. If the exchange rate is 7.500, the customer should pay the bank a sum of US$2,666,667 (20 million/7.50) at maturity. The net settlement amount between the customer and the bank would then be US$66,667.

Fundamental Principles

NDSs provide an offshore market hedge against the non-hedgeable risks caused by local capital or foreign exchange market regulations. The NDS principal is swapped at an agreed exchange rate at maturity. Incurring no transaction costs, NDSs are part of off-balance-sheet business.

NDSs have proven to be very effective when the underlying currency is regulated, as with the Korean won, Philippine peso, New Taiwan dollar, or CNY. In the case of longer maturities, the NDS market is more liquid than the forward market.

When entering into an NDS contract, counterparties specify a settlement method, including details on how the spot exchange rate is to be determined one or two working days before settlement. The exchange rate is usually based on information provided by Reuters. The interest on the payable and the principal in controlled currencies are translated into the major currency at the exchange rate, and the difference between the two cash flows is the result of settlement.

CNY NDSs

Introduction to the market

The CNY NDS market is an extension of the CNY NDF market. Most CNY NDSs involve US dollars. A counterparty to a typical CNY NDS contract receives CNY interest at a fixed interest rate and pays US-dollar interest at a six-month floating rate in the inter-bank lending market. Most CNY NDSs are similar to CNY NDFs in that their transactions are settled in US dollars every six months. CNY NDSs are mostly transacted with maturities of up to three years; those maturing within three years are more liquid. CNY NDSs with maturities of over three years should be marked in quotations. The face value of a standard CNY NDS contract is US$3 million.

Historical Data

The main differences between CNY NDSs and CNY NDFs are that the former have longer maturities and are more sensitive to fluctuations in CNY exchange rates. Figure 14.1 illustrates the three-year CNY NDS rates and the corresponding single currency (US$) swap rates, as well as the spreads between them from January 2000 to January 2003. The exchange rates of CNY cross-currency swaps (CNY CCSs) dropped steadily from the second quarter of 2000 to January 2003.

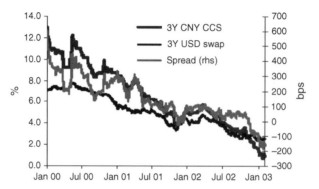

FIGURE 14.1   Three-year CNY NDS rates and three-year US-dollar swap rates, 2002–03
Source: Feng 2003: 6.

CNY NDS Rates

Figure 14.2 shows the market trend of CNY NDS rates from October 2002 to April 2004. The rates fluctuated in the same way as CNY NDF rates, reaching their lowest, –1.725 percent, in October 2003. The most obvious difference is that CNY NDS rates were at their lowest at almost exactly the same time that the premium peaked (at 4,900), signaling record high pressure for the CNY to revalue. CNY NDS rates declined from October 2002 to November 2004.

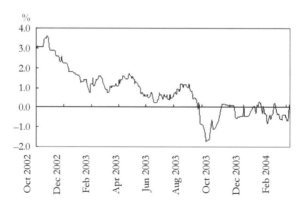

FIGURE 14.2   One-year CNY NDS rates, October 2002–April 2004
Source: Feng 2003: 6.

The figure suggests that, since CNY NDS rates were obviously different from CNY CCS rates, the CNY CCS market may be the better reflector of CNY appreciation pressure. However, given the lack of daily trading volume data for either, it is hard to be definitive about this. On July 2005, reforms were made to CNY exchange rates. Subsequent movements in one-year CNY NDS rates are shown in Figure 14.3.

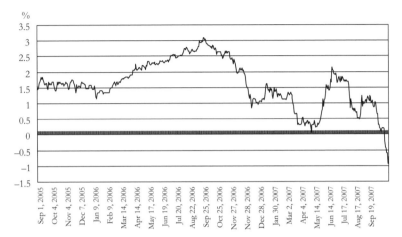

FIGURE 14.3 Post-reform one-year CNY NDS rate movements, August 2005–October 2007
Source: Reuters.

Turnover

Despite the market not releasing any turnover data for CNY NDSs, the Bank for International Settlements (BIS) reported the average daily turnover of CNY foreign exchange products for the first time in April 2004. According to the BIS data, the average daily turnover of CNY swaps was US$4 million for that month, with an annual turnover of about US$1 billion (250 trading days × 4). We note that forwards also cover net settlement products such as NDFs. While the BIS data is highly authoritative, the CNY swap turnover should include CNY NDFs.

The BIS posted average daily data of CNY swaps which indicated that they accounted for 7.4 percent of the CNY average daily turnover in April 2007. As the average daily turnover in April was US$9 billion in April 2007, we can conclude that the average daily turnover of CNY swaps was only US$670 million at that time. Based on this turnover figure, the total amount for 2007 was only US$166.5 billion, representing only 52.8 percent of the CNY swap turnover of US$315.58 billion. Therefore, it is difficult to extrapolate the turnover of offshore CNY NDSs from the BIS data.

APPLICATION

NDSs can help to meet the diverse needs of customers. For example, they may be used to convert major currency loans to non-deliverable currency loan portfolios with fixed outlays. In addition, they allow customers to manage different cash flows and time and undertake financing in the most effective currencies (for example, US dollar, euro, or yen) by artificially converting monetary assets in controlled currencies into major circulation currencies. They also allow asset managers to invest in overseas markets with appropriate knowledge of their capital gains and currency risks.

Hedging

CNY NDSs may be used to achieve clients' specific goals, lowering the risk of portfolio mismatches. Possible portfolios include matching physical assets with liabilities, matching asset-risk exposure with principal, and matching fixed exchange rate/asset rollover date with liabilities. The following scenarios will illustrate the applications of CNY NDSs.

Foreign Currency Asset Swaps   An American investment fund buys CNY2 billion CNY bonds. Because it borrows US dollar loans, the fund would like to receive a bond return in US dollars.

CNY-denominated investments are exposed to risks of CNY exchange rate appreciation and CNY interest rate hikes. To hedge these risks, the fund swaps the fixed CNY interest for US dollar-denominated interest based on inter-bank rates in a CNY NDS transaction with ABC Bank. The transaction structure is as follows:

The CNY debt investment amounts to CNY2 billion. The principal is converted into US dollars at the spot exchange rate at the outset of the transaction. If the CNY/US$ spot exchange rate is 6.830:1, the corresponding principal denominated in US dollars is 2/6.830 = US$0.29283 billion.

The fund will pay ABC Bank the fixed CNY interest at the settlement date. Since the swap is non-deliverable, the interest will be converted into US dollars at the spot exchange rate (fixed rate). ABC Bank will pay interest on the principal of US$0.29283 billion at the six-month inter-bank rate.

When the CNY NDS matures, the principal swaps at the same time. The fund pays ABC Bank the fixed interest on CNY2 billion and receives the converted US dollars. This is the difference between US$0.29283 billion and the interest.

Foreign Exchange Swaps   In foreign exchange swap transactions, a trader can sell one currency under spot delivery and buy another currency under future delivery. A foreign exchange swap involves two currencies. For example, selling HK dollars equates to buying US dollars, while buying HK dollars equates to selling US dollars. A swap can be regarded as borrowing one currency and simultaneously lending another currency.

Swaps are generally used to reduce the volatility risk of short-term exchange rates. For example, if an American dealer wants to invest in seven-day yen certificates of deposit (CDs), he can buy yen in the spot leg and invest these funds in short-term CDs, while selling yen in the forward leg. During the CDs' validity period, the American investor may avoid loss by selling forward yen when the US dollar appreciates against the yen. Dealers may also change the maturity structures of the whole currency position.

The swap market is part of the foreign exchange market and has a huge trading volume. In April 2007, the average daily trading volume of the entire foreign exchange market reached US$3.21 trillion, including currency swaps of US$1.714 trillion. Swaps are usually used for short-term contracts. This US$1.714 trillion also includes US$1.329 trillion of swaps with a maturity of no more than seven days, which accounts for 66 percent of the total.

FOREIGN EXCHANGE FORWARD SWAPS

In foreign exchange forward-swap transactions, a dealer can sell one currency under future delivery and buy another currency under delivery in a more distant future. Thus, a foreign exchange forward swap has two forwards.

Non-deliverable Foreign Exchange Forward Swaps

Non-deliverable foreign exchange forward swaps involve one controlled currency (such as the Korean won and the CNY) and another major currency (such as the US dollar or the euro). As the name implies, these swaps are based on no-principal settlement since the non-deliverable currency is converted into the major currency at an agreed forward exchange rate.

CNY Non-deliverable Foreign Exchange Forward Swap Rates

In addition to CNY NDSs, there is another swap in the offshore market: the CNY non-deliverable foreign exchange forward swap, at maturities of three months, six months and 12 months, as shown in Figure 14.4.

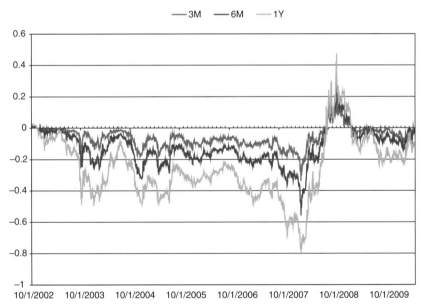

FIGURE 14.4 Three-month, six-month, and one-year CNY non-deliverable forward swap rates, October 2002–October 2009
Source: Chinabond.

The CNY NDF rates in Figure 14.2 and the CNY non-deliverable forward swap rates in Figure 14.4 are surprisingly similar. The one-year NDF had a record high premium of 4,900 points on October 7, 2003 as shown in Figure 14.2, while the CNY non-deliverable forward-swap rate reached its peak of –49.13 percent on October 6 that year. These similarities are not surprising, since the political, economic, and financial information influencing the CNY NDFs and the CNY non-deliverable foreign exchange forward swaps is the same.

Figure 14.4 also shows the three-month, six-month, and one-year CNY non-deliverable forward swap rates for the subsequent period to July 2010. During late 2008 and early 2009, the CNY non-deliverable forward swap rates became positive for a short time as, with the worsening of the financial crisis, market expectations switched from appreciation of the CNY to fears that it would devalue in order to support Chinese exports. Later in 2009, as these fears declined and the US dollar weakened as a result of the Federal Reserve's policy of quantitative easing, market sentiment switched back to the expectation that the CNY would appreciate and the NDF forward swap rates became negative again.

Trading Volumes

As with CNY swaps and CNY NDFs, the market released no turnover data for CNY non-deliverable foreign exchange forward swaps. As noted earlier, the BIS data on which we have to rely do not cover CNY non-deliverable foreign exchange forward swaps and other similar products. However, according to the BIS data released in April 2004, given an average daily turnover of CNY swaps of US$9 million, the annual trading volume would be US$2,250 million (9 × 250 trading days).

Maturities and Market Participants

Of the US$9 million average daily trading volume in April 2004, US$2 million were in swaps that would mature within seven days. Swaps worth US$5 million were traded with other financial institutions, while the remaining US$4 million was traded with the brokers reporting to the BIS. We can infer from this that foreign institutions were more involved with CNY foreign exchange swaps than with CNY non-deliverable swaps.

CONCLUSION

In this chapter, we have introduced two types of CNY NDSs: the non-deliverable CNY CCS and the CNY non-deliverable foreign exchange forward swap. Swaps provide investors with an effective tool to hedge risks and provide access to information on the possibility of CNY appreciation. Movements in these swap rates are very similar to those of CNY NDFs described earlier, because they are both influenced by the same economic, financial, and, in particular, political factors.

CHAPTER 15

Non-deliverable CNY Interest Rate Swaps

INTRODUCTION

Offshore non-deliverable CNY interest rate swaps are contracts under which the two sides agree to exchange the fixed rate and floating rate according to the agreed amount of the principal in the same currency at a certain period of time in the future, and use the US dollar as the settlement currency. The first such swap transaction was completed in August 2006.

These swaps are designed for enterprises and financial institutions that cannot access the mainland's financial market to manage their interest rate risk. Swap transactions are conducted mainly through banks with a price offer to a broker to make the deal. Therefore, the exchange platform provided by the broker is the key trading medium. Major market participants are overseas-domiciled banks or their branches. Enterprises and institutions such as investment funds transact through banks but do not use brokers' exchange platforms directly.

Floating interest rates include the one-year CNY term deposit interest rate; the seven-day repo fixing rate and the one-day fixing rate in China's inter-bank market; and the one-day, seven-day, and three-month Shibor. Of these, using the seven-day repo fixing rate as a floating leg in transactions is the main product. Products linked to the one-year term deposit rate were traded more actively during the initial development of the market, but demand has weakened recently. Shibor-linked products were first marketed in 2007, but their trading has not been consistently active. Now, the market focuses on seven-day repo interest rate swap products, with a daily average turnover of about CNY1 billion (about US$130 million), for terms of primarily one year, three years, and five years.

Figure 15.1 describes the trends of fixed payment of non-deliverable CNY interest rate swaps (with Shibor as the underlying interest rate) for terms of six months, one year, and three years, as well as six-month Shibor interest rates since 2007. As can be seen from this, the longer the term, the greater the contract risk and the higher the risk premium and fixed payable interest rate. That the non-deliverable CNY interest rate swap leads the Shibor trend is a good reflection of interest rate expectations.

Obviously, factors affecting the CNY interest rate will also affect the trends for these swaps. As a result, the economic climate has become one of the most important factors affecting the movements of the swaps. For example, amid the booming global economy in 2007, China's GDP growth reached a record high of 13 percent, increasing expectations of higher domestic interest rates. This in turn continuously drove up the fixed payment of non-deliverable CNY interest rate swaps; the situation reversed when the financial crisis began to affect the real economy. From this chart we can see that since December 2008, Shibor has

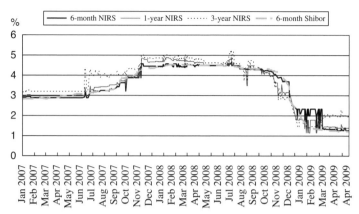

FIGURE 15.1 Non-deliverable CNY IRS trends, January 2007–April 2009
Source: Bloomberg.

declined sharply, from about 4.5 percent to 1.2 percent, and fixed payment of one-year swaps has simultaneously declined from 4.5 percent to 1.4 percent. However, swap movements did not stabilize until the economic crisis bottomed out.

DOMESTIC AND OFFSHORE SWAPS

The offshore non-deliverable CNY interest rate swap market has the following characteristics *vis-à-vis* its domestic counterpart.

Curve Differentiation

During the initial development of the market, there was no difference between domestic and offshore CNY interest rate swap curves. With increasingly active trading and a growing market, the two curves began to separate. In general, the offshore curve has been above the domestic one. On November 1, 2007, the maximum basis spread between the two curves was 29 basis points; it then slid from this peak to zero on November 22, and even became inverted in subsequent years. This was largely a consequence of the participation of different entities in the two markets, as well as diverse views on the mainland interest rate market. In addition to interest rate swaps, investors in China may also look to CNY interest rate-linked bonds, deposits, and lending products, among others. Prices of these products have a major bearing on domestic interest rate swap prices, but as foreign investors do not have other domestic interest rate-linked products for hedging or portfolio management, swap transactions are largely based on their judgment of interest rate movements. This is another reason for a higher offshore CNY interest rate swap curve.

More Active Trading in the Overseas Market

The overseas market operates under a more sound legal system which has developed transaction mechanisms in place and more experienced participants. These factors have enabled it to offer a smaller quotation range of about five basis points. The volume of quotations in the overseas market is typically over CNY100 million, compared with that of about CNY50 million in the domestic market. Furthermore, the overseas market has more average daily transactions and larger turnovers.

Movements of Domestic Interest Rates Under the Influence of Overseas Market Fluctuations

Movements of domestic interest rates are affected by overseas market fluctuations to a large extent. As can be seen from Figure 15.1, the overseas market is more sensitive to interest rates than the domestic market. Therefore, changes in interest rate expectations are reflected in prices more quickly. The domestic market will follow the changes in the overseas markets to a smaller degree. In other words, the overseas market is more influential.

CONCLUSION

Offshore non-deliverable CNY interest rate swaps were launched half a year later than their domestic counterparts. However, the overseas market has developed more rapidly, thanks to the growing demand for CNY products from foreign institutions. As the overseas market is more sensitive to economic information, overseas interest rates have also become a guiding factor in domestic interest rate movements. With the growing internationalization of the CNY, this impact will be increasingly felt in China and will, in turn, help develop the domestic market.

CHAPTER 16

Stock Index Futures and Options

Stock index futures and options are some of the most important derivatives in the international financial market, the transaction volume of stock index futures being second only to interest rate futures. Amid rapid economic growth in mainland China, more and more domestic enterprises are listing in Hong Kong. There is the H-shares Index and related futures and options on these Hong Kong-listed mainland enterprises, while there are stock futures, options, and warrants on some of these companies. Such products are becoming increasingly important derivative products on underlying mainland assets.

CONCEPT OF STOCK INDEX FUTURES AND OPTIONS

Stock Indices

The development of financial innovation has led to the presence of a great variety of index-linked products, such as stock index futures and options, options on stock index futures, exchange-traded funds (ETFs), stock index warrants, and stock index funds, which are actively traded and have become an important force in the financial market. All of these index-linked products are based on the underlying stock index. Nowadays, a number of stock indices are widely used in the market, the most important and widely used being the series published by Dow Jones & Company, the Standard & Poor's Group, and the FTSE Group. The primary uses of stock indices are listed below.

As a Macroeconomic Barometer   Stock prices can reflect the most up-to-date information available on listed companies' activities, their operations, and management, and the effects of macroeconomic policies on their operating results. As a collection of prices of a basket of constituent stocks, stock indices are commonly used as one of the indicators of the conditions of macroeconomic development and the impacts of the implementation of macroeconomic policies. Traditional macroeconomic indicators such as inflation rates, unemployment rates, and import and export volumes are not as current and easily available as stock prices. As a result, stock prices and stock indices have become powerful macroeconomic barometers.

As a Benchmark of the Stock Market   As the yield of a stock index can be regarded as a benchmark of the overall performance of the stock market, it can be used to assess the returns on different assets against the yields of government bonds, gold, and other assets for the same period. Thanks to their simple and representative nature, stock indices are often the news media's first choice in reporting overall fluctuations in the financial market.

As a Stock Market Indicator   A stock index is an overall description of the price changes of the entire stock market or a group of stocks, representing the trend and magnitude of price changes in a designated range and time with respect to the base period. It offers investors an overall measurement of the stock performance of listed companies to forecast trends of price movements and formulate appropriate investment strategies. Different types of stock indices have been developed in response to a huge demand for measuring the overall performance of the stock market.

As a Basis for Innovative Financial Products   Many innovative financial products—stock index futures and options, and options on stock index futures, for example—are designed based on changes in the market as a whole, rather than on changes in individual stock prices. These products would not have been issued without corresponding stock indices. Furthermore, products such as index funds, ETFs, and index warrants and options are totally reliant on stock indices.

As a Basis for Technical Analyses   Technical analyses based on stock indices offer necessary information about market trends and benchmarks to help traders and fund managers in their investment decisions.

As a Basis for Calculating Market Risk and Individual Stock Beta   The capital asset pricing model (CAPM) and modern portfolio theory are based on necessary market information, including market risk (determined by the standard deviation of market returns) and the correlation between the returns of individual stocks and that of the market. Stock price indices form the basis used in the calculation of market parameters including market risk and individual stock beta.

Concept and Characteristics of Stock Index Futures

A stock index future is a special kind of futures contract. Its underlying asset is a basket of stocks represented by a stock index. At maturity, the contact will be settled in cash for the difference between the price of the stock index on the maturity date and at the initial transaction. For example, S&P 500 Index futures are based on the underlying S&P 500 Index, which represents 500 constituent stocks, each carrying the same weighting as in the index.

Stock index futures owe their success on the world's major futures exchanges to the following strengths over corresponding spot markets:

Standardization of Contracts   As with other types of futures, stock index futures are standardized in their maturities, quantities, and prices in that investors need not match with a counterparty to open or close out a position. Although there are stock index futures of different maturities in the market, contracts with the shortest period to maturity are the most heavily traded with the largest outstanding positions because longer-term contracts can be achieved by rolling short-term contracts.

Liquidity   These are the most active investment tools being traded by participants all over the world and offer ample liquidity for investors. Standardization and defined maturities mean that stock index futures offer position-holders a simple way to hedge their positions with counterparties. Given the huge transaction volume of future contracts, the introduction of "mini" futures has further enhanced the liquidity of stock index futures.

Cash Settlement System   In theory, stock index futures represent a basket of stocks at each settlement. For instance, S&P 500 Index futures should represent a basket of 500 stocks at each settlement. Since this is not realistic, cash settlement is required by stock exchanges. Upon settlement, a party to the futures contract has to pay cash for the difference between the price changes during the holding period to another party, rather than settling by stocks.

Leverage Effect   High leverage results from the margin trading system of futures trading. For a 5-percent initial margin on a futures contract, the leverage can reach 20 times (0.2 percent). High leverage lowers the initial investment of the futures contract and leads to a higher risk than the corresponding spot market.

Low Transaction Cost   Transaction costs of futures contracts are calculated based on the number of contracts entered into, and are lower than the handling fees for trading the corresponding basket of stocks, which are calculated based on the amount of stocks traded. The increased popularity of online trading of futures contracts greatly reduces manpower costs. Coupled with the already low commission fee, returns to investors are maximized.

Efficient Hedging Tool   Futures contracts can be hedged anytime the market is open. Since the underlying assets of stock index futures cover the major global stock markets, market fluctuations in other parts of the world may cause significant losses on futures contracts after market close. With the automatic trading system, futures contracts can be hedged even after market close, thus reducing transaction risks.

Elimination of Counterparty Risk   Futures contracts are settled through exchange clearing houses. Therefore, contract holders need not worry about the ability of counterparties to pay.

Short Selling Mechanism   Although most stock exchanges provide a short-selling mechanism, a number of developing markets, including those in China, do not permit short selling of equity shares. The short selling feature of stock index futures is especially appealing to traders in these markets.

Daily Settlement System   As with other types of futures transactions, stock index futures are marked-to-market and settled every day. This system limits the risk exposure of investors within a certain range and helps bring stability to the market.

Minimization of Risk   Risk minimization is a key consideration in all investment strategies. As mentioned above, most stock indices are composed of stocks of many large companies, and are thus less likely to be affected by market volatility. Furthermore, since futures transactions require huge capital, retail investors are unlikely to be able to manipulate the entire market. Therefore, index futures are tools to protect investors amid market volatility and to maximize their profits. Investors can use index futures to reap profits in bullish or bearish markets.

Concept and Characteristics of Stock Index Options

An option is a right to buy or sell in the future. An option buyer pays an option premium to an option seller in return for the right, without obligations, to buy or sell a specific quantity of underlying assets at an agreed price in a future period (for American options) or at a point in the future (for European options). Stock index options are options that use a particular stock index as their underlying asset. For example, the underlying assets of S&P 500 Index futures are the 500 stocks represented by the S&P 500 Index.

The asymmetric payoff structure of stock index options offers investors a new channel for investments, broadens the choice of investments, and is suitable for various investment initiatives, trading purposes, and hedging needs. It also offers investors the possibility of higher returns. The effects of using stock index options to track movements in a stock index are illustrated below.

An option is an effective risk management tool. The underlying asset of an option can be based on the spot market or futures market. Therefore, options can be used to hedge spot assets and futures positions. When hedging the spot or futures positions by using options, investors will not bear the risk of margin calls. Selling options can lower the cost of holding positions or enhance returns. Combinations of options with different strike prices and maturity dates can be used in different hedging strategies, depending on the investor's preferences.

Options provide investors with more investment opportunities and strategies. In futures trading, investment opportunities only arise from price changes. If the price moves in a small range in a consolidation period, investment opportunities are few. By contrast, investors can make money in options trading no matter whether futures prices are amid a bullish or bearish market, or a consolidation period. Futures trading can only be based on price changes, whereas options trading can be based on spot price changes or volatility rates by using option spread, butterfly, and straddle strategies.

Options can offer greater leverage. Compared with margins on futures transactions, just a lower premium can achieve the same effect of holding the same number of futures contracts. Leverage of options can help investors to use limited capital to obtain higher returns. Of course, investors may lose more option premiums when there are adverse changes in the market.

H-SHARES AND THE H-SHARE INDEX

H-shares are the shares of China-incorporated companies listed on the Hong Kong Stock Exchange (HKEx), and are priced and transacted in Hong Kong dollars with the face value in CNY. The first H-share was listed in Hong Kong in 1993, while the Indexes Company Limited started to compile the Hang Seng China Enterprises Index (HSCEI), also called the H-share Index, for H-shares in August 1994. The Hang Seng H-share In-dex consists of all the H-shares included in the Hang Seng Composite Index (HSCI), which covers the 200 largest (by market capitalization) Hong Kong-listed companies, which account for 90 percent of the stocks on the Main Board of the HKEx. As at April 30, 2010, the Hang Seng H-share Index consisted of 43 H-shares, accounting for 96.4 percent of the total H-shares by market capitalization, and is therefore able to reflect the movements of major H-shares.

As at the end of May 2009, of the 150 H-shares listed on the HKEx, 110 were listed on the Main Board, while the remaining 40 were listed on the Growth Enterprise Market (GEM). The market capitalization of these 150 H-shares reached HK$3,575.17 billion (US$458.4 billion), accounting for 26.15 percent of that of all stocks listed on the HKEx. Thanks to China's rapid economic development, the H-shares market has become a major component of Hong Kong's stock market. The annual transaction volume of H-shares listed on the Main Board increased from a mere HK$33 billion (US$4.2 billion) in 1993 to HK$5,152.8 billion (US$660.6 billion) in 2009, contributing about 45 percent of the total transaction volume. Tables 16.1 and 16.2 show details of the market capitalization, market share, and transaction volumes for the period 1993–2010.

According to these tables, the H-share market has become more active since 2003, driving up the H-share Index and reaching a peak by the end of October 2007. During the period, the Index increased from 2,000 points in January 2003 to a high of 20,400 points, representing an average annual growth rate of 59 percent. Since the major H-share compa-nies are located in mainland China and investors of the H-share market are mainly large international financial institutions, movements of the H-share market reflect the view

TABLE 16.1 Market capitalization and market share of H-shares listed on the Main Board of the HKEx, 1993–2010

Year	Market Capitalization (HK$ million)	Market Share in Gross Market Capitalization (%)	Year	Market Capitalization (HK$ million)	Market Share in Gross Market Capitalization (%)
1993	18,228.70	0.61	2002	129,248.37	3.63
1994	19,981.32	0.96	2003	403,116.50	7.36
1995	16,463.77	0.70	2004	455,151.75	6.87
1996	31,530.63	0.91	2005	1,280,495.01	15.78
1997	48,622.01	1.52	2006	3,363,788.46	25.39
1998	33,532.66	1.26	2007	5,056,820.09	24.62
1999	41,888.78	0.89	2008	2,720,188.76	26.53
2000	85,139.58	1.78	2009	4,686,148.75	26.37
2001	99,813.09	2.57	2010*	4,527,584.78	25.24

*Up to April 2010.
Source: www.hkex.com.hk.

TABLE 16.2 Transaction volume and market share of H-shares listed on the Main Board of the HKEx, 1993–2010

Year	Transaction Volume (HK$ million)	Market Share (%)	Year	Transaction Volume (HK$ million)	Market Share (%)
1993	33,037.82	3.01	2002	139,711.41	9.50
1994	34,208.97	3.32	2003	501,496.87	22.12
1995	17,291.65	2.27	2004	933,860.83	27.49
1996	24,890.36	1.93	2005	949,155.23	26.46
1997	297,769.58	8.48	2006	2,521,764.08	39.26
1998	73,538.68	4.61	2007	7,748,899.57	46.93
1999	102,788.51	5.80	2008	6,130,592.75	48.53
2000	164,309.62	5.74	2009	5,152,805.63	44.56
2001	245,201.03	13.47	2010*	1,560,158.65	39.54

*Up to April 2010.
Source: www.hkex.com.hk

of international investors on China's economic development. In addition, this is closely related to CNY appreciation from 2003 onwards.

As illustrated in Figure 16.1, the H-share Index has grown much faster than the Hang Seng Index since 2003. As will be explained below, the main contributing factor was the inflow of funds arising from overseas, expectations of CNY appreciation, in addition to other fundamental factors.

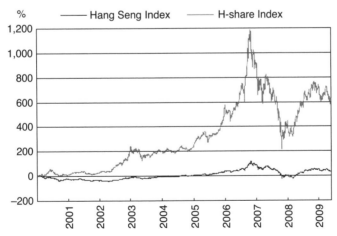

FIGURE 16.1 Comparison between H-share Index and Hong Kong Index, 2001–2010
Note: For purposes of standardized measurement, the comparison is based on the growth of the Hang Seng Index and H-shares Index relative to the respective figures of January 2, 2003.
Source: Bloomberg.

FUTURES PRODUCTS WITH H-SHARES AS THEIR UNDERLYING ASSET

H-share Index Futures

H-share Index futures were rolled out on December 8, 2003. They offer opportunities for investors to gain from the general movements of H-shares, and can be used to hedge H-share positions. Investors may also use them to gain from the diverse movements between the HSCEI and the Hang Seng Index. Table 16.3 provides a summary of H-share Index futures contracts, while Table 16.4 shows the transaction volume of H-share Index futures since 2003.

TABLE 16.3   Summary of H-share Index futures contracts

Item	Contract Terms
Underlying index	Hang Seng China Enterprises Index
Hong Kong Automated Trading System (HKATS) code	HHI
Contract multiplier	HK$50 per index point
Minimum price volatility	1 index point
Contract months	Spot month, the next calendar month, and the next two calendar quarter months
Pre-market opening period	9:15 a.m.–9:45 a.m. and 2:00 p.m.–2:30 p.m.
Trading hours	9:45 a.m.–12:30 p.m. and 2:30 p.m.–4:15 p.m. (expiring contract month closes at 4:00 p.m. on the last trading day)
Last trading day	The business day immediately preceding the last business day of the contract month
Final settlement price	Rounded down to the nearest whole number, the average of quotations taken at (i) five-minute intervals from five minutes after the start of, and up to five minutes before the end of, the continuous trading session of HKEx; and (ii) the close of trading on HKEx on the last trading day.

Source: www.hkex.com.hk.

According to Table 16.4, the transaction volume of H-share Index futures has been high since their launch in 2003. As at May 27, 2010, the average daily transaction volume of H-share Index futures was 60.1 percent of that of Hang Seng Index futures, and was a lot more than the average daily transaction volume of mini Hang Seng Index futures (see below). Moreover, the transaction volume and open position of H-share Index futures increased rapidly year after year. Even amid the global financial crisis, the transaction volume of futures contracts in 2008 was still higher than that in 2007. Based on these figures, H-share Index futures are regarded as important futures contracts on the HKEx.

TABLE 16.4 Transaction volume of H-share Index futures, 2003–2010

| Year | Days of Transaction | Number of Contracts Traded | | Number of Outstanding Unsettled Contracts |
		Daily Average	Total	
2003	15	3,196	47,941	6,299
2004	247	7,060	1,743,700	22,418
2005	246.5	8,027	1,978,673	35,125
2006	247	19,759	4,880,470	59,345
2007	245	44,271	10,846,277	91,786
2008	243	59,428	14,440,965	96,120
2009	247	50,077	12,394,116	74,324
2010*	98	51,907	5,086,919	119,908

*Up to May 27, 2010.
Source: www.hkex.com.hk.

Mini H-share Index Futures

Mini H-share Index futures were launched on March 31, 2008. The contract value of each future is one-fifth of that of an H-share Index future. Mini H-share Index futures are effective trading and hedging tools for those wanting to use less capital to track the H-shares market. They can also be used together with standard H-share Index futures and options (see www.hkex.com.hk).

The underlying index of the mini futures is still the HSCEI in connection with H-shares. Contract months are the same as for H-share Index futures, that is, spot month, the next month, and the subsequent two calendar quarter months. Because of the trading convenience of the Mini H-share Index, its transaction volume has increased rapidly and, as at June 15, 2009, was higher than the total transaction volume in 2008.

Other Index Futures with H-shares as the Underlying Asset

With the deepening reform of China's financial sector, Hong Kong-listed mainland banks and insurance companies have attracted the attention of an increasing number of investors. In response, Hang Seng Index Company Limited launched the Hang Seng China H-Financials Index in November 2006, covering all the financial stocks in the HSCEI. In April 2007, the Hong Kong Futures Exchange launched the Hang Seng China H-Financials Index futures based on this index.

FTSE/Xinhua China 25 Index futures target Hong Kong-listed shares of mainland companies. These products were launched in May 2005 by the Hong Kong Futures Exchange, based on the FTSE/Xinhua China 25 Index (illustrating movements of 25 Hong Kong-listed mainland companies) compiled by FTSE/Xinhua Index Limited. However, in December 2008, the Hong Kong Futures Exchange terminated the transactions of both because of weak market demand.

OPTIONS WITH H-SHARES INDEX
AS THE UNDERLYING INDEX

H-share Index Options

In June 2004, the Hong Kong Futures Exchange launched European-style H-share Index options based on the HSCEI to meet the demand of investors. Table 16.5 gives a summary of H-share Index option contracts. As with the spot and futures markets, they are valued at and transacted in Hong Kong dollars. There are two types of contracts short-dated options, which are more actively traded, and long-dated options.

TABLE 16.5 Summary of H-share Index option contracts

Item	Standard Options		Flexible Options
Underlying Index	Hang Seng China Enterprises Index		
HKATS code	HHI		XHH
Contract multiplier	HK$50 per index point		
Minimum fluctuation	One index point		

Contract months	Short-dated options:
	    Spot, next two calendar months and next
	        three calendar quarter months
	Long-dated options:
	    the next three months of June and December
			Any calendar month
			    not further out than
			    the longest term of
			    expiry months that
			    are available for
			    trading

Exercise style	European		
Option premium	Quoted in whole index points		
Strike prices	Short-dated options:		Within ±30% from the
	Index points	Intervals	opening price of the
	Below 2,000	50	spot month futures
	At or above 2,000 but below 8,000	100	contract on the day of request, or the range
	At or above 8,000	200	of the prevailing
	Long-dated options:		highest and lowest
	Index points	Intervals	strike prices available
	Below 4,000	100	among the contract
	At or above 4,000 but below 8,000	200	month requested to be created and all
	At or above 8,000 but below 12,000	400	other existing contract months with
	At or above 12,000 but below 15,000	600	longer expiry terms on the day of request,
	At or above 15,000 but below 19,000	800	whichever range is the largest
	At or above 19,000	1,000	
Trading hours	9:45 a.m.–12:30 p.m. and 2:30 p.m.–4:15 p.m. (expiring contract month closes at 4:00 p.m. on the expiry day) For flexible index options, no request of series creation is acceptable within the last 30 minutes before market close		

TABLE 16.5 (*Continued*)

Item	Standard Options	Flexible Options
Expiry day	The business day immediately preceding the last business day of the contract month	
Official settlement price	The average of quotations taken at (i) five-minute intervals from five minutes after the start of, and up to five minutes before the end of, the continuous trading session of SEHK; and (ii) the close of trading on the HKEx on the last trading day	
Transaction costs	Exchange fee HK$3.50 Commission levy HK$0.80 Commission rate negotiable	

Source: www.hkex.com.hk.

H-share Index options had a thin transaction volume in their initial launch period. They have rapidly developed since the end of 2005, when a majority of participants in the spot and futures markets have used different kinds of option strategies to hedge their H-share positions and create their preferred risk/return structure. Figures 16.2 and 16.3 show daily transaction volumes and unsettled positions since the launch of H-share Index options, respectively. The transaction volumes shown in Figure 16.2 are adjusted by the 10-day moving average. The line "H-share Index options/Hang Seng Index options" in Figure 16.3 represents the proportion of unsettled H-share Index options to unsettled Hang Seng Index options. As illustrated in the charts, the transaction volume and unsettled positions of H-share Index options increased rapidly from 2005 and the unsettled positions were comparable to those of the Hang Seng Index options in the most active period.

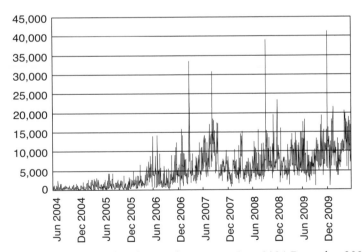

FIGURE 16.2 Transaction volumes of H-share Index options, June 2004-December 2009
Source: Bloomberg.

FIGURE 16.3 Ratio of unsettled H-share Index options to unsettled Hang Seng Index options, June 2004-March 2010

Source: Bloomberg.

APPLICATIONS OF H-SHARE INDEX FUTURES AND OPTIONS

Stock index futures and options provide equity investors with good hedging tools and are important channels for investments in the world's stock markets. Since the values of stock index futures and options are consistent with price movements in the underlying stocks, the return on stock index futures investments is the same as that on underlying stocks. In addition, investors do not incur actual costs and opportunity costs of purchasing and holding stocks, or pay taxes on their shareholdings. Consequently, stock index futures and options are widely used and actively traded by:

- Fund managers: Fund managers use them to hedge investments and reallocate asset portfolios of funds to facilitate trading and lower investment cost.
- Professional traders: Professional traders arbitrate discrepancies between futures and options market volatility and spot markets. Brokers, underwriters and securities companies hedge their positions on newly-issued securities with stock index futures and options.
- Retail traders: The reduction in the size of standard stock index futures and options contracts has enabled retail investors to trade stock index futures.

Stock index futures and options are widely used for hedging and cash flow management purposes. They are also commonly used for trading and arbitrage activities. As the composition of participants varies across different exchanges, trading also varies in its applications. For H-share Index futures, 50 to 60 percent of their gross transaction volume from 2002 to 2008 was used for trading purposes, 25 to 45 percent was used for hedging, and the remainder was used for arbitrage. For H-share Index options, 45 to 65 percent of their gross transaction volume from 2005 to 2008 was used for trading purposes, 25 to 35 percent for hedging, and the remainder for arbitrage. Table 16.6 provides a summary of the three major applications of stock index futures and options traded on the Hong Kong Futures Exchange from 2002 to 2009.

TABLE 16.6 Major applications of stock index futures and options traded on the Hong Kong Futures Exchange, 2003–09

Product	Year	Trading	Hedging	Arbitrage	Total
H-share Index futures	2003/2004	62.1	28.9	9.0	100
	2004/2005	46.2	44.9	8.9	100
	2005/2006	54.8	31.7	13.5	100
	2006/2007	53.2	34.0	12.9	100
	2007/2008	55.2	32.2	12.5	100
	2008/2009	43.7	40.8	15.5	100
H-share Index options	2005/2006	62.4	28.4	9.2	100
	2006/2007	55.0	28.5	16.5	100
	2007/2008	46.2	35.9	17.9	100
	2008/2009	58.4	34.0	7.5	100

Source: www.hkex.com.hk.

Since the launch of H-share Index options, the proportion of arbitrage trading has increased year-on-year. This suggests that more investors intended to achieve greater returns on CNY appreciation by investing in H-share Index derivatives, after China embarked on its exchange rate reform in July 2005. The relationship between the H-share market and CNY appreciation will be dealt with below.

RELATIONSHIP BETWEEN THE H-SHARE INDEX, ITS RELATED DERIVATIVES, AND CNY APPRECIATION

As we saw in earlier chapters, the CNY was under pressure to revalue from 2002. In subsequent years, especially in the two years following the reforms of 2005, the CNY continuously appreciated against the world's major currencies, including the US dollar. With increasing expectations of CNY appreciation in overseas markets, there was an influx of international capital intended to cash in on the simultaneous appreciation of capital and the CNY. Although the CNY has been freely convertible under China's current account since 1996 (to meet IMF requirements), that account still lacks a certain openness, with strict controls on capital inflow and outflow. Against the background of CNY appreciation from 2003, international capital could not easily obtain CNY for investment through normal channels. As Hong Kong-listed H-shares are based in China, international capital has tried to indirectly invest in China by investing in H-shares and their related derivatives in the hope of reaping double profits from economic growth and CNY revaluation.

Table 16.7 clearly illustrates the correlation between the proportion of foreign institutional investors and major historical events. Before the launch of H-share Index futures and options, the Hang Seng Index derivatives provided a key platform for foreign institutions to speculate on the CNY and China's economy. When the Asian financial crisis abated in 1999,

TABLE 16.7 Investor composition in the Hong Kong Stock Index derivatives market, 1997–2009 (%)

Year (July–June)	Market-maker	Free Transactions Among Exchange Members	Local Retail	Local Institutions	Foreign Retail	Foreign Institutions
		Hang Seng Index Futures				
1997/1998	—	9.00	43.70	16.50	4.50	26.30
1998/1999	—	5.90	47.10	19.10	1.60	26.30
1999/2000	—	6.00	46.60	23.50	1.40	22.50
2000/2001	—	7.00	56.00	12.00	2.00	23.00
2001/2002	—	12.00	42.00	13.00	4.00	29.00
2002/2003	—	16.00	36.00	8.00	1.00	39.00
2003/2004	—	20.00	35.00	8.00	3.00	34.00
2004/2005	—	17.00	30.00	10.00	2.00	41.00
2005/2006	—	21.00	29.00	9.00	3.00	38.00
2006/2007	—	24.00	30.00	8.00	3.00	35.00
2007/2008	—	21.00	32.20	6.10	4.40	36.20
2008/2009		20.00	31.80	9.10	4.70	34.50
		Hang Seng Index Options				
1997/1998	29.20	3.40	18.10	12.30	1.00	36.00
1998/1999	10.70	9.80	21.50	27.10	0.50	30.40
1999/2000	28.90	1.40	21.80	16.10	0.70	31.10
2000/2001	19.00	1.00	38.00	30.00	1.00	11.00
2001/2002	23.00	2.00	29.00	31.00	3.00	12.00
2002/2003	23.00	5.00	21.00	27.00	1.00	23.00
2003/2004	25.50	7.20	18.70	24.50	0.70	23.40
2004/2005	23.20	6.00	21.10	21.10	1.20	27.40
2005/2006	32.10	8.40	22.00	18.20	2.00	17.30
2006/2007	39.30	7.20	15.10	13.50	1.00	23.90
2007/2008	47.30	8.70	16.10	5.10	2.60	20.20
2008/2009	42.20	8.80	19.90	11.90	2.60	14.60
		H-share Index Futures				
2003/2004	2.20	15.00	28.50	11.70	3.00	39.70
2004/2005	2.10	12.40	23.80	10.50	2.40	48.80
2005/2006	0.40	15.40	27.70	12.80	2.90	40.80
2006/2007	—	18.00	28.30	8.40	2.40	42.90
2007/2008	—	17.60	24.70	6.10	2.70	48.90
2008/2009	—	22.30	16.90	7.00	4.60	49.20
		H-share Index Options				
2005/2006	19.30	6.50	17.90	26.10	1.80	28.40
2006/2007	18.80	9.20	10.10	18.30	1.10	42.50
2007/2008	23.40	11.50	13.10	13.30	2.90	35.80
2008/2009	21.60	12.30	14.50	20.50	3.10	27.90

Source: HKSE's Derivatives Market Transaction Surveys.

international financial institutions also terminated massive short selling transactions in the Hong Kong market, and their trading volume share in the Hang Seng Index fell and then stabilized. Along with the increased pressure for the CNY to revalue in 2002 and 2003, foreign institutions once again speculated on the CNY in the Hong Kong stock market, and their trading volume share in the Hang Seng Index futures and options increased year by year. In 2003 and 2004, H-share Index futures and options products were sought after by institutional investors as soon as they were launched. The trading volume share of these products reached over 40 percent in the second year after their launch, and accordingly their share in Hang Seng Index products declined. The share of the Hang Seng Index futures dropped by 5 percent in 2003 and 2004 and the share of the Hang Seng Index options dropped by 10.1 percent in 2005 and 2006. This change highlights that foreign institutions used Hang Seng Index products and then H-share Index products to indirectly speculate on CNY appreciation. It also explains the stable correlation between H-share Index futures and options and CNY exchange rates amid increasing pressure to revalue the CNY.

Although the US sub-prime mortgage crisis broke out in 2007, its impact outside of the United States remained limited until the first quarter of 2008. Stable emerging markets, such as China, were still considered attractive as a safe haven for international investment funds. Table 16.7 shows no signs of large-scale capital repatriation by foreign institutions. However, as the sub-prime crisis developed into a global economic and financial crisis, many international financial institutions reported losses, and became more likely to withdraw their overseas investments to bail out their parent companies. The table shows a slight fall in foreign institutions' share of Hang Seng Index futures for the 2008/2009 period, at 34.5 percent compared to 36.2 percent for the 2007/2008 period, and a significant fall in foreign institutions' share of Hang Seng Index options in the 2008/2009 period, at 14.6 percent compared to 23.9 percent in 2006/2007.

A-SHARE STOCK INDEX FUTURES

After preparations lasting around a decade, A-share stock index futures trading was finally launched on April 16, 2010 on the China Financial Futures Exchange (CFFEX) in Shanghai, marking an important milestone in the development of the domestic financial derivatives market. The A-share stock index futures contracts are based on the underlying China Securities Index (CSI) 300 index, an index consisting of 300 major stocks trading on both the Shanghai Securities Exchange and the Shenzhen Securities Exchange. Interested readers may refer to the official website of China Securities Index Co., Ltd. (www.csindex.com.cn) for detailed issues of the CSI 300 Index. Individuals are required to have a minimum of CNY500,000 (US$73,206) to open an account, while initial margins are set at between 15–18 percent. Interested readers may refer to the official website of the CFFEX for detailed descriptions of the A-share stock index contracts (www.cffex.com.cn).

The launching of A-share stock index futures has been a success, as shown in Figure 16.4. A moderate average daily trading volume of less than 200,000 within the first three weeks from April 16 to May 6, 2010, increased significantly to around 250,000 from May 16 to May 22, and it increased further to above 300,000 from May 23, 2010.

The success of A-share index futures can also be measured by comparing their trading value to the trading value of underlying shares. The total trading value of A-share futures in its first full month, May 2010, reached CNY4.72 trillion (US$0.69 trillion), 44 percent

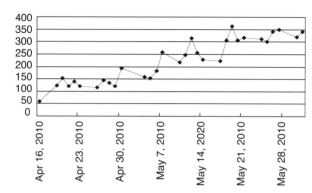

FIGURE 16.4   Trading volume of A-share stock index futures in CFFEX, April 16–May 31, 2010 (thousand contracts)

Source: www.cffex.com.cn.

greater than the corresponding total share trading value of the two securities exchanges— that is, CNY3.27 trillion (US$0.48 trillion). With more investors and institutions expected to enter the A-share index futures market in the future, the trading value is very likely to be a few times greater than the corresponding total of A-shares trading value in mainland China in 2010 and beyond.

As the A-share index futures market is still in its infancy, with limited data available, it is not yet possible to study the market thoroughly or compare it with the H-share index futures market in Hong Kong. The successful launch of A-share index futures contracts adds necessary risk management tools for investors, and it will help the stock market to develop steadily in the future.

CONCLUSION

Amid China's rapid economic development and increased listings of mainland enterprises in Hong Kong, H-shares have provided international capital with important access to asset investments in China. H-share Index futures and options, as well as futures, options and warrants based on individual H-shares marketed by the Hong Kong Futures Exchange, offer investors more tools to meet their various needs. Since H-shares are issued by companies based in mainland China, movements of the H-share Index and transaction data of H-share Index futures and options are closely related to CNY exchange rates. As a result, the H-shares market has become an important overseas venue to reflect expectations regarding the appreciation and depreciation of the CNY.

The CFFEX was established in Shanghai in September 2006, after many years of preparation. The stock index futures contracts have been designed and tested based on the Shanghai-Shenzhen 300 Index, an index of 300 major stocks listed in the Shanghai Stock Exchange and Shenzhen Stock Exchange. On January 8, 2010 the State Council gave in-principle approval for the launch of stock index futures in mainland China. The successful launch of A-share index futures since April 16 marks a very important milestone in the development of China's financial market and risk management, and will accelerate the development of other types of exchange-traded derivatives such as interest rate futures, foreign exchange futures, and so on.

Four

The Internationalization of the CNY and Development of CNY Markets

The internationalization of the CNY is a long, slow process which is closely related to the development of China's domestic economy and the process of financial reform, as well as the development of the international economy and market changes. Although it is difficult to outline a specific timetable for this in the next few years, we can gauge the importance of the financial market in the process by analyzing the liquidity of major international currencies and their products. Based on this analysis, we can better understand the basic approaches of CNY product innovation in the future.

To date, we have analyzed both onshore and offshore CNY products and their markets. Knowing the basic conditions of these markets, we will now discuss the potential for the internationalization of the CNY and how onshore CNY markets should develop as part of that process.

CHAPTER 17

Major International Currencies and Their Foreign Exchange Market Liquidities

Before discussing the internationalization of the CNY, it is necessary to understand the composition of the major international currencies and their foreign exchange market liquidities because this may shed some light on the internationalization process and the requirements for the corresponding development of the CNY market.

THE IMF'S SPECIAL DRAWING RIGHTS

The composition of major international currencies is clear from the constituent currencies of the special drawing rights (SDRs) created by the International Monetary Fund (IMF). In the 1980s and 1990s, SDRs were composed of five major currencies: the US dollar, the German mark, the Japanese yen, the French franc, and the British pound. Table 17.1 sets out the weightings of these SDR currencies in 1985 and 1996. There was little change in the period, except that the weighting of the US dollar fell 1 percent, while the yen increased 1 percent. From the beginning of 2002 onward, the euro gradually replaced the individual currencies of the European Union's member states, a process that was completed in July of that year. For the purposes of Table 17.1, the combined weightings of the mark and the franc are taken to represent the weighting of the euro, leaving the respective weightings of the four remaining SDR currencies as follows: the US dollar at 39 percent, the euro at 32 percent, the yen at 18 percent, and the pound at 11 percent.

TABLE 17.1 Weightings of constituent currencies of the IMF's SDRs (%)

Currency	US$	Mark	Yen	Franc	Pound
Weighting in 1985	40	21	17	11	11
Weighting in 1996	39	21	18	11	11

Source: IMF website (www.imf.org).

COMPOSITION OF MAJOR INTERNATIONAL RESERVE CURRENCIES

Table 17.2 sets out the total global foreign exchange reserve, as well as the identifiable foreign exchange reserve and their proportions, from 1995 to the third quarter of 2009. The identifiable foreign exchange reserve refers to the amount of assets in identifiable foreign currencies. The difference between the total foreign exchange reserve and the identifiable foreign exchange reserve is "the reserve in unidentifiable foreign currencies." Such assets are "equity" in unidentifiable foreign currencies. The world's total foreign exchange reserve soared 321.8 percent in 10 years, from US$1.782 trillion at the end of 1999 to US$8.087 trillion at the end of 2009, with an annual compound growth rate of 16.3 percent. At the same time, the unidentifiable reserve increased 4.31 times, from US$1.380 trillion at the end of 1999 to US$4,567 trillion at the end of 2009, with an average compound annual growth rate of 12.7 percent. The unidentifiable reserve as a percentage of the total increased from 22.8 percent to 43.5 percent over the same period.

Table 17.2 shows that the US dollar has been the major reserve currency, with assets accounting for more than 71.5 percent of the total in 2001. Yet, the proportion of US dollar assets over total global assets has largely fallen from 2001 to 2009. The fall in US dollar

TABLE 17.2 Total global foreign exchange reserve assets and the contributions of major reserve currencies 1995–2009 (US$ billion)

Year	1995	Proportion (%)	1999	Proportion (%)	2001	Proportion (%)	2004	Proportion (%)
Type of reserve								
Total foreign exchange reserve	1,389.8	100.0	1,782.1	100.0	2,049.9	100.0	3,748.4	100.0
Identifiable foreign exchange reserve	1,034.2	74.4	1,379.7	77.4	1,569.5	76.6	2,655.1	70.8
US$	610.3	59.0	979.8	71.0	1,122.4	71.5	1,751.0	65.9
€	21.9	2.1	402.4	29.2	480.4	30.6	1,093.3	41.2
£	21.9	2.1	39.8	2.9	42.4	2.7	89.5	3.4
¥	70.1	6.8	87.9	6.4	79.2	5.0	101.8	3.8
CHF	3.5	0.3	3.2	0.2	4.4	0.3	4.4	0.2

Year	2005	Proportion (%)	2007	Proportion (%)	2008	Proportion (%)	2009	Proportion (%)
Type of reserve								
Total foreign exchange reserve	4,303.0	100.0	6,682.5	100.0	7,321.6	100.0	8,086.8	100.0
Identifiable foreign exchange reserve	2,843.5	66.1	4,119.2	61.6	4,210.6	57.5	4,566.8	56.5
US$	1,902.5	66.9	2,641.6	64.1	2,699.1	64.1	2,837.8	62.1
€	683.8	24.0	1,082.3	26.3	1,112.2	26.4	1,250.0	27.4
£	102.2	3.6	192.7	4.7	168.8	4.0	194.2	4.3
¥	101.8	3.6	120.5	2.9	131.9	3.1	137.7	3.0
CHF	4.1	0.1	6.4	0.2	5.8	0.1	5.3	0.1

*Note that while the Swiss franc (CHF) is also a reserve currency, its importance is insignificant as its proportion fell from 0.3 percent of the total identifiable foreign exchange reserve at the end of 1999 to 0.1 percent in 2009.
Source: IMF COFER March 31, 2010.

assets from 57.5 percent in 2008 to 56.5 percent in 2009 is mirrored by corresponding rises in euro assets. With the European debt crisis going on and likely to worsen, US dollar-denominated assets are likely to resume their rise back up to 60 percent in 2010 or so, while euro-denominated assets will likely fall back toward 25 percent in the same period.

The 15-year downturn in the Japanese economy is the main reason for the sliding share of yen assets, which has resulted in the decline in the international status of the yen. The proportion of yen assets declined steadily from 6.8 percent in 1995 to 3.0 percent in 2009. While the United Kingdom's GNP is a little over half that of Japan's, pound sterling assets surpassed yen assets in 2005 thanks to the position of London as an international trading center for foreign exchange and inter-bank derivative products. The rapid growth of the UK property market was another driving factor. As the impact of the financial crisis diminishes, the international status of the pound will be further adjusted to an appropriate level.

STATUS OF MAJOR INTERNATIONAL CURRENCIES IN THE INTERNATIONAL FOREIGN EXCHANGE MARKET

Distribution of Trading

Accurate annual data for the foreign exchange market is unavailable as it is dominated by over-the-counter (OTC) transactions. The most authoritative data available are the daily average figures for April released by the Bank for International Settlements (BIS) every three years. The latest data available are from April 2007 (for details, see www.bis.org). From these, we have calculated the combined share of the four major international reserve currencies in the market, which fell from about 80 percent in 2001 to 77.4 percent in 2007, or from 85.0 percent to 80.8 percent if the Swiss franc is included.

The CNY only accounted for 0.25 percent of the transactions in the global foreign exchange market in 2007, which was incompatible with China's 6.2 percent share of the world's GDP. This indicates that the development of the Chinese foreign exchange market is still in its early stages, and there is a long way to go if the CNY is to become a truly international currency.

Exchanges Between Major Currencies

Table 17.3 sets out the exchange amounts between major currencies and their proportions from 2001 to 2007. It indicates that the exchanges between the four major currencies still dominate the market, with exchanges between the US dollar and other currencies accounting for nearly half of the market share. The share of the exchanges between the euro and other major currencies remained stable from 2001 to 2007.

Geographical Distribution of Transactions

Table 17.4 lists the 16 most active countries or regions in foreign exchange trading from 1995 to 2007. From 1998 to 2007, the United Kingdom's share of the market stayed above 30 percent, and continued to grow. Nonetheless, the pound only accounted for less than

TABLE 17.3 Exchange amounts between major currencies and their proportions, 2001–07 (US$ billion)

	2001		2004		2007	
	Amount	Proportion (%)	Amount	Proportion (%)	Amount	Proportion (%)
US$/EUR	354	30	501	28	840	27
US$/JPY	231	20	296	17	397	13
US$/GBP	125	11	245	14	361	12
US$/AU$	47	4	90	5	175	6
US$/CHF	57	5	78	4	143	5
US$/CA$	50	4	71	4	115	4
US$/SEK					56	2
US$/Other currency	195	17	292	16	572	19
US$/All currencies	1,059	90	1,573	89	2,659	86
EUR/JPY	30	3	51	3	70	2
EUR/GBP	24	2	43	2	64	2
EUR/CHF	12	1	26	1	54	2
EUR/Other currency	21	2	39	2	112	4
EUR/All currencies	441	38	660	37	1,140	37
Exchanges of other currency	26	2	42	2	122	4
Exchanges of all currencies	1,173	100	1,773	100	3,081	100

Note: The total percentage for each year is 200% as every transaction involves two currencies.
Source: www.bis.org.

TABLE 17.4 Geographical distribution of international foreign exchange transactions, 1995–2007 (%)

	1995	1998	2001	2004	2007
UK	29.5	32.4	31.2	31.3	34.1
US	15.5	17.9	15.7	19.2	16.6
Switzerland	5.5	4.2	4.4	3.3	6.1
Japan	10.3	6.9	9.1	8.3	6.0
Singapore	6.7	7.1	6.2	5.2	5.8
Hong Kong	5.7	4.0	4.1	4.2	4.4
Australia	2.5	2.4	3.2	3.4	4.2
France	3.7	3.7	3.0	2.7	3.0
Germany	4.8	4.8	5.5	4.9	2.5
Denmark	2.0	1.4	1.4	1.7	2.2
Canada	1.9	1.9	2.6	2.2	1.5
Russia	n.a.	0.4	0.6	1.2	1.3
Belgium	1.8	1.4	0.6	0.8	1.2
Luxembourg	1.2	1.1	0.8	0.6	1.1
Sweden	1.3	0.8	1.5	1.3	1.1
Holland	1.7	2.1	1.9	2.0	0.6

Source: BIS 2007.

10 percent of the transactions in the market, indicating that the majority of transactions were related to the US dollar and the euro.

Table 17.4 shows that the combined foreign exchange transactions of Germany, France, Switzerland, Denmark, Russia, Belgium, Luxembourg, Sweden, and Holland accounted for less than 20 percent of the world total.

Also noteworthy is Japan's contribution in this regard. Although it has maintained its status as the second-largest economy for many years, its share of foreign exchange transactions has been on the decline in recent years, falling to 6 percent in 2007, significantly lower than its share of GDP (8.2 percent). It is also worth mentioning Hong Kong and Singapore, East Asia's main financial centers. While their respective GDP figures were less than 0.5 percent of the world total, these two cities hold a considerable position in the global foreign exchange market. In particular, though Singapore's economy was less than 5 percent of Japan's in 2007, its share of trading in the international foreign exchange market was only marginally lower. This is a clear demonstration of Singapore's importance in East Asia's foreign exchange market.

MAJOR CURRENCIES IN THE INTERNATIONAL FOREIGN EXCHANGE DERIVATIVES MARKET

The BIS data include foreign exchange spot, forwards and swaps data. Traditional spot transactions no longer dominate the market, as they did up until the early 1990s, and have been replaced by swaps as the major product in the foreign exchange market. Spot trading now accounts for around one-third of the total. To gain a full picture of the global foreign exchange market, we need to look at the derivative products of various major currencies.

Market Share of Foreign Exchange Products

Table 17.5 details the distribution of foreign exchange spot, forward and swap products of the world's 28 major currencies in April 2007. The total spot transactions of all currencies accounted for 32.6 percent of the total foreign exchange trading; forward trading accounted for 11.7 percent and swap trading 55.6 percent. The spot trading of the US dollar, the most important currency in the world, accounted for less than 30 percent of total US-dollar foreign exchange trading. This proportion is lower than that of the total spot trading of all currencies. However, the proportion of its swap trading was close to 60 percent, significantly higher than that of the total swap trading of all currencies. On the contrary, the shares of swap trading in the more traditional euro and yen were relatively low, with their proportions of spot trading higher than the United States and even the total spot trading of all currencies.

CNY spot trading accounted for more than 60 percent of all CNY foreign exchange trading in 2007, and its forward trading passed 30 percent—more than most other countries in this regard. However, its share of swap trading was just 7.4 percent, which is a further indication of low liquidity and the immaturity of CNY instruments for managing foreign exchange risk.

TABLE 17.5 Share of daily average trading volume of spot, forward and swap products of major currencies in April 2007 (%)

	Spot	Forward	Swap
US$	29.7	10.9	59.4
EUR	36.9	12.1	51.1
JPY	40.4	12.1	47.5
GBP	32.5	10.0	57.4
CHF	42.2	10.1	47.7
AU$	25.7	10.0	64.3
CA$	29.7	11.8	58.6
SEK	20.7	10.0	69.3
HK$	18.4	7.0	74.6
NOK	18.4	9.7	71.9
NZ$	29.4	11.3	59.3
MXP	37.4	11.7	50.9
SGD	22.5	7.9	69.6
KRW	44.7	29.4	25.9
ZAR	19.9	12.1	68.0
DKK	21.8	10.3	67.9
RUB	70.7	5.0	24.3
PLN	20.0	10.9	69.1
INR	42.6	27.5	29.8
CNY	61.4	31.3	7.4
NTD	47.1	40.6	12.3
BRL	50.2	47.3	2.5
HUF	34.1	15.7	50.2
CZK	23.8	20.9	55.3
THB	18.9	13.3	67.8
TRY	61.4	11.4	27.2
PHP	36.9	32.5	30.5
IDR	43.7	39.3	17.0
All currencies	32.6	11.7	55.6

Note: Adjustments have been made for duplicate domestic and cross-border transactions.
Source: BIS.

Foreign Exchange Forwards and Swaps Compared

Table 17.6 details the position balance of foreign exchange forwards, swaps, and options from 2001 to April 2007. The table shows that the share of the position balance of US-dollar forwards and swaps continued to decline in the period, but remained above 40 percent of the total. The proportion of euro forward and swap transactions was relatively stable. Yen forward and swap transactions kept falling, while pound-sterling transactions continued to rise. These movements are consistent with the changing trend in the currencies' weightings as international reserve currencies.

Table 17.6 also shows a divergence in the product structure of different countries' foreign exchange markets. For example, while the respective shares of US-dollar and euro options were roughly similar to their shares of forwards and swaps in the period, yen options

TABLE 17.6   Position balance and duration of global foreign exchange derivative products* (US$)

| | Total** | | | Of Which | | | | | |
| | | | | Forward and Swap*** | | | Option | | |
	April 2001	April 2004	April 2007	April 2001	April 2004	April 2007	April 2001	April 2004	April 2007
Total	20,435	31,500	57,597	17,577	24,702	43,898	2,824	6,789	13,662
By currency									
US$	18,341	28,402	47,793	15,977	22,024	37,418	2,364	6,378	10,376
EUR	7,325	11,726	21,355	6,181	9,248	16,204	1,144	2,478	5,151
JPY	4,888	7,265	12,155	3,918	5,178	7,106	970	2,088	5,048
GBP	2,912	5,078	8,931	2,553	4,013	7,700	359	1,065	1,232
CHF	996	1,590	3,451	869	1,276	2,424	127	313	1,027
CA$	885	1,261	2,604	789	1,044	2,183	96	217	421
AU$	762	1,583	3,056	588	1,169	2,344	174	414	712
SEK	561	877	1,601	533	790	1,434	29	88	167
Other	4,199	5,216	14,246	3,746	4,663	10,984	386	538	3,189
By maturity date**									
Less than 1 year	15,906	24,706	43,838	10,848	18,618	33,233	2,456	6,089	10,605
1–5 years	3,293	4,712	9,783	2,543	4,114	7,080	321	598	2,702
Above 5 years	1,206	2,067	4,216	1,022	1,966	3,842	47	101	375

*Adjustments have been made for duplicate transactions among dealers.
**Including "other" instruments. The calculation of each transaction by two currencies results in the aggregate trading amount by currency twice the actual total trading amount.
***Including direct forwards and foreign exchange swaps.
****The combined and total trading amounts of all components may not match, given the lack of complete maturity data.
Source: BIS.

were higher by more than 10 percent, and the pound-sterling options balance was significantly lower than its share of forwards and swaps.

International Currencies in the Interest Rate Derivative Market

Interest rates are the decisive market factor that influences the entire financial market and even the overall economy. The active level of its interest rate derivative products is, to a large extent, a reflection of a currency's international status. Table 17.7 details the daily average trading volume of forward rate agreements (FRAs) and interest rate swaps of major international currencies in April from 2001 to 2007.

The volume of euro FRAs was significantly higher than US-dollar FRAs in 2001 and 2004 but was lower in 2007. As for the amount of interest rate swaps, the euro surpassed the US dollar from 2001 to 2007, indicating that the OTC trading of euro interest rate derivative products was more active than US-dollar products. This is a key area where the euro outperforms the US dollar. The British pound was more active than the yen in the trading of FRAs and interest rate swaps.

TABLE 17.7 Daily average trading in OTC derivative markets (US$ billion)

| | Total | | | Of Which | | | | | |
| | | | | Forward Rate Agreement | | | Swap | | |
Currency	April 2001	April 2004	April 2007	April 2001	April 2004	April 2007	April 2001	April 2004	April 2007
US$	152	347	532	39	59	98	100	195	322
EUR	231	461	656	48	116	66	173	288	528
JPY	27	46	137	9	0	4	16	35	110
GBP	37	90	172	12	25	42	23	59	124
CHF	6	10	19	2	2	4	4	7	14
CA$	6	8	15	1	2	1	4	5	12
AU$	8	12	19	4	5	3	4	7	14
SEK	5	13	33	4	9	18	1	4	13
Other	17	38	103	10	15	22	6	21	74
Total trading volume	489	1,025	1,686	129	233	258	331	621	1,210

Note: Adjustments have been made for duplicate domestic and cross-border transactions.
Source: BIS.

DEGREES OF INTERNATIONALIZATION IN THE FOREIGN EXCHANGE MARKET

Having discussed the status of major international currencies in the global foreign exchange market, we now expand our discussion to include other major currencies. Table 17.8 provides a comparison of the respective performances in foreign exchange trading of the four major international reserve currencies and those of other countries and regions. This is expressed both as a percentage share of the total trade and the GDP of the respective countries.

TABLE 17.8 Foreign exchange trading and GDP of major countries and regions, 2007 (%)

Currency	Share of Foreign Exchange Trading in 2007	Share of GDP in 2007	Difference Between Share of Foreign Exchange Trading and GDP	Share of Foreign Exchange Trading/Share of GDP
US$	43.2	25.4	17.8	169.9
EUR	18.5	27.5	−9.0	67.3
JPY	8.3	8.1	0.2	101.9
GBP	7.5	5.0	2.5	150.0
CHF	3.4	0.8	2.6	425.0
Total of 5 reserve currencies	80.8	66.8	14.0	121.0

TABLE 17.8 (*Continued*)

Currency	Share of Foreign Exchange Trading in 2007	Share of GDP in 2007	Difference Between Share of Foreign Exchange Trading and GDP	Share of Foreign Exchange Trading/Share of GDP
AU$	3.4	1.5	1.9	223.3
CA$	2.1	2.4	−0.3	87.5
SEK	1.4	0.8	0.6	175.0
HK$	1.4	0.4	1.0	350.0
NOK	1.1	0.7	0.4	157.1
NZ$	1.0	0.7	0.3	135.7
SG$	0.7	0.3	0.4	216.7
Total of 7 currencies	11.0	6.4	4.6	171.1
MXP	0.7	1.6	−1.0	40.6
KRW	0.6	1.8	−1.3	30.6
RUB	0.4	2.4	−2.0	16.7
INR	0.4	2.2	−1.9	15.9
CNY	0.3	6.2	−6.0	4.0
BRL	0.2	2.4	−2.2	8.3
Total of 6 currencies	2.4	16.6	−14.2	14.5
Total of the last 4 currencies	1.2	13.2	−12.0	9.1

Source: The percentages of foreign exchange trading are derived from Table 17.3 and the percentages of GDP are calculated from the 2007 GDP data released by the World Bank in 2008.

The table shows that, with the exception of the Canadian dollar (CA$), the share of foreign exchange trading of the second-tier currencies significantly exceeded the share of GDP of the corresponding countries or regions. Among them, the Hong Kong dollar's share of foreign exchange trading represented 350 percent of the city's share of GDP, underlining the importance of Hong Kong as a regional financial center. The high ratios recorded by both the Australian dollar (AU$) and the Singapore dollar (SG$) reflect their prominence in the Asia Pacific region. It is clear, too, from the rapid development of the seven second-tier currencies that they are catching up with the five major reserve currencies.

THE CURRENCIES OF MAJOR DEVELOPING COUNTRIES

In Table 17.8 the CNY is grouped with the currencies of five other major currencies, all of which recorded a share of trading lower than their respective share of GDP. The CNY's share of foreign exchange trading was especially low. The "Last 4 currencies" mentioned in the table is a reference to the currencies of Brazil, Russia, India and China, commonly dubbed the "BRIC" economies. In 2007, the aggregate amount of foreign exchange trading of these four currencies accounted for only 1.2 percent of the world total, 12 percent lower than the BRIC's combined share of global GDP.

Of the 18 major currencies cited, the CNY has the lowest ratio (4 percent) of foreign exchange trading share to GDP share, less than half the second-lowest [the Brazilian real (BRL) at 8.3 percent] and about one-quarter of that of the Indian rupee (INR). This indicates a significant gap in China's economic development and the urgent need to raise the CNY's international status.

YUAN AND RUPEE COMPARED

As we saw earlier, the difference between the daily average trading amounts of the CNY and the INR was only 0.2 percent, which appears insignificant at first glance. However, a closer analysis reveals substantial differences. Table 17.9 gives the daily average trading amount of the two currencies, compares their spot, forward, and swap transactions as a proportion of GDP, and shows their respective foreign exchange trading amounts per unit of GDP. In April 2007, the daily average trading amount of the INR was US$34 billion, 3.8 times that of the CNY. INR forwards and swaps developed better, with INR spot trading accounting for much less than 50 percent of the total. CNY transactions, on the other hand, were still dominated by spot trading, which accounted for more than 60 percent of the total. The share of swap trading was a mere 7.4 percent, compared to the 29.8 percent of the INR. In GDP terms, China conducted US$69 million of foreign exchange trading for every US$1 billion of GDP, which is just 9.5 percent of India's figure of US$730 million in the same period. India's foreign exchange trading amount per unit of GDP was equivalent to half of the world level of US$1.477 billion, while China's was a mere 4.6 percent.

TABLE 17.9 Foreign exchange trading and GDP of China and India (US$ billion)

	Total (Daily Average)	Spot	Forward	Swap	GDP in 2007	Foreign-exchange Trading Amount Per GDP Unit
China	9	5.53	2.82	0.67	3,380	0.069
India	34	14.48	9.35	10.13	1,171	0.073
World	3,210	1,005	362	1,714		
China's share (%)	0.3	0.5	0.75	0.04		
India's share (%)	1.1	1.4	2.5	0.57		
CNY (Product composition) (%)		61.4	31.3	7.4		
INR (Product composition) (%)		42.6	27.5	29.8		
World (Product composition)		32.6	11.7	55.6	543,470	1.477

Source: The foreign exchange data come from the BIS and the GDP data come from the World Bank.

In addition to the differences in the activity levels of their products, India has developed a relatively mature market for exchange-traded stock derivative products, such as stock index futures and options, as well as individual stock futures, providing effective tools for managing risk. These products are still absent in the mainland stock market.[1]

CONCLUSION

From our analysis of the composition and status of a range of currencies from developed and developing economies, we have established that the international status of reserve currencies is evidenced in foreign exchange trading and reserve holding. They play dominant roles in spot, forward, and swap trading in the international foreign exchange market. The currencies of other major developed countries or regions play a role equivalent to or greater than their own economic status. The currencies of most major developing countries do not match their corresponding economic status, indicating a need for them to raise their international status.

After developing for more than a decade, and particularly since the implementation of the plan to improve the CNY exchange rate formation mechanism in July 2005, China has made considerable advances in both market mechanism and product innovation. China has launched forward foreign exchange, foreign exchange swaps, FRAs, and interest rate swaps and improved their liquidity. To enhance the financial market, China not only needs to compare its current and historical performance, but also to close the gap that exists between it and the financial markets of other countries and regions. The above analysis shows that China's foreign exchange and interest rate markets lag a long way behind those of major developed countries, and even trail most other major developing countries' markets. Although many foreign exchange and interest rate products have been launched, their liquidity remains rather low. As a result, the markets cannot function fully. The absence of foreign exchange options also reveals inadequacies in the range of exchange-traded derivative products.

Rome was not built in a day. While acknowledging her great achievements, China should pursue scientific development and learn from the successful experiences of developed and other developing countries to avoid failures. China should formulate short-, medium-, and long-term plans for improving the financial market, launching financial products, and further refining regulatory mechanisms that will enable the market to function fully. Only then can finance serve the real economy and build a solid foundation for the internationalization of its currency.

ENDNOTE

1. A detailed analysis of the gaps between the development stages of the two countries' financial markets is beyond the scope of this chapter. Readers interested in the topic may wish to refer to Zhang Guangping and Yang Jian's *Indian Financial Reforms and Experiences for China to Learn*, 2008 (research sponsored by the Asian Development Bank).

CHAPTER 18

Lessons from the Internationalization of the Yen

The process by which a currency becomes truly international is both lengthy and complex. It involves macroeconomic aspects such as economic development, trade growth and monetary policy. It is also inextricably linked with trade settlements and capital account liberalization, as well as capital market development, and regulation. Each country has its own economic and financial system, market structure and regulatory framework, and the steps and sequences in the promotion of capital account liberalization are different. However, we can draw on and learn from the experience of countries which have undergone the process, though many of the measures they have adopted may not be directly applicable.

Japan was the first non-Western nation to become a developed country after World War II and the yen became established as one of the world's major reserve currencies. Although it is extremely difficult to forecast when the CNY will achieve a similar position, it is instructive to map its progress against the internationalization of the yen.

After World War II, Japan embarked on liberalizing its trade, foreign exchange, and capital accounts in sequence. These preparations spanned decades and paved the way for the yen to become a major international currency. China can draw invaluable lessons from Japan's experience, applying what has been good and avoiding the mistakes it has made along the way.

THE YEN AS AN INTERNATIONAL RESERVE CURRENCY

Japan became the world's second-largest economy in 1968. That was also the year that the US Congress repealed the requirement for the dollar to be backed by gold. The yen became an international reserve currency shortly after the world floating currency regime was established in March 1973. The yen represented just 0.5 percent of identifiable international reserves in 1975.

We looked briefly at the changes in major international reserve currencies in an earlier chapter. Table 18.1 shows the changes in the yen's contribution to these currencies from 1970 to the third quarter of 2009. This reached a peak of 8.7 percent in 1991 but then declined to below 5 percent in 1997. Following a short-lived rebound in 1998 and 1999, it fell again and has remained flat at around 3.2 percent from 2006.

TABLE 18.1 The yen's contribution to identifiable international reserve currencies, 1970–2009 (%)

Year	Proportion	Year	Proportion	Year	Proportion
1970	0.0	1987	6.9	1999	6.4
1975	0.5	1988	7.0	2000	6.1
1977	2.5	1989	7.3	2001	5.0
1978	3.3	1990	8.1	2002	4.4
1979	3.6	1991	8.7	2003	3.9
1980	4.4	1992	7.7	2004	3.8
1981	4.2	1993	7.7	2005	3.6
1982	4.7	1994	7.9	2006	3.1
1983	4.9	1995	6.2	2007	2.9
1984	5.7	1996	5.5	2008	3.1
1985	7.5	1997	4.8	2009	3.0
1986	6.9	1998	5.1		

Source: IMF annual reports (for data from 1970 to 1998) and COFER (for data after 1999).

The rapid expansion prior to 1985 was attributable mainly to rapid growth in demand for yen reserves as a result of a significant pressure for the yen to revalue against the US dollar. Although the Japanese government took various measures to promote the internationalization of the yen from the late 1990s, this slowed down rather than accelerated because of an economic downturn that spanned more than 10 years.

THE YEN'S ROLE IN TRADE SETTLEMENTS

One of the most basic functions of an international currency is trade settlements. In order to prepare for the 1964 Tokyo Olympic Games, Japan implemented a number of major national projects including the famous Shinkansen Super Express Train in the early 1960s. In 1968, Japan surpassed West Germany to become the world's second-largest economy. From the late 1960s, Japan began to push for the yen to be used in international trade settlements and, by the early 1970s, the Japanese currency was playing a significant role in this.

Table 18.2 shows the proportions of yen-settled import and export trades in Japan from 1970 to 1998. In 1970, the figures were as low as 0.3 percent and 0.9 percent, respectively. However, by 1980 the proportion of yen-settled exports had surged to 29.4 percent. From 1980 to 1985, this rose to a record high of 39.3 percent, and remained at above 30 percent. From 1980 to 1998, yen-settled imports recorded a widening share, although this was only about half that of yen-settled exports.

Regional Differences in Yen-settled Trade

Yen-settled trades had markedly different proportions for various regions. According to Table 18.2, from 1985 to 2000, yen-settled export trades with Southeast Asia had the largest share of about 50 percent, while exports to the EU had about 40 percent. The smallest

TABLE 18.2 Japan's yen-settled international trades, 1970–98 (%)

	Exports to:				Imports from:			
	World	US	EU	Southeast Asia	World	US	EU	Southeast Asia
1970	0.9	—	—	—	0.3	—	—	—
1975	17.5	—	—	—	0.9	—	—	—
1980	29.4	—	—	—	2.4	—	—	—
1985	39.3	19.7	51.3	47.3	7.3	9.2	27.3	11.5
1987	33.4	15.0	44.0	41.1	10.6	11.6	26.9	19.4
1988	34.3	16.4	43.9	41.2	13.3	10	26.9	17.5
1989	34.7	16.4	42.2	43.5	14.1	10.2	27.7	19.5
1990	37.5	16.2	42.1	48.9	14.6	11.6	26.9	19.4
1991	39.4	16.5	42.0	50.8	15.6	11.2	31.4	21.6
1992	40.1	16.6	40.3	52.3	17.0	13.8	31.7	23.8
1993	39.9	18.0	41.0	52.5	20.9	13.8	45.0	25.7
1994	39.7	19.4	40.9	49.0	19.2	13.3	38.6	23.6
1995	37.6	17.5	37.2	44.7	22.7	21.5	44.8	26.2
1996	35.2	15.9	36.1	46.3	20.6	16.4	46.1	24.0
1997	35.8	16.6	34.3	47.0	22.6	22.0	49.3	25.0
1998	36.0	15.7	34.9	48.4	21.8	16.9	44.3	26.7

Source: Sato (1998).

proportion by region was in respect of the United States, reflecting the unrivalled dominance of the US dollar.

The proportions for yen-settled imports were significantly smaller, largely because Japan imported mostly energy and raw materials which were mainly priced in US dollars. The proportions for yen-settled imports from respective regions were the highest for the EU, followed by Southeast Asia and United States (the lowest).

Other Comparisons

Table 18.3 shows the proportions of local currency-settled import and export trades from 1980 to 1997 for six major developed countries: Japan, United States, United Kingdom, Germany, France, and Italy. Japan had the lowest proportions among them. Even in the late 1980s before Japan's economic bubble burst, the proportions of yen-settled trades were notably smaller than the other currencies.

Table 18.4 illustrates major currencies used for export trade settlements in recent years. The proportions of Japan's US dollar-settled exports were significantly higher than Germany, France, and the United Kingdom, while those of its yen-settled exports were much smaller than these countries. However, its US-dollar-settled exports were markedly smaller than those of Australia, South Africa, Canada, Korea, and Pakistan, while its yen-settled exports were higher than these countries.

The proportion of yen-settled trades was low because the US dollar and the pound sterling were mostly used for international trade settlements. The choice of trade settlement

TABLE 18.3 Proportions for local currency-settled import and export trades among major developed countries (%)

Exports	1980	1988	1995	1997
Japan	29.4	34.3	36.0	35.8
US	97.0	96.0	—	—
UK	76.0	57.0	—	—
Germany	82.3	81.5	74.8	—
France	62.5	58.5	—	49.2
Italy	36.0	—	—	38.0
Imports	**1980**	**1988**	**1995**	**1997**
Japan	2.4	13.3	22.7	22.6
US	85.0	85.0	—	—
UK	38.0	40.0	—	—
Germany	43.0	52.6	51.5	—
France	33.1	48.9	—	46.6
Italy	18.0	—	—	38.0

Source: Ministry of International Trade and Industry (MITI).

TABLE 18.4 Settlement currencies in export trades (%)

Countries	Germany	France	UK	Japan	Australia	South Africa	Canada	Korea	Pakistan
Euro	57.7	49.5	21.0	8.5	0.9	17.0	—	4.9	4.0
US$	26.6	37.9	27.8	51.2	67.4	52.0	70.0	85.5	91.4
Local currency	57.7	49.5	49.0	36.3	28.8	25.0	23.0	≪9.2	≪4.6

Note: These are average values from 2002–04 for Germany; from 1999–2003 for France, Japan, Australia, and Korea; from 1999–2002 for the United Kingdom; from 2003 for South Africa; from 2001–2003 for Pakistan; and from 2001 for Canada
Source: Kamps (2006).

currencies depends largely on the costs to hedge against exchange rate risk, which are in turn determined by the market liquidity of hedging instruments such as foreign exchange forwards, futures, options or swaps. Also, Japan's trades were mostly carried out by established trading companies, which were more experienced than their trading partners in controlling exchange rate risk. As a matter of preference, Japanese producers settled export trades in the same currency used for settling imports to maintain stable production and reduce the risk of fluctuations in external demand arising from exchange rate volatility.[1]

GRADUAL RELAXATION OF EXCHANGE CONTROLS

Shortly after World War II, Japan's trade and capital accounts were under strict controls that lasted for decades. (It enacted the *Foreign Exchange and Foreign Trade Control Law* in 1949 and the *Foreign Investment Control Law* the following year.) With the gradual stabilization of its balance of payments, Japan began to liberalize the current account first and then the capital account.

In opening up its capital accounts, Japan gradually relaxed import restrictions to the point where, in 1963, only 192 products remained subject to import restrictions. In 1964, Japan accepted Article 8 of the International Monetary Fund (IMF) Accord by further liberalizing its current account, when only 66 products, including rice, were still under import restrictions. However, the amount of foreign exchange kept by Japanese traveling abroad was still strictly controlled. By the late 1990s, the limit on foreign currency carried abroad was extended to 5 million yen (US$50,000). The liberalization of exchange controls over Japan's capital account started in the 1970s. In 1980, Japan passed a new *Foreign Exchange and Foreign Trade Control Law*, also known as the *Foreign Exchange Law*. This was a combination of the original 1949 law and the *Foreign Investment Control Law* enacted in 1950. In principle, the law aimed to foster free international trade, fully opening up the current account while keeping a considerable portion of the capital account under control. In May 1997, significant changes were made to the *Foreign Exchange Law*, including the abolition of advance reporting systems for capital transactions and replacing them with post-transaction reporting systems. At this point, Japan's capital account was very much liberalized.

Features of Japan's Liberalization of Exchange Controls

Japan's liberalization of exchange controls was characterized by capital-inflow controls. Until the 1970s, the government tried to reduce its foreign debts to a minimum. Protecting domestic industries from foreign control had been its prime concern and, for a long time, it had placed more emphasis on the purchase or transfer of technology patents than on foreign direct investments (FDIs). Japan lifted its current account controls in 1964, but adopted an incremental approach on foreign direct investments until 1980. Therefore, Japan's rapid economic growth during the 1950s and 1960s did not rely on foreign direct investments, but the full utilization of high domestic savings played an important role.

Capital inflows and outflows were mostly channeled through banks. Foreign banks in Japan which met a certain standard were also allowed to operate and were required to report to the central bank on a regular basis, which helped maintain a good database on the balance of international payments and made capital flow regulations easier. Finally, the liberalization of international capital flows and the relaxation of domestic financial controls were almost synchronous to largely prevent arbitrage in domestic and foreign markets. This approach to liberalization has great significance for China's current approach to internationalizing its currency.

JAPAN'S CAPITAL ACCOUNT LIBERALIZATION

The capital account liberalization has both positive and negative effects on the stability of a financial system, and thus many countries are cautious about opening up their capital accounts. Having discussed the opening up of Japan's capital account in general terms, we now focus on several specific areas that reveal more clearly the process and characteristics of the liberalization process.

Foreign Exchange Systems

From 1949 to 1971, Japan maintained a fixed exchange rate of ¥360 to US$1. This was altered to ¥308 for a short period before the introduction of the floating exchange rate system in 1973. From 1973 to 1998, the exchange rates had significant fluctuations, but overall the yen appreciated against the dollar. In 1984, Japan's foreign exchange market abolished its long-standing trading measures of requiring forward foreign exchange transactions backed by real trade demand. Prior to the lifting of these measures, forward transactions in Japan had to be made for the sole purpose of hedging.

One of the most important elements of Japan's foreign exchange monitoring system was that authorized foreign exchange banks were required to report cross-border transactions to regulators on time. The government emphasized the importance of minimizing the impact of the international activities of foreign banks on the domestic market. Therefore, restrictions on the translation of foreign currencies into the yen were revoked in 1984. Regulations on each bank's net foreign exchange positions (total daily spot and forward limits) remain valid today, which is rare in developed countries. In 1986, Tokyo established an offshore market with the requirement to split onshore and offshore transactions.

Authorized foreign exchange banks were required to notify their foreign-related business to the central bank, both in advance and afterwards, and submit all relevant data to regulators for monitoring.

Securities Investment

The *Foreign Investment Control Law* of 1950 allowed non-residents to invest in Japanese securities—albeit with a significant number of restrictions, including those on industries and the share of investments. In 1980, foreign investors were allowed to invest fully in Japanese securities through designated securities companies. Japanese investments in foreign securities began in 1970, when non-residents started to issue yen-denominated bonds ("Samurai" bonds) in Tokyo. Initially, only sovereign states or international institutions could issue Samurai bonds in the capacity of non-residents. Foreign private companies were allowed to issue these bonds in Japan in 1979 and outside Japan in 1984. The yen-bond issue required issuers to comply with certain standards for credit ratings and financial status. Domestic investors were allowed to invest in overseas securities through mutual funds as early as 1970, and were allowed to do so fully through designated securities companies in 1980.

Foreign Direct Investments

In 1980, FDIs of banks and securities firms (other than special industries such as fishery, pearl cultivation, leather, leather production and processing, textiles and processing, weapon production, and drug production) and foreign investment of other industries could, in principle, be processed within a day. In times of rapid economic development, Japan focused on technology aspects in FDIs, while non-residents investing in or acquiring Japanese securities were also subject to restrictions on both industries and Japanese securities investments.

Emergency Regulation

Emergency regulation refers to the regulatory approach to capital account transactions under special conditions. Special conditions would arise when there were difficulties in maintaining the balance of payments, when the yen's exchange rates fluctuated drastically, or when foreign markets caused serious adverse effects on financial and capital markets in Japan.

The liberalization of capital accounts is a very complex issue. Issues regarding residents' foreign loans, foreign trade, foreign exchange dealings, as well as technical designs of other transactions between residents and non-residents are beyond the scope of this chapter.

OVERVIEW OF JAPAN'S PROMOTION OF YEN INTERNATIONALIZATION

In previous sections, we briefly introduced the gradual liberalization of foreign exchange and capital accounts in Japan to pave the way for the internationalization of the yen. Table 18.5 presents a list of the major events involved in the internationalization process since 1980.

TABLE 18.5   Major events in yen internationalization since 1980

1980	December	The *Foreign Exchange and Foreign Trade Control Law* is fully revised to promote free trade in principle.
1983	November	The Japan-U.S. Yen-Dollar Committee is established.
1984	April	The principle of real demand for foreign exchange futures is revoked, and only forward exchange transactions continue to be based on actual import and export demands.
	May	The Japan-U.S. Yen-Dollar Committee releases a report entitled "Current Status and Prospects for Financial Liberalization and the Internationalization of the Yen."
	June	Restrictions on the conversion of foreign currencies into the yen are lifted (and spot foreign exchange positions were once regulated), while short-term euro–yen loans to residents are allowed.
	December	Lead manager positions for euro–yen bonds are open to foreign institutions.
1985	March	The Council on Foreign Exchange and Other Transactions issues a report entitled "Internationalization of the Yen."
	April	Withholding income taxes on euro–yen bonds issued by domestic institutions are abolished.
	September	The Plaza Accord is signed.
1986	April	Eligibility requirements for issuance of euro–yen bonds by foreign institutions are relaxed, and credit ratings are used to determine issuers' eligibility for bond issuance.
	May	The *Foreign Exchange and Foreign Trade Control Law* is partially revised, and offshore markets are set up.
1987	February	The Louvre Accord is signed.
	June	"Outlook for the Liberalization and Internationalization of Financial and Capital Markets" is released.

TABLE 18.5 (*Continued*)

	July	Eligibility requirements for issuance of euro–yen bonds by domestic institutions are relaxed, and credit ratings are used to determine issuers' eligibility for bond issuance.
	November	Restrictions on the holding of euro–yen commercial papers (CPs) by non-residents are lifted.
1989	April	The Tokyo International Financial Futures Exchange is established.
	May	Euro–yen medium- and long-term loans to residents are allowed.
	June	Eligibility requirements for issuance of euro–yen bonds by foreign institutions are further relaxed (and credit ratings are no longer considered). Restrictions on the holding of euro–yen bonds (with maturities of less than four years) by non-residents are lifted.
	July	Restrictions on overseas foreign currency deposits held by residents are lifted (and approval is no longer required for gross amounts equivalent to ¥5 million or less for individual investment accounts).
1990	July	Restrictions on overseas foreign currency deposits held by residents are lifted (and approval is no longer required for gross amounts equivalent to ¥30 million or less for corporate and individual investment portfolio accounts).
1993	April	The Ministry of Finance's *Administrative Guidance on Prohibiting Japanese banks' Overseas Subsidiaries from Being Lead Managers for Overseas Public Offering of Securities by Japanese Companies* (measures taken amid strong market volatility for a period of five years) is abolished.
	July	Eligibility requirements for issuing euro–yen bonds by foreign institutions are fully revoked.
1994	January	Eligibility requirements for issuing foreign bonds by domestic institutions and Samurai bonds by foreign institutions are eased. Restrictions on sovereign euro–yen bond repurchase are abandoned.
	July	Eligibility requirements for issuing yen-denominated foreign bonds are relaxed.
1995	April	Approval and reporting procedures for euro–yen and domestic bonds issued by non-residents are eased.
	August	Restrictions on repurchase of issued euro–yen bonds by foreign institutions are abolished.
1996	January	Eligibility requirements for issuing domestic bonds by foreign institutions are eliminated.
	April	The deadline period for repurchasing euro–yen bonds issued by domestic institutions is shortened from 90 days to 40 days, and the restrictions on issuing euro–yen CPs are abandoned (and the rules on bringing CPs into Japan are also eliminated).
1997	May	The revised *Foreign Exchange and Foreign Trade Control Law* is promulgated.
	June	The Financial System Research Council submits a report entitled "Regarding the Reform of the Japanese Financial Market", and the Securities and Exchange Council releases an article entitled "Comprehensive Reform of the Securities Market."
1998	April	The revised *Foreign Exchange and Foreign Trade Control Law* is enforced. Restrictions on repurchasing issued euro–yen bonds by domestic institutions are revoked.
	June	The Financial System Reform Bill is enacted.
	December	The Financial System Reform Bill is enforced.

Source: www.mof.go.jp.

Although the Japan-U.S. Yen-Dollar Committee and the Council on Foreign Exchange and Other Transactions released their respective reports in 1984 and 1985, Japan took a cautious approach towards internationalizing its currency during a period of more than 10 years after the mid-1980s. The Japanese government was preoccupied with addressing a large number of bad debts and related economic and financial issues arising from the bursting of Japan's economic bubble in the late 1980s. In the late 1990s, especially after the outbreak of the Asian financial crisis, Japan came to realize that promoting the internationalization of the yen could expand its influence in East Asia and reduce the regional market risk to ensure Japan's economic and financial market stability. However, in light of objections from the United States and the IMF, it had to abandon the proposed internationalization. As Japan endured a nearly decade-long recession, internal and external factors combined to thwart its plans.

FUNDAMENTAL WORK ON REFORMING THE FINANCIAL SYSTEM

To promote the internationalization of its currency effectively, the Japanese government undertook some major measures to improve the infrastructure of its domestic financial market. These are reviewed below.

Increased Liquidity of Short-term Government Bonds

As part of its reform initiatives, the Japanese government enhanced liquidity of short-term government bonds in 1999 to allow easy access for foreign investors to this market. Increased liquidity enabled foreign and domestic investors to manage yen assets through risk-free government bonds. In April 1999, Japan launched a short-term, yen-bond auction system.

Formation of the Yen Yield Curve

As part of the fundamental work on restructuring its entire financial system, Japan formed and refined the market price-based interest rate curve according to which various financial assets were priced. Prior to March 2000, it separately launched one-year, five-year, and 30-year government bonds to enhance their maturity profiles for a smooth and reliable interest rate curve.

Exemption from Income Tax

To increase government bond liquidity, in 1999 Japan exempted interest income on government bonds from income tax and abandoned transaction taxes. These measures enhanced the liquidity of Japanese government bonds.

OTC PRODUCTS IN JAPAN

Overall, the Japanese inter-bank market and the over-the-counter (OTC) derivatives market have lagged far behind developed markets in Europe and America. In this section, we will describe Japan's inter-bank market activity.

Trading of the Yen in International Foreign Exchange Markets

As we saw in Chapter 17, the proportion of the yen's average daily turnover remained at around 23 percent from 1992 to 2001, but continued to decline after 2001. This demonstrates that the Japanese government's active promotion of yen internationalization in the late 1990s did not achieve its goals. According to the corresponding Bank for International Settlements (BIS) data prior to 1992, the proportion of the yen's average daily turnover from 1982 to 1989 was much higher than in the 1990s, reflecting that the yen had carried much more weight before the bursting of Japan's bubble economy. Since Japan was not well prepared for yen internationalization despite its rapid economic growth in the 1980s, yen trading was restricted. However, the late 1990s saw a gloomy economy and distressed financial system in Japan when measures were gradually put in place to promote internationalization, resulting in a continued decline in yen trading.

Establishment of the Tokyo Offshore Market

In October 1985, Japan's Council on Foreign Exchange and Other Transactions agreed to set up an offshore market in Tokyo in 1986 to push for the internationalization of the yen. In June 1986, the Japanese Ministry of Finance announced operational guidance to the Tokyo offshore market, in which no more than 5 percent of funds in offshore bank accounts could be used in onshore operations, while the onshore flow of funds was to be subject to the same margin requirements as for onshore accounts. Equally, onshore funds could not freely flow into the offshore market. There was to be stringent registration and related requirements to prevent capital flows between onshore and offshore markets. Foreign banks in Tokyo were critical of these regulatory requirements. Because corporate and personal tax was still levied on Tokyo's offshore market, these requirements were less attractive to foreign enterprises than those in place in Singapore and Hong Kong. Even compared to New York, where municipal and state taxes were exempted, Tokyo's concessions were not generous enough. Foreign banks also complained of Tokyo's over-stringent monitoring of fund flows between offshore and onshore markets. Handicapped by these strict regulations, the Tokyo offshore market failed to promote internationalization of the currency.

DERIVATIVES TRADING

Japan's well-established commodity futures market, Osaka Dojima Rice Market, began trading in 1730 (see Schaede 1989), more than a century earlier than the Chicago Board of Trade. Nevertheless, the development of Japan's futures industry in modern times—even amid its rapid economic growth—was far from satisfactory. Futures products were not traded in Japan until the mid-1980s, more than a decade later than in the United States. With the Japanese foreign exchange futures and stock index futures as examples, this section will briefly describe the development of the domestic derivative exchange.

Development of Foreign Exchange Futures Market

In 1972, when the Chicago Mercantile Exchange (CME) offered the world's first foreign exchange futures contracts, yen–dollar futures were the earliest-launched product.

By 2008, the annual turnover of these contracts on the CME reached ¥2,010 trillion (about US$18.8 trillion), 12.57 times the total amount of yen-denominated imports and exports in the same period. Foreign exchange futures were not launched in Japan's newly-established Tokyo Financial Futures Exchange until 1989, with lower liquidity than the United States. Yen futures trading on the CME became increasingly active against thin yen/US-dollar futures trading in Japan, where there was a total of only 800 transactions from 2003 to the end of 2005. As a result of the low turnover, the Tokyo Futures Exchange stopped yen/US dollar futures trading in 2006; thereafter, the world's yen futures contracts were all executed on the CME.

Development of the Stock Index Futures Market

Though in a slightly better situation than foreign exchange futures, Japanese stock index futures also left much to be desired. They were launched successfully in the United States as early as 1982. As the most innovative and dynamic regional financial center, Singapore also launched futures based on the Nikkei 225 Index in 1986, which were well-received by the market. At that time the Japanese government was worried that the cash settlement of stock index futures might be risky, and therefore created the world's first stock index futures delivered in shares, which ultimately proved a failure. In 1987, the Osaka Stock Exchange launched the Osaka Stock Futures 50, but this also ended in failure. Two years after the Singapore Exchange introduced Japanese stock index futures, Japan also introduced the cash settlement Nikkei 225 stock index futures in Osaka in September 1988. Initially, the Singapore Exchange's liquidity was relatively low, but because of errors committed by the Japanese in establishing these features in Osaka, the trading of Nikkei stock index futures on the Singapore Exchange overwhelmingly exceeded that in Osaka. From January 1990 to August 1993, the Osaka Stock Exchange increased futures margins on four consecutive occasions, while Singapore lowered similar margins five times. This led to a position where margins in Osaka were more than double those in Singapore, which also had lower commissions and transaction costs. As a result, major participants in the Nikkei market relocated to Singapore in a period of just a few weeks, resulting in a serious shortage of market liquidity for Singapore. The situation remained the same until the late 1990s, when the Japanese government instituted remedial measures.

TOKYO AS AN INTERNATIONAL FINANCIAL CENTER

In November 1996, the then Prime Minister Ryutaro Hashimoto introduced moves to reform the financial system that were designed to transform Japan's financial market into an international financial market like New York and London by 2001. This marked the start of the so-called Japanese Big Bang. Excessive market regulation meant that Japan's financial market had long lagged far behind New York and London in foreign exchange and securities, in particular. There were three core guiding principles for Japan's reform:

- Freedom: to liberalize access to financial products and their pricing to ensure different market principles could be implemented and complied with.

- Justice: to set out clear rules and greater transparency with a view to establishing a fair and reliable financial market.
- Globalization: to upgrade legal, accounting, and regulatory systems to cope with the age of internationalization and to bring them in line with international standards.

The reform would provide public investors and financial consumers with more financial products and services to meet their needs. Expanding the scope of services offered by banks and securities firms would provide greater convenience for customers. Though the reform was forward-looking, its timing was unfortunate. With the bursting of Japan's bubble economy, most Japanese financial institutions had been preoccupied with huge bad debt for a very long time. In view of this, Japan should have first moved to stabilize its financial system before any expansion and development.[2] Because of its poor positioning and over-ambitious strategic objectives, Tokyo failed to achieve its goal and even now still lags far behind New York and London.

CONCLUSION

In this chapter, we briefly discussed the liberalization of yen trade settlement and of the capital account, and the major initiatives entailed in the internationalization process. Knowledge of Japan's initiatives from the 1970s onwards can lead China to a clearer understanding of its own current situation and enable it to draw on Japan's experience in a number of respects. First of all, Japan's approach of focusing on science and technology and technology transfer for luring FDIs is meaningful to China's current economic restructuring. Selective and more effective application of foreign investments can lead to better use of high domestic savings for economic growth. Secondly, in promoting currency internationalization, the financial market infrastructure must be upgraded for sustainable, sound market development. Thirdly, reform policies should be well-organized for better internal and external coordination and cooperation. Fourthly, off-shore market accounts must be effectively separated from onshore market accounts for a better segregation of domestic and overseas markets. Fifthly, approval, verification and necessary data collation in respect of foreign-related business must be sought to prepare for cross-border business and financial supervision. Finally, great attention should be paid to tracking and monitoring cross-border transactions. Of course, this list is by no means exhaustive.

There are also a number of Japanese failures that China can learn from. First of all, Japan lagged behind other developed countries in financial liberalization because it prioritized trade over finance, and overemphasized the treasury role of government bonds, rather than their financial functions. Secondly, Japan missed the best chance to internationalize the yen because it liberalized its finance and capital account behind schedule and did not push strongly enough for internationalization until the late 1990s. It took no practical action in this regard during the late 1980s and early 1990s when its economy accounted for up to 60 percent of the US economy. It was not until the late 1990s that the Japanese government started to consider taking active steps to reform its distressed financial system, when the effect of the bursting of Japan's economic bubble was significant. Subsequently, when the Asian financial crisis broke out in 1997, Japan then pushed further for yen internationalization. Thirdly, the Japanese government undermined the yen's value and role as an international reserve currency by suppressing appreciation and confining the exchange rate against the US dollar within a certain range to facilitate exports. This suggests that despite its coordinated domestic and foreign policies for the internationalization of its currency, Japan still lacked comprehensive research and strategic initiatives, thus leading to long-lasting policy conflicts and missed opportunities. These are lessons that China would do well to heed.

ENDNOTES

1. Detailed explanations of the reasons for the low percentages of yen settlements are beyond the scope of this chapter, and interested readers may like to refer to Taguchi (1982), and Tavlas and Ozeki (1991).
2. See Fukukawa (1997).

CHAPTER 19

The Current Status of the CNY Internationalization Process

Thanks to three decades of reform and opening-up, China has recorded remarkable and enviable economic achievements, rapidly attaining the status of a leading world economy. Though China's economic output accounted for only 1.8 percent of the world's total economic output in 1978, this surged to 8.5 percent in 2009, and Chinese GDP is expected to surpass 9 percent of the world's total GDP in 2010, making China the world's second-largest economy in 2010. China is expected to have become the world's largest exporter and second-largest importer in 2009. Amid the prevailing international financial crisis, China has been attracting increasing global attention.

In earlier chapters, we have discussed the world's major currencies and their roles, and the lessons to be learned from Japan's experience in striving to internationalize its currency. This chapter will look at the current status of China's move to internationalize the CNY and the future directions its development might take.

Despite China's continued economic strength, the CNY has still not attained international status comparable to China's economic standing. Only through a steady, incremental process towards internationalization can China assert an influence commensurate with its economic standing.

GENERAL SITUATION

Over the past few years, China has adopted a very prudent approach towards financial liberalization. The CNY has yet to become fully convertible under the capital account. Since the 1990s, China has increasingly converged with the global economy, with the import and export trade as a proportion of GDP soaring from around 30 percent to a record high of 60 percent. In addition, as part of its foreign exchange management reform, the country has undertaken obligations under Articles 2, 3, and 4 of Section 8 of the International Monetary Fund (IMF) Accord, with a view to establishing free convertibility of the CNY under the current account.

In the wake of the 1997 financial crisis in East Asia, scholars have made a thorough study of the risk arising from global capital flows. When emerging markets come under speculative raids, capital restrictions can play the role of a temporary firewall. China has also exercised discretion in its approach to the free convertibility of the CNY. From 2003, it has gradually relaxed its capital controls. In particular, domestic foreign exchange regulators have lessened the pressure for the CNY to revalue by relaxing local restrictions on the use of foreign exchange. To date, there is still no specific timeframe for the free convertibility of the CNY.[1]

Though it is not freely convertible, the CNY has been used outside China by government departments or the private sector as a store of value. However, it has yet to become an anchor for other currencies and the internationalization process will remain in its infancy until the CNY becomes fully convertible.

USE OF CNY IN TRADE

In July 2009, China launched a pilot scheme to allow import and export trades to be settled in CNY. In fact, the use of the CNY for settlement of border trades and other transactions with neighboring countries began unofficially years before. The CNY is said to be "freely circulated" in Pakistan, Vietnam, Myanmar, and Laos, enjoying "almost the same" status as the US dollar. In 2004, around 90 percent of China's border trade with Mongolia was settled in CNY. For border trades with Vietnam, North Korea, and Russia, the figures were around 81 percent, 45 percent, and 15 percent, respectively.[2] We will return to this subject later in the chapter.

In general, as a proportion of domestic money supply and total foreign trade, the amount of CNY in circulation arising from international trade remains low. Apart from exchange and payment in tourism, non-neighboring Asian countries, Europe, and the United States have not used the CNY as the settlement currency. As border trade represents only a small share of China's overall trade and the Chinese government has not released any data on CNY-settled trades, it is difficult to estimate the full extent of the use of the CNY in trade settlement. With the expansion of CNY-settled trades, it is expected that official data on these activities will be released in the future, allowing for further comparison and analysis.

CURRENT CNY APPLICATIONS IN HONG KONG

Since the return of Hong Kong to China in 1997, the economic relationship between the mainland and Hong Kong has become ever closer. As an international financial and shipping center, Hong Kong provides an excellent financing platform for well-performing Chinese business entities, and serves as an effective gateway for mainland exports. At the same time, the enormous mainland market presents unprecedented opportunities for Hong Kong enterprises. All of this puts Hong Kong at the forefront of the internationalization process, while becoming a springboard for international speculative capital entering China.

Following China's reform and opening up, Hong Kong has become the most important source of its foreign direct investment (FDI), and one of its most important trading partners. Thanks to its unique status within China and the implementation of the Closer Economic Partnership Arrangement (CEPA) with the mainland, Hong Kong has become the most active offshore CNY market.

Implementation and Changes of Related Policies

At the end of 2003, as approved by the State Council, the People's Bank of China (PBC) agreed to arrange settlement for personal CNY business in Hong Kong. Following the official launch of CNY business in Hong Kong in January 2004, local shops and automatic teller machines (ATMs) started to accept debit and credit cards issued by mainland banks. Later that year, Hong Kong banks were permitted to provide CNY deposit, exchange, and remittance services and to issue CNY debit and credit cards to Hong Kong residents for use on the mainland.

In November 2005, the PBC announced the following five-pronged approach to broaden the scope of local CNY business:

- Allowing the PBC Shenzhen Central Sub-Branch to accept deposits from clearing banks for CNY business in Hong Kong.
- Relaxing requirements for closing positions between the CNY and the HK dollar by increasing the limit on personal CNY (banknotes) exchanges from the equivalent of CNY6,000 to the equivalent of CNY20,000; expanding the list of designated local CNY exchange operators to cover those engaged in transportations, communications, medical and education industries; and allowing designated shops to convert their CNY deposits maintained in participating banks into HK dollars.
- Increasing the maximum daily remittance limit of Hong Kong residents from CNY50,000 to CNY80,000.
- Clearing Hong Kong residents' personal CNY checks issued by clearing banks; these non-transferable personal checks can be used to draw up to CNY80,000 from each account per day to pay for consumer expenditures in Guangdong province.
- Raising the credit limit of CNY100,000 for each CNY card issued by Hong Kong banks.

DEPOSITS

When Hong Kong banks began to take CNY deposits from February 2004, CNY deposits soared, recording a seven-fold increase by July 2007. Growth was particularly strong in the period up to July 2005, when CNY deposit interest rates were higher than HK-dollar rates and there were strong expectations of CNY appreciation. A period of slower growth followed, when expectations eased and HK-dollar rates rose. In October 2007 after the stock market plunge, CNY deposits surged to a record level of CNY77.675 billion (US$11 billion) in May 2008, before gradually dropping to CNY50 billion (about US$7.1 billion).

As at June 2009, there were 40 licensed banks (including major local retail banks) operating CNY business in Hong Kong, accounting for 13.2 percent of all local banks and 28.8 percent of licensed banks.

Remittances

Since customers prefer remittance to carrying cash to mainland China, remittance services have expanded steadily. As at the end of 2005, Hong Kong residents had remitted CNY1 billion (US$120 million) to mainland China, with an average transaction amount of CNY41,344 (US$5,000). However, remittances to Hong Kong from the mainland were insignificant.

Debit and Credit Cards

Following the introduction of related business in January 2004, mainland visitors increased their use of CNY debit cards and credit cards in Hong Kong. As at the end of 2005, their consumption using CNY cards in Hong Kong reached HK$7.2 billion, and their withdrawals from ATMs amounted to HK$2.2 billion. Their credit card consumption reached an average of HK$2,800 for each transaction. The use of bank cards in Hong Kong made consumption more convenient for mainland visitors. From mid-2004 to the end of 2005, Hong Kong residents consumed and withdrew from ATMs a total of CNY0.37 billion in mainland China using CNY debit cards and credit cards issued by Hong Kong banks.

CNY Foreign Exchange Futures

According to the *China Securities Journal*, Paul Chow, CEO of the Hong Kong Stock Exchange (HKEx), announced on December 13, 2006 that the exchange's board of directors had approved in principle a resolution on the proposed introduction of CNY foreign exchange futures products, and that the HKEx planned to consult the market over this proposal and to launch CNY futures products by mid-2007. As at the time of writing, however, CNY foreign exchange futures have yet to be launched, although the HKEx does mention in its 2010–12 strategic plan that the development of new products, including derivatives, linked to the increasing internationalization of the yuan remains a priority.

CNY BONDS IN HONG KONG SAR

Leveraging technical strengths and flexibility in its capacity as an international financial center, Hong Kong has witnessed a fast-growing CNY bond market.

Market Development

With the approval of the State Council, in January 2007, the PBC, in conjunction with the National Development and Reform Commission, announced its *Interim Measures for the Administration of Domestic Financial Institutions to Issue CNY Bonds in Hong Kong*. The measures were designed to expand and regulate CNY bond issuance in Hong Kong by Chinese financial institutions.

The measures confined approval to issue CNY bonds to policy banks and commercial banks legally established in China (excluding the Hong Kong and Macau SARs and Taiwan). Confining bond issuance to reputable policy and commercial banks with higher credit standards was designed to ensure the smooth and orderly development of the business.

The first issue of CNY bonds by a mainland financial institution in Hong Kong took place between June 27 and July 6, 2007, when the China Development Bank (CDB) issued 3 percent two-year CNY bonds to institutional and individual investors in Hong Kong. The maximum amount of bonds issued was CNY5 billion (US$648 million), including a retail bond issuance at a minimum of CNY1 billion (US$130 million). The minimum subscription threshold for individual investors was CNY20,000 (US$2,590).

Since then, several mainland banks have issued CNY bonds in Hong Kong with a combined amount of over CNY20 billion (US$2.59 billion). Nevertheless, Hong Kong's slack bond market (it has a lower trading volume than, for example, Singapore) has dampened the enthusiasm of these institutions for issuing bonds locally. In 2009, the global financial crisis dealt a heavy blow to the Eurozone, Japan, and South Korea. Furthermore, the US 10-year bond yield has reached only about 2 percent in recent years, leaving a large amount of capital idle. As Hong Kong has entered a zero-interest rate era, foreign banks have recently become more eager to issue CNY bonds, marking a new wave of local issues.

On July 23, 2009, the Bank of East Asia (China) Limited (BEA China), a mainland subsidiary of the Bank of East Asia (BEA), issued 2.8 percent two-year CNY4 billion (US$586 million) bonds, of which CNY2.8 billion (US$410 million) was issued to retail investors. BEA therefore became the first non-Chinese bank to issue CNY bonds in Hong Kong through its mainland subsidiary. Given expectations of CNY appreciation and the limited size of its issue, BEA China's bond issuance was highly sought-after in the local bond market, with a subscription of CNY6.3 billion (US$922 million).

Following in BEA China's footsteps, HSBC Bank (China) Company Limited (HSBC China) issued CNY3 billion (US$439 million) of CNY bonds in Hong Kong in 2009.

Over the past two years, the Bank of China (BOC) has issued a total of CNY6 billion (US$872 million) in bonds in Hong Kong. It has also released a plan to issue bonds worth CNY10 billion (US$1.453 billion) by the end of 2010. Because of the limited supply of such bonds, CNY bond issuance in Hong Kong has been well received by investors, and both Chinese and foreign banks are optimistic about the financing market in Hong Kong.

Standard Chartered Bank (SCB) has received approval to issue CNY 3.5 billion (US$510 million) bonds in mainland China, making it the first foreign bank to do so. DBS Bank has also expressed its interest in a similar venture but has yet to make a formal application.

According to published financial statements of foreign banks in China for 2008 and the first quarter of 2009, it seems that their businesses have not been greatly affected by the financial crisis; some have even enjoyed a positive turnaround, though capital remains tight. Issuing CNY bonds in either China or Hong Kong will undoubtedly ease their capital shortages, as well as greatly reduce the financing costs of their business in China.

Through issuing CNY bonds in Hong Kong, mainland institutions have gained vital experience in bond pricing, rating, and other aspects which, in turn, has helped develop China's own bond market. Now that Hong Kong is expanding its CNY bond market and offering a greater variety of CNY investment products, investors will have more incentive to continue to hold the CNY. This has undoubtedly marked a milestone in developing Hong Kong as an offshore CNY center.

CNY FUTURES ON THE CME

The Chicago Mercantile Exchange (CME), the world's major exchange for foreign exchange futures and options, launched CNY non-deliverable futures with a contract size of CNY1 million (US$125 million) in August 2006. Although yen and euro contracts were also launched, trading has been almost exclusively in CNY/US-dollar contracts.

Trading has been extremely thin, with respective annual trading values of US$0.539 billion, US$2.222 billion, and US$1.042 billion being recorded for the three years from 2007 to 2009. The total trading value in the first half of 2010—US$0.147 billion—was just 25.9 percent of that of the same period in 2009. The low volatility of the exchange rates has obviously contributed to this but there are other reasons beyond the scope of this book for the low market liquidity.

CNY-SETTLED CROSS-BORDER TRADES

The use of a local currency for foreign-trade settlement is the most basic feature of the currency's internationalization, as the Japanese example clearly illustrates. Further to our earlier discussion on the recent use of CNY in trades with neighboring countries and regions, we now describe the state-driven, CNY-settled, cross-border trades in China during 2009.

In the early 1990s, China began to use the CNY for trade settlements with some neighboring countries and, by the end of 2008, the PBC had signed CNY settlement agreements with the central banks of Vietnam, Mongolia, Laos, Nepal, Russia, Kirghizia, North Korea, and Kazakhstan. In May 2009, Brazilian President Luiz Inacio Lula Da Silva suggested that China and Brazil should stop using the US dollar for bilateral trades and use their own currencies instead. Later that year, Premier Wen Jiaobao disclosed that a scheme for trial CNY trade settlements had already been formulated and would be implemented as soon as it had received State Council approval.

In the wake of the global financial crisis, the PBC signed currency swap agreements with the central banks of Hong Kong, Korea, Malaysia, Indonesia, Belarus, and Argentina for a gross amount of CNY650 billion (US$94.5 billion). These currency swaps will pave the way for CNY trade settlements.

In April 2009, the State Council implemented trial CNY settlements for cross-border trades between mainland cities (including Shanghai, Guangzhou, Shenzhen, Zhuhai, and Dongguan) and Hong Kong/Macau. This was an important step towards promoting the CNY as a settlement currency.

With the promulgation of the *Administrative Measures for the Trial Program for CNY-settled Cross-border Trades* and the release of the PBC's *Implementation Rules on Administrative Measures for the Trial Program for CNY-settled Cross-border Trades* in early July 2009, China has taken the first step towards CNY internationalization. The trial program was kicked off in Shanghai a few days later when the Shanghai Silk Group Co., Ltd. (the exporter), Zhong Ye Trading (HK) Co., Ltd., and the Bank of Communications (the clearing bank for cross-border remittances by the exporter) completed the first CNY-settled trade deal.

CNY-settled cross-border trades have remained inactive so far: PBC data released in January 2010 show a total of only CNY4.066 billion (US$0.595 billion) for the first six months of the scheme. Of this total, exports amounted to CNY0.96 billion (US$0.14 billion) and imports to CNY3.1 billion (US$0.45 billion), which together accounted for a mere 0.027 percent of China's total foreign trade for 2009. It is clear from this that CNY-settled cross-border trades still have a long way to go.

The trial program is now subject to further refinement. All parties involved—regulators, enterprises, and banks—need time to study the arrangements and coordinate their activities.

The pilot enterprises are currently confined to certain regions and further support systems and measures are being formulated.

The purpose of holding CNY is also of extreme importance for accepting CNY to settle trades simply because the availability of CNY investment largely determines the willingness to accept the CNY. Therefore, policies such as entrance to the CNY money market, bond market, or stock market have to be coordinated if the CNY is to be more willingly accepted. What is more, the development of CNY foreign exchange derivatives is also of great importance, as holders of CNY or CNY assets can hedge their CNY foreign exchange risk conveniently when these markets have sufficient liquidity. It would be difficult to promote CNY-settled foreign trades without providing appropriate investment locations and foreign exchange risk management instruments. We believe that CNY-settled cross-border trades will prove effective in China in the near future with further development of the domestic financial market and risk management instruments.

POTENTIAL FOR USE IN FOREIGN EXCHANGE RESERVES

If the use of a local currency for trade settlements represents the most fundamental role of the currency's internationalization, its use as a reserve currency—the last and the most difficult obstacle to clear—will also serve that ultimate objective. The value of a global reserve currency depends on the size of the issuing country's economy, the role of its financial market, and its policy stability. It is pleasing to note that China has made good progress towards establishing the CNY as a reserve currency.

The governments of India and the Philippines have accepted the CNY as a convertible currency for exchange rate purposes. In November 2005, the Reserve Bank of India (the central bank) announced adjustments to the exchange rate index to include the CNY in its currency basket. A year later, the Philippines Monetary Board announced that it would start accepting the CNY as a reserve currency of the Central Bank of the Philippines from December 1, 2006.[3]

In response to China's initiatives to promote the internationalization of its currency, many countries and regions have expressed their intention to use the CNY for their foreign exchange reserves. In June 2009, a representative of Russia's central bank was reported as saying that the bank believed that the CNY might become a suitable reserve currency for Russia.[4] Malaysia's central bank, too, may use CNY-denominated assets, among others, for foreign exchange reserves.[5] Taiwan's premier, Liu Chao-shiuan, is also reported as saying that Taiwan might consider using the CNY for foreign exchange reserves in light of the unprecedented progress in cross-straits relations.[6]

In September 2009, the IMF and the PBC signed an agreement under which the PBC would purchase around US$50 billion-worth in IMF notes. The agreement is the first of its kind and offers China a safe investment instrument. It will also boost the IMF's capacity to help its membership—particularly the developing and emerging-market countries—to weather the global financial crisis, and facilitate an early recovery of the global economy.[7] The important thing to note here is that the purchase was to be transacted using the CNY, rather than US dollars from the Chinese foreign reserve. This will certainly promote the CNY's international status as a reserve currency in the coming years.

Liberalization of CNY Capital Items

In the six years since the Chinese government's internationalization initiatives began, it has broadened the limits on cross-border capital transactions selectively and incrementally, expedited trial CNY trade settlements, and is gradually realizing capital account convertibility.

In 2009, on the eve of the G20 financial summit held in London, PBC Governor Zhou Xiaochuan suggested broadening the application of the IMF's special drawing rights, with a view to creating a super-sovereign international reserve currency. Echoing this suggestion, the EU, Russia and India have also called for reforms of the international monetary system by reducing the dominance of the US dollar.

In 1996, China achieved CNY current account convertibility and opened up its capital account in a proactive and orderly manner. Presently, around 20 to 30 of the 43 capital-transaction items provided by the IMF are subject to few or no limitations. Conditions for full convertibility include a sound macroeconomy, a comprehensive domestic financial system, risk management awareness, and management capacity of enterprises and financial institutions; a stable international balance-of-payments position; mature approaches to domestic macroeconomic control; and effective control over cross-border capital flows.[8]

With due regard to its own circumstances, China has set out sequences for opening up its capital account: relaxing inflow and then outflow controls; deregulating direct investments and then equity investments; relaxing controls over, first, long-term capital flow and then short-term capital flow; deregulating financial institutions and then non-financial institutions and individuals; as well as deregulating real transactions and then non-real transactions.[9]

According to the PBC's *2007 Report on the International Financial Markets,* China will relax controls over capital-item transactions selectively and gradually, and introduce and develop capital market instruments with a view to realizing the convertibility of CNY capital items systematically and under effective risk control. In August 2009, all enterprises, whether private or state-owned, have been permitted to supplement their capital through overseas lending, and to use CNY to buy foreign currencies for overseas investments. Although there are still no specific plans or timeframes for realizing the CNY's free convertibility, these developments demonstrate China's commitment to the liberalization of its capital items.[10]

Controlling Cross-border Capital Flows

In a research paper[11] published shortly after the financial crisis broke out in 2008, Carmen M. Reinhart and Vincent Reinhart had this to say about the movement of capital across borders:

> *A pattern has often been repeated in the modern era of global finance. Global investors turn with interest toward the latest "foreign" market. Capital flows in volume into the "hot" financial market. The exchange rate tends to appreciate, asset prices to rally, and local commodity prices to boom. These favorable asset price movements improve national fiscal indicators and encourage domestic credit expansion. These, in turn, exacerbate structural weaknesses in the domestic banking sector even as those local institutions are courted by global financial institutions seeking entry into a hot market.*

Such comments largely capture what has happened in most developing countries with inflows of international capital. These capital influxes turn out to be a useful organizing device for understanding the swings in investor interest in foreign markets as reflected in asset price booms and crashes, and for predicting sovereign defaults and other crises. Swings in international capital flows are the major reason for most of the financial booms and crashes of the past few decades. China, of course, is no exception in this regard.

China's experimental CNY-settled cross-border trades will certainly expand in scope and will eventually be implemented across the board. However, the pilot program has indirectly prompted international capital inflows and outflows. From 2004 to 2007, China enjoyed an average annual trade surplus growth of more than 100 percent. Scholars and experts acknowledge that even without strong promotion of CNY-settled cross-border trades, massive amounts of foreign capital had flowed into China to take advantage of the country's liberalization of trade items, thus pushing up the level of its fixed asset investment in respective years.[12] Nevertheless, China's economy was hard hit by an exodus of foreign capital from the fourth quarter of 2008 and the first quarter of 2009.

Greater access has been granted for foreign capital flows into China following trade settlements in CNY. Without increased control, China's economy and its financial market will come under increasing influence from cross-border capital flows. In view of this, China needs to upgrade its CNY management system, implement and improve supporting measures, and establish a monitoring and preventative framework to establish the necessary controls. Oversight and prevention will continue to be key tasks in light of greater access to China for foreign capital flows amid the gradual liberalization of capital items in the coming years. Given the full liberalization of capital items sometime in the future, China should also continue to put in place a system for monitoring capital flows, which is indispensable in ensuring China's economic stability.

CONCLUSION

By comparison with the process and results of the internationalization of the Japanese yen, it is clear that China's efforts to promote the CNY as an international currency are still in their infancy. However, China has a number of conditions in its favor. It has large amounts of foreign exchange reserves in US dollars, which means that, for investors, holding the CNY is somewhat similar to holding US dollars. Furthermore, unlike Japan, China has trade deficits with many Asian countries, allowing the CNY to flow more easily into these markets. The internationalization of the CNY is certain to proceed further, but this should be implemented in a steady, planned, and orderly manner. To achieve stability in this process, it is very important for China to keep a firm control over cross-border capital flows. Otherwise, the foreign capital flows can deal a heavy blow to the Chinese economic and financial systems, as evidenced late in 2008 and early in 2009.

ENDNOTES

1. See He Fan (2009).
2. See Liu Mingzhi (2008).

3. China Review News Agency, Hong Kong.
4. See http://rusnews.cn, June 10, 2009.
5. *Wall Street Journal*, June 22, 2009.
6. In an exclusive interview with Dow Jones Newswire on August 6, 2009, as reported by Xinhua News Agency.
7. For details, see the IMF website at http://www.imf.org.
8. See Wei Benhua's report on www.chinanews.com, November 9, 2004.
9. See Wei Benhua's report in *Securities Times*, July 1, 2004.
10. See He Fan (2009).
11. "From capital flow bonanza to financial crash" at: http://mpra.ub.uni-muenchen.de/11866.
12. See Li Dongping (2008).

CHAPTER 20

Market and Product Trends Under the Internationalization of the CNY

Currency internationalization requires adequate liquidity in the issuing country's foreign exchange and capital markets to facilitate investments and transactions. It also requires plenty of risk management and hedging instruments in the financial market to give full play to a currency's settlement, trading, and reserve functions. Here, we examine the scale of the foreign exchange market and its main products for the past 10 years since China's currency has attained a certain level of internationalization.

CNY INTERNATIONALIZATION AND DEVELOPMENT NEEDS FOR THE FOREIGN EXCHANGE MARKET IN 2020

As we saw in Chapter 17, the key indicator of a currency's status is its place in the international currency system. The liberalization of capital accounts is an important, but not essential, condition of international currencies in the early stages. Chapter 18 showed how, two decades before Japan fully liberalized its current and capital accounts, the yen already took up 3.6 percent of the identifiable international reserves in 1979, a level not seen since 2006. Another key feature of an international currency is its status in the international foreign exchange market. The settlement, trading, and reserve functions of a currency cannot be exerted fully without a flourishing foreign exchange market. While the CNY will certainly become an international reserve currency by 2020, it is difficult to forecast accurately its share of international reserves. In this section, we will estimate the scale of the CNY foreign exchange market in 2020, based on reasonable assumptions about the CNY's share in that market and China's anticipated share of world GDP.

Key Assumptions

Table 17.8 showed the respective contributions of 18 currencies to the global foreign exchange market and the contributions of their respective countries' share of world GDP in 2007, which reflects the degree of internationalization of these currencies relative to their economic scale. In this section, we will estimate the projected scale of the CNY foreign exchange and other major markets and their corresponding average annual growth rates in 2020.

As we saw in Chapter 1, China's share of the world's economy rose from 4.6 percent in 2004 to 8.5 percent in 2009, an average growth of 0.78 percent. Assuming that this grows at

0.5 percent annually from 2010 to 2020, it should account for around 14 percent of the world's GDP in 2020. Based on the Bank for International Settlements (BIS) statistics on the global triennial foreign exchange market we referred to earlier, we calculate that for the three 12-year periods from 1989 to 2001, 1992 to 2004, and 1995 to 2007, the average annual growth rates of the international foreign exchange market were 6.1 percent, 7.2 percent, and 8.6 percent, respectively. From 2004 to 2007, excessive leverage and speculation in the market led to significantly higher growth in these three years than any other previous three-year period. In addition, the impact of the financial crisis can be expected to trigger deleveraging adjustments in the development of the market. It is therefore reasonable to assume that from 2007 to 2020, the forex market will continue to grow at an average of 7.2 percent annually. Based on this assumption, we calculate that average daily trading will reach US$7.9 trillion in April 2020. Assuming the respective ratios of the CNY's share in the global foreign exchange market and the foreign exchange share of the world's economy to be in the order of 24 percent and 80 percent from 2007 to 2020, we can calculate the overall scale of the CNY foreign exchange market in 2020 and its expected average annual growth rate from 2007 to 2020. The results are as shown in Table 20.1.

TABLE 20.1 Anticipated scale and growth rates of the CNY foreign exchange market by 2020 given five different estimates for China's share of global foreign exchange trading (US$ trillion)

China's Share of Global foreign exchange Trading/GDP Share in 2020 (%)	25	35	56	59	80
Weighting of China's foreign exchange market in the global foreign exchange market (%)	3.5	4.9	7.8	8.3	11.2
Scale of China's foreign exchange market (in US$ trillion)	69.1	96.8	154.8	163.1	221.1
Average annual growth rate of trading on China's foreign exchange market (%)	30.1	33.6	38.5	39.0	42.3
Average annual growth rate of spot trading on China's foreign exchange market (%)	26.9	30.3	35.1	35.6	38.8
Average annual growth rate of forward trading on China's foreign exchange market (%)	26.7	30.1	34.9	35.4	38.6
Average annual growth rate of swap trading on China's foreign exchange market (%)	49.3	53.2	58.9	59.5	63.3

Sources: Calculated based on BIS statistics, 1989 to 2007, and the assumptions stated above.

Main Outcomes

Table 20.1 shows that by 2020, when the ratio of the CNY's share in the global foreign exchange market and China's share of the world's GDP is only 25 percent, the world share of CNY foreign exchange trading would be about 3.5 percent, slightly higher than that of the Swiss franc (3.4 percent in 2007 as shown in Table 17.8). The scale of the CNY market will be US$69.1 trillion at an average annual growth rate of 30.1 percent from 2007 to 2020. If the percentage of the CNY in the global market and China's share of the world's economy reaches 35 percent in 2020, the world share of CNY foreign exchange trading would be about 4.9 percent, and the scale of the CNY market would be US$96.8 trillion, at an average annual growth rate of 33.6 percent. Thus, as long as the ratio of the CNY's share in the global foreign exchange market and China's share of the world's GDP is above 25 percent, the percentage of CNY trading in the foreign exchange market will rank fifth, higher than that of the Swiss franc and closer to the level of international reserve currencies.

If, by 2020, the CNY's proportion in the global market and China's share of the world's economy reach 56 percent (11.3 percent lower than the level of the euro in 2007 when the extent of euro internationalization was not fully reflected), the scale of the CNY foreign exchange market will be US$154.8 trillion, at an average annual growth rate of 38.5 percent from 2007 to 2020. CNY foreign exchange trading would claim a 7.8-percent share of global foreign exchange trading to become the fourth major international currency.

If, by 2020, the CNY's proportion in the global foreign exchange market and China's share of the world's economy reach 59 percent (8.3 percent lower than the level of the euro in 2007), the market scale will be greater than US$163.1 trillion, at an average annual growth rate of at least 39 percent from 2007 to 2020. CNY foreign exchange trading as a proportion of global foreign exchange trading will be greater than 8.3 percent, making it the third major international currency after the US dollar and the euro.

As China's foreign exchange market is still in its infancy, it is realistic to believe that the ratio of the CNY foreign exchange trading to China's share of world GDP would be around 35 percent in the 13 years from 2007 to 2020; in which case, the CNY would be in the top four of the major international currencies.

Development Trend of Foreign Exchange Spot, Forwards, and Swaps Markets

The liquidity of foreign exchange markets is an important indicator of the extent of a currency's internationalization. This is because the settlement function of a currency cannot be fully exerted without a flourishing foreign exchange market; neither can the trading and reserve functions be performed normally. Similarly important are flourishing foreign exchange forwards and swaps markets, as these are key instruments with which international traders hedge their risk. Cross-border trading cannot be settled effectively without a highly liquid foreign exchange derivatives market. Here, we use the results from Table 20.1 to estimate the scale of the CNY forwards and swaps markets from 2007 to 2020.

As we saw from Table 17.9, CNY spots and forwards trading accounted for 61.4 percent and 31.3 percent, respectively, of the total foreign exchange trading in 2007, 28.8 percent and 19.6 percent higher than the corresponding world levels, indicating that China's foreign exchange trading still mainly comprised traditional spots and forwards trading. Forex swaps only accounted for 7.4 percent, which was 48.2 percent lower than the world level, indicating that China's swaps market remained in the early stages of development. Assuming that the proportions of CNY spots, forwards, and swaps trading reach 40 percent, 20 percent, and 40 percent, respectively (closer to the world level by 2020), we can use the results in Table 20.1 to calculate the average annual growth rates for each. The results are shown in the second half of Table 20.1, and we can conclude that the required average annual growth rate of swaps will be 20 percent-plus higher than those of spots and forwards trading.

DEVELOPMENT REQUIREMENTS FOR THE CAPITAL MARKET

The extent of a capital market's development is another major factor determining a currency's internationalization. If the depth and breadth of capital markets have not reached a certain level, it will be difficult for currency holders to find instruments and markets for investment.

The domestic bond market is the foundation for developing China's capital market. For many years, treasury bonds (the functions of which need further exploration) have been used in public finance to facilitate the implementation of international economic policies. Although progress has been made in constructing the yield curve of CNY treasury bonds, the liquidity of the secondary bond market remains low and the exchange and over-the-counter (OTC) bond markets remain largely disconnected. Furthermore, corporate bonds represent a relatively low percentage. To promote the sustainable development of the capital market and strengthen the infrastructure, measures such as refining the yield curve as well as introducing corporate rating mechanisms, are indispensable. Only by implementing a series of effective support measures and increasing the liquidity and efficiency of the CNY bond market can foreign and domestic institutions be tempted to actively participate in the China market and help promote the steady internationalization of the CNY.

The stock market is a key component of the capital market and a main channel through which people accumulate property income and financial wealth. However, wild fluctuations in the market and an exceedingly high turnover rate are detrimental to the normal exercising of the stock market's capital function, that is, the role of the stock market in supporting steady and continual development of the economy. The data show that the turnover rate (the ratio of the annual trading amount to the market value) of China's stock market is significantly higher than that of major developed countries and most other developed and developing countries and regions, indicating a significantly stronger speculative inclination over investment. If China's degree of securitization (the ratio of the stock market value to GDP) gradually reaches 100 percent in 2020, then the market value of the domestic stock market would be approximately CNY90 trillion (US$15 trillion). Such a high level of financial wealth would have a great impact on effectively stimulating consumption, accelerating economic structural transformation, and promoting steady economic development, as well as accelerating the process of CNY internationalization.

UNIQUE ROLE OF HONG KONG

China's quest towards the internationalization of the CNY enjoys the advantages brought by the international position occupied by the Hong Kong financial industry. As we saw in Chapter 17, though Hong Kong's GDP only accounted for 0.4 percent of the world total, its foreign exchange trading amounted to 1.4 percent of the world total in 2007; at 350 percent of its GDP share in the world, it was second only to the Swiss franc. Hong Kong has made great contributions to China's reform and opening-up in finance, trade and market development and will continue to play an important role in the process of CNY internationalization.

As we have seen, the non-deliverable forwards, swaps, and options markets in Hong Kong have given rise to flourishing overseas CNY transactions in the past decade. These markets reflect the enthusiasm of foreign institutions to speculate on CNY appreciation. They have a significant impact on the domestic CNY foreign exchange market and, to a large extent, form the overseas CNY foreign exchange market. Proper use of these markets will have a positive effect on CNY internationalization.

Hong Kong has a relatively mature stock market structure that makes use of stock index futures and options, individual stock options, and subscription warrants as risk management tools. In particular, the H-share index futures and options launched gradually since 2003 have direct reference value for the development of such markets in mainland China.

In addition, Hong Kong, with its many international financial institutions, has proven to be a good choice for issuing and promoting overseas CNY bonds. Because the CNY is already in use in Hong Kong, the arrangement of CNY trade settlement there will be of benefit to it as a pilot center for CNY capital settlement in the future. Mainland China can observe the results of various cross-border CNY businesses in the open environment of Hong Kong for reference for further opening-up in the future.[1]

Hong Kong's experience in dealing with the 1997 East Asian financial crisis, its position as an international financial center, its legal system, and its mature markets provide significant advantages that China can use to promote the CNY internationalization process.

CNY AND YEN: INTERNATIONALIZATION PROCESSES COMPARED

In Chapter 18 we looked at the process by which the yen became established as an international currency. The Japanese experience should prove instructive for China's strategy as it undergoes the same process.

As noted earlier, yen-settled trading accounted for 0.9 percent of Japan's exports and 0.3 percent of its imports back in 1970. Although no accurate data on the trading settled in the CNY are available now, we estimate from the data reviewed in Chapter 19 that the ratios are much lower than the corresponding 1970 levels in Japan. That is, CNY trade settlement lags behind the yen by about 40 years.

A comparison of the adoption of floating exchange rate mechanisms shows similar results. Japan adopted such a mechanism in 1973. Although China's system from July 2005 contains improvements, it is not yet a floating exchange rate mechanism in the international sense. Even if it were considered as such, it would still lag behind Japan by 32 years.

A further point of comparison is the time at which the respective current accounts were liberalized. Japan's current accounts were fully liberalized by 1980, while China formally accepted the obligations set in Sections 2, 3 and 4 of Article 8 of the IMF Accord in December 1996, and realized free exchange of the CNY in its current accounts. Once again, Japan was years ahead in this regard.

Similar results are found in comparing the opening-up of the two countries' capital accounts. Japan began to invest in foreign securities in 1970. Foreign investors could invest in Japanese securities through assigned Japanese securities firms from 1970 and have been free to invest since 1980. In comparison, foreign investors were permitted to invest in China through the Qualified Foreign Institutional Investors (QFII) scheme in 2003, and domestic investors were permitted to invest in foreign securities through the Qualified Domestic Institutional Investors (QDII) scheme in 2006.

In 1970, non-residents in Japan were permitted to issue "Samurai" bonds and, from 1979, foreign private companies were also permitted to issue yen bonds in Japan. In China, non-residents have been able to issue CNY bonds only since 2005.

Japan has unique ways of attracting and managing foreign direct investment (FDI). In the period of rapid economic growth, Japan's attitude to FDI was technology-oriented and private savings were thus utilized effectively. China has been actively attracting FDI since the beginning of the reform process, with loose policies for investment in the processing and real estate industries. As a result, China has accumulated trillions in US-dollar reserves, with low investment returns from international markets. Meanwhile, it continues to attract more FDI.

Another useful point of comparison is in foreign exchange forward trading. Japan abolished the requirement that such trading be restricted to hedging purposes as long ago as 1984. China has not changed this requirement since it came into effect in 1997.

Finally, we compare the two countries' supervision of banks conducting foreign business. Japan has plenty of experience in this respect. The supervision on each bank's net foreign exchange position (that is, the daily limits on spots and forwards) remains in force now, which is rare, even in most other developed countries. The offshore market set up in Tokyo in 1986 is also required to separate onshore and offshore trading. Furthermore, authorized banks are required to inform Japan's central bank before and after such trading, and provide information on foreign businesses to facilitate supervision. Strict supervision of domestic and foreign banks conducting foreign business ensures that all related business, especially cross-border capital flows, is recorded. While China also has relevant supervisory requirements for offshore banking and other foreign business, it still needs to improve its supervision of cross-border capital flows.

From the above it is clear that China has a lot of catching up to do in some areas.

Accelerating Financial Innovation

Regardless of the duration of the impact of the financial crisis on the global economy, China will continue to follow the path of the market economy, the development of which should comply with the market principles and rules of investment, production, and consumption. Decision-making in investment and production requires price information from both the spot and futures markets. Spot prices reflect current demand and supply, while future demand and supply can only be reflected in the forward or futures markets. Therefore, having launched spot markets for commodities, equities, foreign exchange, and bonds, China needs corresponding forward and futures markets and measures to increase market liquidity. The good news is that the State Council has given in-principle approval for the launching of stock index futures in the first half of 2010. This will not only add one more instrument for the capital market but also accelerate financial innovation in the years to come. Having these futures and forward markets in place will help to give China a clearer picture in planning its future production and investment requirements.

The prices of all assets—commodities, equities, foreign exchange, and bonds—are uncertain and subject to market risk. These uncertainties are not always reflected in the spot and forward markets. Experience in the international markets since the 1970s shows that options markets can best reflect the uncertainty of asset prices. Without price information from options markets—that is, the implied uncertainty of asset prices—we cannot determine accurately the uncertainty of future asset prices from historical price data. The implied volatility of options markets is an important market parameter that cannot be reflected in spot, forward and futures markets. This information is essential in understanding the trend of future asset prices. Therefore, China has to actively promote the development of the forward and futures markets alongside that of the spot market, and set up an options market in the near future.

Finance provides an important impetus for economic development, and sustained economic development needs support from both direct and indirect investment. Although China's capital market has developed to some extent, the financial sector is still mainly based on indirect financing. A sound banking system and a healthy capital market are required to maintain steady and sustained economic growth. This requires financial innovation to continuously push it forward. Financial innovation is also needed for economic restructuring and industrial upgrading. The impact of the financial crisis shows that China's economy must undergo structural transformation and strengthen its capacity for scientific and technological innovation. The development of high-tech industries requires the support of a well-developed financial system if they are to serve the real economy more effectively.

FINANCIAL INNOVATION FOR DIVERSE INVESTMENT

The report of the Seventeenth Communist Party of China (CPC) Central Committee of 2007 clearly pointed out the goal "to create conditions for more people to own income-generating properties." This goal can only be achieved by providing diverse investment products through financial innovation. After 30 years of reform and opening-up, China's GDP has grown at an average annual rate of 9.8 percent and its per capita GDP at 14.6 percent. From the end of 1999 to the end of 2008, the average annual growth rate of China's savings deposits was 15.7 percent. Over that period, its savings deposits remained high, at about 74 percent of GDP, and this has laid a solid foundation for both consumption and investment. If part of these savings is to be channeled into investment, there have to be diverse and personalized products for investors to choose from. The design and development of investment products can only be accomplished through financial innovation. Varied investment products allow investors to make choices based on their risk appetite.

Demand for more diversified products will also rise in the international marketplace as the Chinese economy continues its steady growth and the CNY develops into an international currency. Although there is a variety of products offering various levels of risk in the international markets, they may not fit the investment and risk appetite of domestic investors. It is therefore the responsibility of both domestic and international institutions to develop products to meet the specific and increasing needs of domestic investors.

RISK MANAGEMENT INSTRUMENTS AND TRADING PLACES

Need for Risk Management

Risk management has become an important part of international financial trading. We have looked at a range of foreign exchange risk management instruments—from traditional forwards and swaps and their variations, to options and swap options based on interest rates, and stocks, commodities, and related indexes. Some of these products, such as credit default swaps, have exacerbated the financial crisis. Over-speculation in other products also resulted in excessive trading in the years leading up to the crisis, as evidenced by the compound annual growth rate of 25.8 percent in futures trading value from 2000 to 2007 and 40.1 percent in the same period for all options trading. Yet the value of futures trading declined by 1.2 percent from 2007 to 2008, and by a further 37.1 percent in the first three quarters of 2009, and options trading declined by 3.8 percent from 2007 to 2008 and 40.1 percent in the first three quarters of 2009 compared with the same period in 2008. However, no serious problems have occurred in the trading of exchange-traded derivatives products—financial futures and options—before or after the financial crisis, indicating that these products have some market functions and risk-mitigation capabilities.

As the judgments of different market participants often vary in degree and even in direction, they hedge their risks using exchange-traded futures and options to decentralize or distribute the risks through the use of risk management tools. Spot markets only reflect the current demand and supply and cannot provide information on future demand and supply. Futures markets reflect the future demand and supply of all kinds of markets, with participants voting with their capital to determine market factors such as future prices, exchange rates, and interest rates. They are indispensable components of a market economy and financial markets, and no other mechanisms can provide better market information in this respect. Options markets reflect another type of future information for all kinds of markets with participants voting with their capital to determine the uncertainty of market factors such as prices, exchange rates, and interest rates at a specific time in the future. Such information cannot be provided by other markets and are essential for risk management.

After more than 10 years of exploration and practice, China's commodity futures market has made considerable advances. In 2009, the trading of domestic commodity futures amounted to CNY130.5 trillion (US$19.1 billion), 381.3 percent of that year's GDP, providing a bourse for the commodity market to hedge risks. However, China still lacks some important commodity futures such as crude oil futures and financial futures. Financial products that are common in the global market—stock index futures, interest rate futures, and stock futures, for example, not to mention various kinds of options—are still unavailable in China. To promote steady internationalization, China should gradually launch and improve these markets.

Need for Hedging Instruments

In any market economy, all product prices are influenced by and fluctuate with macro-economic factors at home and abroad, and are subject to various market risks. Factors such as interest rates, foreign exchange rates, and inflation increase the market risk of financial assets. Faced with a wide range of market risks, investors need appropriate risk management instruments to hedge their risks. Risk management is achieved through products such as forwards, futures, swaps, and options, without which it will be difficult to hedge risk. After exploring and practicing for more than a decade, the commodity futures market has many products and is increasingly active. As at the end of 2009, the total trading volume of the three futures exchanges accounted for 46.6 percent of world trading volume. The turnover of China's commodity futures was as high as 194.6 percent of that year's GDP, with the risk management function gradually emerging. However, in the absence of commodity options, the market's risk-hedging function cannot develop fully. There is also a lack of financial futures and options. Although CNY forward settlement and sale was launched as early as 1997, and foreign exchange forwards and swaps, interest rate swaps, bond forwards, and forward rate agreements have been developed in recent years, the turnover of these products remains low, making it difficult for their hedging role to function fully. As China's exchange rate mechanism continues to improve, interest rates gradually liberalized, and dependence on international market increases, market risks will become the major risk for investor. Only by systematically improving the turnover of the foreign exchange and interest rate forward and swap markets, and gradually introducing futures and options for foreign exchange, bonds, and equities, can investors effectively hedge these risks to allow the markets to develop steadily.

Need to Implement Risk Management Models

The risk management practices of the international financial market of over more than a decade have shown that establishing and implementing risk management models is essential to gaining an accurate understanding of the risks of a department, a sub-branch/branch or the entire company. The New Basel Capital Accord requires the banking industry to implement a risk management model that covers market risk, credit risk, and operational risk. The implementation of any risk management model requires effective market parameters to compute effective results. In this case, it requires the parameters of spot market prices and those from the futures and options markets. Therefore, if futures and options markets are not active enough, it will be difficult to implement a risk management model and even more difficult to achieve the desired results.

Need for Domestic Institutions Investing Overseas to Manage Foreign Exchange Risk

Since the establishment of the QDII program in 2006, dozens of domestic and foreign commercial banks, fund companies, securities firms, and insurance companies have provided overseas investment services for domestic customers. With the progressive liberalization of the capital account, demand from domestic enterprises and individuals for overseas investment will gradually increase. In addition to investing in overseas securities, China also encourages enterprises to go abroad and expand overseas. Both overseas securities investment and FDI involve exchange rate risk. Managing and avoiding this risk is an important consideration in overseas investment. Although China's foreign exchange forward and swap market has achieved remarkable progress in recent years, its turnover remains low and cannot meet the hedging needs of enterprises and customers. It is therefore necessary to improve the liquidity of existing products in the foreign exchange market, and introduce other CNY risk management tools. Only the steady development of exchange-risk management can steer the financial market onto a track of healthy growth.

Need for Foreign Institutions Investing in China to Manage Foreign Exchange Risk

Since the introduction of the QFII scheme at the end of 2002, almost 50 foreign institutional investors have received approval to invest in domestic securities. Like QDIIs, QFIIs have to manage exchange rate risk for their investments in China. As China's controls on the capital account are gradually loosened, both QFII and QDII businesses will gradually increase. However, the lack of mature foreign exchange risk management products will continue to impose considerable restraints on these businesses.

CREATING INNOVATIVE CNY PRODUCTS: A MATTER OF URGENCY

As discussed in Part II of this book, many new CNY products have been introduced into mainland China in the past few years and have enjoyed reasonable growth. Despite this, however, their liquidity has generally been low, and the weight of trading value has been significantly lower than China's corresponding GDP weight as a proportion of global GDP. Thus, it is highly necessary to further promote product and market innovation. Compared with international markets, Chinese markets are still in their infancy, with domestic transactions accounting for less than 1 percent of the world total. This figure does not fit China's world economic status. Even allowing for the fact that there has been excessive leverage and speculation in the international market in recent years, China's share of the transaction amount is still significantly lower than its contribution to world GDP. There is still a big gap between China's financial markets and those of developed countries, and even those of major developing countries such as India.

As mentioned above, many products common in the international market are still unavailable in China. In view of the lack of exchange-traded and OTC products, the low turnover of the domestic financial markets and the low capacity for product innovation among domestic financial institutions, domestic CNY wealth management products requiring higher technological input are mostly designed by foreign financial institutions. China needs to enhance the innovation of financial products, especially CNY products. It should take concrete measures to increase the liquidity of existing markets while accelerating the improvement of the domestic system through enriching the mix of available products.

FINANCIAL INNOVATION FOR PROMOTING SHANGHAI AS AN INTERNATIONAL FINANCIAL CENTER

At the end of April 2009, the State Council published a series of "opinions" on, among other things, its plans to promote Shanghai as an international financial center, a move designed to serve both the city and the strategic development of the nation as a whole. By 2020, Shanghai will be developed as an international financial center that reflects China's economic strength and the international status of the CNY.

Although it is difficult to accurately sum up the impacts of the financial crisis on the global economy, lower financial leverage and a decline in financial wealth are likely to lower the average growth rate of the US economy in the years to 2020. China's model of export-oriented development will be affected accordingly and its average growth rate will likely be lower than in the 10 years up to 2009 when its GDP and nominal GDP grew at average annual rates of 9.87 percent and 15.73 percent, respectively. Despite the financial crisis, China's economy managed to maintain a growth rate of about 10 percent in 2010 and there are grounds to expect GDP and nominal GDP to maintain average annual growth rates of between 8 percent and 10 percent, respectively, in the years up to 2020. As calculated earlier, China's economy should be around CNY90 trillion (about US$ 15 trillion) by 2020. Sustained and steady economic growth is usually accompanied by continued currency appreciation. Even if the CNY appreciates only 2 percent year-on-year against the US dollar up to 2020, China's GDP should be around US$16 trillion. Assuming US nominal GDP maintains a growth rate of 5 percent year-on-year (from 1996 to 2008, it was 5.2 percent), China's GDP will be equivalent to around 70 percent of the US economy in 2020, laying a solid economic foundation for Shanghai as an international financial center.

As China's economy continues its steady development, the internationalization of the CNY is inevitable. According to GDP data in Table 1.10, China's GDP in 2009 was US$150 lower than Japan (the difference was only US$75 billion if we use the newly updated GDP figure of China released by the National Bureau of Statistics of China on July 2, 2010). With an annual GDP growth rate about 10 percent in 2010, China is likely to replace Japan as the world's second-largest economy in 2010. However, of the 18 major world currencies, the CNY was still ranked seventeenth in global foreign exchange trading volume and eighteenth in its ratio of foreign exchange trading to GDP weight, which is highly incongruent with China's current status. Thus, the acceleration of CNY internationalization is extremely important to the construction of the proposed Shanghai international financial center.

The higher the level of CNY internationalization, the higher the demand from both domestic and foreign investors for a domestic capital market and CNY products, and the higher the corresponding requirement for risk management. In other words, the gradual internationalization of the CNY requires a more mature market for CNY products in China. Such a market can be established step by step by creating innovative CNY products. With the rapid expansion of the economy and gradual and steady internationalization, the CNY is expected to become a major international currency by 2020. To develop mature capital markets and banking business that match the status of its economy, China has to learn from foreign experience, and develop a variety of products with turnover comparable with international levels.

STRENGTHENING SUPERVISION OF CROSS-BORDER CAPITAL FLOWS

Empirical studies on cross-border capital flows in 181 countries from 1960 to 2007 (Reinhart and Reinhart 2008) show that cross-border capital "first flows into emerging countries, then reverses the situation and flows out, making it hard for these countries to adjust." The memory of the negative impacts that international capital flows had on East Asian countries and regions during the Asian financial crisis in 1997–98 is still vivid, and was especially so during the recent global financial crisis. Yu Yongding (2009) pointed out that "if the CNY is internationalized and capital flows out freely, the small-scale domestic capital market would be easily influenced by international markets." He also said that "China's capital market is immature, with a low financial depth and low market capacity. Thus it cannot stand the lash of capital inflows and outflows."

Back in May 2008, four months before the financial crisis broke out, China's vice-premier, Wang Qishan, pointed out that China should "improve forex management, refine the related laws and regulations and strengthen the regulation on cross-border capital flows."[2] In March 2009, Premier Wen Jiabao clearly pointed out that China had to "strengthen the monitoring and management of cross-border capital flows to maintain the stability and safety of the financial system."[3] A new channel for cross-border capital flows is available with the opening up of every item in the capital accounts in future. China will gradually open up its capital items, and if the supervision and controls over cross-border capital flows are not firmly in place, the newly opened channels will, to some extent, be substitutes for unopened channels, and weaken the control on unopened capital items. China has to conduct in-depth research on these matters and formulate contingency measures to lessen the impacts of external factors on its financial system and macroeconomy.

If China fails to have a clear picture of the relatively simple situation before it opens up new channels and fails to put countermeasures in place, it will merely compound the problems it will face when more channels are opened.

CONCLUSION

The internationalization of a currency is supported by the strength and trade volume of its related economy, and the maturity level of its foreign exchange and capital markets, substantially affecting the extent to which its currency can play an international role. The sustainable development of China's economy will provide a solid foundation for CNY internationalization, with the rising weighting of China's GDP to the global economy and the corresponding trend for the CNY to appreciate, creating a favorable environment for the CNY to become a major international currency. On top of these macroeconomic factors, endeavors to improve the foreign exchange and capital markets, to develop CNY products, to increase the trading and operational efficiency of its markets, and to enhance the competitiveness of financial institutions and controls over financial risk are crucial to the internationalization process.

The internationalization of its currency is a key component of China's strategy to integrate with the world. It requires continued, interactive adjustments and reform of economic and financial systems, as well as enriching domestic CNY products and improving market liquidity. To ensure stable and continued progress, China must formulate a rational medium- to long-term strategic plan, and set up mechanisms to strengthen the monitoring, control and management of cross-border capital flows so that the gradual and steady process will not be unduly disturbed by external factors. If all CNY capital items become freely convertible in the future, these time-tested mechanisms will form important levers for China to mitigate international risks.

We are confident that, with the efforts of so many market participants, policymakers, and supervisors from both China and beyond, the CNY will gradually become internationalized, and the domestic financial markets will develop efficiently to support and serve China's economic growth in the coming decade.

ENDNOTES

1. See "Hong Kong to Become a Renminbi Circulation Center," Margaret Leung, *First Financial Daily*, A5, August 25, 2009.
2. In a keynote speech at Lujiazui Forum, 2008.
3. In the Government Working Report of the National People's Congress and Chinese People's Political Consultative Conference.

Bibliography

Cai, Fang. *Green Book of Population and Labor—Report of China's Population and Labor No.6*, Social Sciences Academic Press (China), 2005.

Feng, Charles. "CNY Offshore NDF and Onshore Bank Bond Markets," Asia Fixed Income Research, Deutsche Bank, 2003.

Fukukawa, Shinji. *Development of the Japanese Big Bang and its Impact*, Dentsu Institute for Human Studies, 1997.

He Fan. "Realistic Choice in CNY Internationalization," *International Economic Review*, 2009.

Kamps, Annette. *The Euro as an Invoicing Currency in International Trade*, European Central Bank Working Paper Series No. 665, August 2006.

Kuramitsu, Yumi. "China Yuan Forward Rate Passes H.K. Peg for 1st Time," *Bloomberg*, October 7, 2003.

Li Dongping. "A Brief Analysis of Falsity of China's Trade Surpluses in Recent Years and Its Impacts on China's Monetary Policies," *International Economic Review* 3, May–June 2008.

Li Hao *et al.* Research Note: "Learning from History," Review and Outlook of China Warrant Market, CITIC Securities, August 22, 2007.

Li Jie and Ma Xiaoping. "Estimate of China's Short-term Capital Inflows: 2001–2006," *Shanghai Finance* 10, 2007.

Liu Mingzhi. *Internationalized Finance—Theories, Experiences and Policies*, 2008: 47–48.

Masunaga, Rei. *The Deregulation Process of Foreign Exchange Control in Capital Transactions in Post-war Japan*, 1997.

Reinhart, Carmen M., and Vincent Reinhart. "From Capital Flow Bonanza to Financial Crash," University of Maryland, 2008. At: http://mpra.ub.uni-muenchen.de/11866.

Sato (1998)

Shaede, Ulrike. "Forwards and Futures in Tokugawa-Period Japan: A New Perspective on the Dojima Rice Market", *Journal of Banking and Finance* 13 (1989): 487–513.

Taguchi, Hiroo. "A Survey on the International Use of the Yen," BIS Working Paper No. 6. Basle: Bank for International Settlements, July 1982.

Tavlas, George S., and Yuzuru Ozeki. "The Japanese Yen as an International Currency." IMF Working Paper WP/91/2. Washington, D.C.: International Monetary Fund, January 1991.

———. "The Internationalization of Currencies: An Appraisal of the Japanese Yen," Occasional Paper 90. Washington, D.C.: International Monetary Fund, January 1992.

Wang Zhihao. "China's Trade: Bermuda Triangle, Accounting Issue or foreign exchange Flows?" in *On the Ground in Asia*, Standard Chartered, Shanghai, October 25, 2006.

Ye Yonggang and Li Yuan Hai. *Forward Settlement and Sales: Market Research on RMB against Foreign Currency Forwards*, Wuhan University Press, 2001.

Yu Xuejun. "Issues on the Current Macroeconomic Circumstances in China," *Global Perspective: Analysis of China's Macroeconomics*, September 1, 2009.

Yu Yongding. "Views on CNY Internationalization," Speech Report of the Shanghai Development and Research Foundation, 2009. At: www.sdrf.org.cn/09.05.13yuyongding.htm.

Zhang, Peter G. *Exotic Options: A Guide to Second-generation Options*, World Scientific Publishing, 1998.

———. *Chinese Yuan Renminbi Products* (2nd ed.) China Financial Publishing House, 2006.

———. *Chinese Yuan Derivative Products* (2nd ed.) (in Chinese), China Financial Publishing House, 2008.

Zhang (2003a)

Zhao Xiao Fan (2006)

Index

THE ILLUSTRATED STORY OF COPYRIGHT